A Winding Road to the Land of Enchantment

Gerald W. Thomas

Contents

Dedication

To my wife, Jean Ellis Thomas.

Acknowledgements

I want thank first my children and grandchildren, who insisted that I provide them "something written down" about Jean's and my life. A "winding road" that started on two ranches in Clark County, Idaho and ended in the "Land of Enchantment." I want to thank Marianne Shipley for the history recounted in her book "A View From Here," which I have drawn upon. I want to thank David Thomas for editing the book and preparing the photos for publication. I want to thank my Air Group 4 buddies for their contributions to the chapters about my service in WWII. And finally, I want to thank my many friends and colleagues at Texas A&M, Texas Tech, and New Mexico State University for the generous assistance they have given my life and career.

Introduction

This journey of Jean and Gerald Thomas to the Land of Enchantment began on ranches in the rugged mountains and valleys of Clark County, Idaho. The raw beauty of the country, the harsh environment and exposure to the Great Depression helped prepare us for challenging and exciting experiences as we traveled the winding road that would eventually lead to the "Land of Enchantment."

The road had an austere beginning as an unpaved lane where the primary mode of travel was by team and wagon. There were many bumps and unexpected detours in the road before we reached the point where Highway 70 intersects the old "Camino Real" at Las Cruces, New Mexico.

This is a look at that journey – a journey as enchanted as the destination.

Gerald and Jean Thomas moved into the President's Residence at
New Mexico State University on August 1, 1970.
Gerald retired from NMSU August 1, 1984.

The President's Residence was designed by Henry C. Trost and built in 1918 for $9,560. A total of ten NMSU presidents lived in the house. The den/living room (shown here) was added by President Roger Corbett. The house was named the Nason House on October 30, 1987 and converted to the Center for Latin American Studies.

Chapter 1

Growing Up: Our Ranch at Small, Idaho

"We crossed the creek to the barnyard."

I was born on a ranch on Medicine Lodge Creek, Small, Idaho on July 3, 1919. My parents Daniel "Dan" Waylett Thomas and Mary Elizabeth Evans were married on May 6, 1917, and they raised six boys. The first four boys (and a cousin) were born in the old log house on the ranch and the last two boys were born in California.

The headquarters for the Dan Thomas Ranch straddled Medicine Lodge Creek. The family living quarters were on the East and the barn, corrals and other livestock facilities were across the bridge to the West. The place was run down when Dan and Mother moved in. They started immediately making improvements. As a young boy I remember the ranch as a wonderful, exciting place with many opportunities to play and explore the buildings and facilities on both sides of the creek.

Our home when I was born consisted of an old log house with one bedroom and closet. The small addition that had been added was inadequate so the folks bought an abandoned dry farm house east of the Steve Green place. Mother's Uncle Seymour Evans and the neighbors helped Dad jack up the house, place logs under it and move it with two 4-horse teams and wagons to our ranch. It was exciting to watch the move which took several days. This house was then attached to the log house and became our kitchen, dining room and a bedroom for Dad and Mother. The attic over the log house was enlarged for a bedroom for the boys and the downstairs of the old log house now served as our living room. Winter heat was provided by a coal stove in the center of the log house. (We hauled coal from Dubois in the wagon.) Mother cooked meals for the family and the hay crew on a large wood stove with a warming oven.

We had a big orchard with several varieties of apples, pears and plums. Large cottonwood trees were along the fenced lane to the north. A "lower orchard" was fenced separately along the creek. The two-hole outhouse was on the fence line between the two orchards. The only building in the lower orchard was a smokehouse for curing meat.

A large cellar and an icehouse were down by the creek. We sawed chunks of ice from the creek when it froze over in the winter. We packed the ice in sawdust from the Johnson sawmill on Middle Creek. After a few years Mother found a small one-room shack on a dry farm to move close to the path by the creek for a wash house, bunk house and a place to hold our cream separator so we did not have to clutter up the kitchen.

Passing through the gate we crossed the creek on the bridge (designed to hold a team and wagon) to go to the farmyard. This is where most of the excitement took place. The large barn had rooms to harness the horses, milk the cows and wean the calves. The hayloft was a great place to play when we were not doing chores. The large corral had a gate down by the creek and one by the barn. Inside the large corral was a "round corral" for breaking horses, and a hay feeder. Livestock could reach creek water from the corral or from the lane which lead to the fields.

Other facilities on the west side of the creek included the blacksmith shop, granary, pig pens, and chicken houses and gates to the hay fields, pastures and "the world beyond." This was the Medicine Lodge Ranch, which had such an impact on the life of the Thomas boys.

The Dan Thomas Ranch on Medicine Lodge – Winter.

Gerald Thomas feeding Buck and Buster. Dan Thomas Ranch, 1940.

Buster (center) was sold while I was serving in the Navy.

The corral was built into the creek to provide water for the livestock.

Benjamin Daniel and Matilda Ann (Waylett) Thomas. Malad, Idaho, Circa 1880s.

Children of Benjamin and Matilda Thomas.
Standing: Rees W., Benjamin H. "Hop," William Henry, Daniel "Dan" W.,
George Dewey. Sitting: Leah, Mabel S., and Leticia (Tish).

Thomas Family Roots

"Grandparents settle in Clark County."

The Thomas roots go back to Carmarthenshire, Wales. My Dad's grandfather, Benjamin Thomas, the son of David and Hannah Thomas, was born February 25, 1820, in Carmarthenshire, South Wales. He and his first wife, Leticia Davies, and their son, Daniel Davies, born September 13, 1847, sailed to the United States in 1849 on the ship *Buena Vista*. One brother, Daniel Thomas, also sailed with them. They were converted to Mormonism, so when they arrived in the United States they joined the George Smith Company and headed west for Salt Lake City, Utah. On their journey, Leticia gave birth to a daughter, Hannah Maria, born on May 13, 1849, on the banks of the Missouri River. Benjamin and Leticia had five more children after arriving in America, Sarah Anne, Mary Jane, David Davies, Benjamin Daniel and Joshua Davis. **(1)**

On March 25, 1856, Benjamin married Susan Roberts in a ceremony performed by Brigham Young. In 1858, Benjamin and his families moved from Salt Lake City to Brigham City, Utah. That same year the Church requested they move south to Dixie, but in Sanpete County Leticia died giving birth to their son Joshua. After the death of Leticia, Benjamin didn't marry again even though it wasn't until March 3, 1887, that the Edmonds/Tucker Act prohibiting multiple wives was enacted. Senator Fred Dubois of Idaho was instrumental in getting this legislation passed.

In April, 1864, Benjamin and his family moved to Malad Valley and began the rigorous process of settling the forbidding but beautiful wilderness. He and Susan were hardy and energetic pioneers. That same year, on September 30th, Susan gave birth to their fourth son, David. Benjamin and Susan's marriage produced 14 children, four born in Brigham City and ten born after they moved to Malad, Idaho. Benjamin died August 16, 1887, at the age of 67, and is buried in the Malad cemetery.

Waylett Roots

Grandmother Thomas` maiden name was Waylett. Her father was William Henry Waylett, born February 13, 1826, in Manchester, Lancaster, England. When he was 26 he left his home and worked as a collier (coal worker) and sailed to America on the *Good Ship Jersey*. On board ship he married Sarah Williams, born November 29, 1825, who was immigrating to America from Denbigh, Wales, with her parents Rees Williams and Leah Jones Williams. Leah Jones parents were Thomas and Margaret Jones, who were also Welch.

William Henry Waylett converted to Mormonism before he left England; so on arriving in America, he and Sarah joined a Handcar Company heading west to Salt Lake City. Their first daughter Leah Marie was born in Salt Lake City on November 8, 1855. In 1857, the family moved to Brigham City where seven more children were born. Then in 1872, the family moved to Malad, Idaho. Matilda Ann Waylett (my grandmother) was born March 17, 1860, in Malad.

The Thomas/Waylett Marriage

"The boys were adept at breaking wild horses to saddle or harness."

My Dad's parents Benjamin D. Thomas and Matilda Waylett were married in 1880, and they lived in Malad, Idaho. In 1884, *"Six years before Idaho Statehood and many years before Clark County was established, the couple moved from Malad to settle on a homestead on the sinks of Medicine Lodge Creek."* **(1)**. They had two children in Malad before the move, Ella Mae (Fayle) and William Henry. Seven more children were born to the couple after this last move: Leah (Leonardson) , Leticia (Small), Daniel Waylett, Rees Waylett, Sarah Mabel (Gauchay), George Dewey, and his twin brother Benjamin Hopson.

---

(1) A biography of Benjamin Thomas was compiled by members of the family in Malad, Idaho. It is interesting to note that the first non-Indian born in the Malad valley was David R. Thomas born September 30, 1864.

John Columbus and Sarah Anne (Schooley) Evans Family, Webster, Kansas, 1915.
Back: Mary Elizabeth, Ina Schooley, Amos Ezra, Beulah Grace, Flora Maye.
Front: Laura Elsie, John Bunyon, Sarah, William, Mona Lucille, Lettie Gertrude.

Evans family members gather at J. C. Evans place to say goodbye
to John C. Evans family. Webster, Kansas, August 29, 1916.

Grandfather Benjamin passed away in 1909 leaving Grandmother Matilda and the children to run the sizable cattle, horse, hay and grain operation. The family had water rights for irrigation from Medicine Lodge Creek. In addition to the hay and grain operation the family owned over 100 head of range horses at one time. Grandmother said, *"The boys were adept at breaking wild horses to saddle or harness."* In later years there were on-going arguments about which of the boys was the best cowboy. Dad's brother, Rees, probably spent more time in the saddle than any of the other Thomas brothers. He was still riding for the Crooked Creek Cattle Association long after World War II. (1897-1967).

In addition to the ranch and farming operation, the Thomas family had the mail contract to Winsper, Crooked Creek and the Reno Ranch.

Evans Family Roots

"We took the train to Idaho Falls."

My mother, Mary Elizabeth Evans Thomas, was born in Brumley, Missouri on April 2, 1897. Her parents were John Columbus Evans and Sarah Anne Schooley Evans. Her maternal grandparents were Obadiah Schooley and Martha Ann Henry. In tape recordings, Mother stated:

"Grandpa Schooley was married before he married Grandmother and had two children. He went to war and fought on the north side even though he lived in a border state. He didn't believe in slavery. He and my Grandmother had eight children as far as I can remember. Aunt Amanda was the oldest, then Irma, Jane, Martha Anne, Sarah (my mother), Mary, Harv and Eliza. Mama and Aunt Mary married brothers. (Mother's Uncle Seymour later lived in Altadena, California.) Mama was from Shoals, Indiana.

"My Father's Father was named Absolom Evans. My Dad's people came from Illinois. My parents must have migrated into Missouri around the same time be-

cause they knew each other when they were young and growing up. My Father used to say that they all, and my mother, too, had good shoes for Sunday, but went barefoot or wore pretty old shoes during the week. They would carry their new shoes in their hands until they got nearly to church and then they would sit down and put on their shoes and stockings."

In 1902, Mary Elizabeth moved from Brumley to Webster, Kansas, with her parents, her brother Amos Ezra, and her sister Flora Maye. Mary was five years old when they moved. Five more children were born to John and Sarah after the move to Webster. They were Beulah Grace, Laura Elsie, Lettie Gertrude, John Bunyan, and Mona Lucille. Mother said:

"My parents were Baptists as were the Schooleys and the Henrys. My father was not a minister, but he was a deacon in the church and a choir leader. He was a good musician."

Mother joined the Baptist Church and was baptized by Reverend Chandler in a pond south of the city (See photo of the minister baptizing in this pond during the winter.)

Mary Elizabeth (my Mother) graduated from the eighth grade in Webster, Kansas, and decided she wanted to be a school teacher. She enrolled at Ft. Hays Normal School. Then, after a summer at the Academy of Stockton, she passed the teachers' examination.

In the spring of 1915, when Mary was 17 years old, she returned home and said to her Dad, *"I want to go west to teach."* She had made up her mind that the salaries were better outside of Kansas. To her delight, her Father said, *"I think we might sell out and go with you. Our neighbor has said he might buy our place. What do you say, Mama?"* Even though they had a good, prosperous farm and eight children, John and Sarah Evans decided that

Mary Evans (Mother) signed her first teaching contract at age 18. The classroom was located in the Ranger Station at Rice, Idaho. Nothing remains at the site today. 1916.

Detail showing Ranger and Mary Evans at Rice Ranger Station.

day to sell their farm and make a new life just like their adventurous and determined daughter.

The Evans family took the train west, intending to go to Oregon. At a stop in Idaho Falls, Idaho, they met a real estate man who informed them that they should look at a homestead relinquishment near Dubois, Idaho. They were informed that the oldest boy, Ezra, was eligible to take out a homestead on his own and he could locate in the same area. This proposition sounded interesting, so they took the train to Dubois.

Mother recalled:

"Daddy found a little four room shack- the only place left in town. We moved in only to find that there were bed bugs behind the paper-covered walls. Mother started cleaning and Father went to look for water to drink. When he came back he said, `They drink this water running by the house. It comes from springs up in the mountains and is very pure` But none of us would drink it. `We will choke first!` We said, `There are cows and a dog standing in the creek.` So Daddy took a bucket and went over to the school house which had the only well in town besides the one at the Depot. Mother didn't get much sleep that night. She finally set the bed posts in coal oil so that we would be safe from the bed bugs."

Moving to their new property, the Evans family bought machinery and broke out the sagebrush land for grain. They were not familiar with the dry Southern Idaho desert conditions. The first year or two they got their seed back, but after that there was no crop worth harvesting. Dry farmers were starving out all over the county. However, the Small, Idaho Post Office was moved to the Evans property and Ezra became the Postmaster while the rest of the family looked for contract work.

Shortly after the move to Idaho, Mary wrote to the County Superintendent inquiring about vacancies for school teachers. Even though she was only 18, she was hired for $70 a month to teach at Rice, Idaho, 25 miles west of the train depot at Ashton. To get to the school, she had to take the train from Dubois back to Idaho Falls, remain over night, take another train to Ashton and then hire a horse rig to go to Rice. The agent at the depot in Ashton called a livery man to take the young school teacher to the remote school at Rice. When the man arrived she was hesitant to go with him. He had tobacco stains in his beard, *"The worst bewhiskered man I had ever seen."* Fortunately, he did not know the way to Rice, so the livery stable found another man to make the trip.

The Rice school was located in one end of the Forest Ranger Station. Mary had eight children in the school and taught six grades. One of the boys was 19, a year older than the teacher. The school day began at 9 am and ended at 5 pm. The homemade benches and desks were made of planks from the local sawmill. Mary said:

"I loved the children and they liked me. The older boys were no trouble. I think they were anxious to learn. I liked the new country. We had six feet of snow that winter."

The next year, Mary was offered a school at Small, Idaho. The log school was five miles south of her parent's house and *"it had store-bought desks."* The number of students varied as people moved in and out of the area. When the weather was pleasant, Mary was able to live with her parents, walking the five miles to school. During bad weather she boarded with Mrs. Matilda Ann Thomas and that is where she met her future husband. It did not take long for one of Mrs. Thomas' sons, Daniel "Dan" Thomas, to fall in love with the beautiful new school teacher his Mother was boarding.

Pond where Mother and other Evans family members were baptized by Rev. Chandler. Caption reads, "Baptizing at Norman's Pond Webster, Kansas. January 21, 1913."

Detail of baptism. Several inches of ice have been chopped to get to the water.

The Cowboy Marries the School Teacher

"It took four horses to pull the car through the lane."

My Dad and Mother were married May 6, 1917, in the Baptist parsonage in Idaho Falls. The newly-weds planned to live on the old Gilliard Ranch that Dan had recently purchased. Dad borrowed a Ford car from his Brother Henry's livery stable in Du-bois to bring his bride home from Idaho Falls. The weather was bad and it took four horses to pull the newly-weds` car through the lane to the log house on the Medicine Lodge Ranch which was to be their home for many years to come.

Mother added:

"Mice – man alive! The walls of the house had two layers of boards filled with dirt. Flora and I papered the ceiling on cheesecloth." Dad said, "When we took over the Ranch there were about 200 dead sheep in the corral. It had been a hard winter. Gilliard had run out of feed so he just let the sheep die. Because of the snow drifts there were even some dead sheep in the hay loft of the barn. I had to haul off tons of manure and all those dead sheep. The next year (1919) was another dry year. No creek water for the alfalfa. We had to live off the sale of horses. We had over 100 head. Good horses too, but we only got $3 a head."

Dan and Mary Thomas, wedding photo, May 6, 1917.

Matilda Ann (Waylett) Thomas.

Amos Ezra and Mary Elizabeth Evans.

John C. Evans family – Webster, Kansas.

Friend and Mary (Evans) clowning around at
Ft. Hays Normal School on Graduation, 1915.

Daniel "Dan" Waylett Thomas. 1917.

Mary's graduation class, Ft. Hays Normal School, September 30, 1915.

Dan Thomas, 1913.

Dan and son Daniel (with friends), Medicine Lodge Ranch, 1918.
This is the original log cabin that was on the homestead.

Dan, Daniel, and Mary, Medicine Lodge Ranch, 1918.

Mary, Walter, and Daniel, 1929.

Mary, Pasadena, 1937.

Gerald with Grandparents Sarah and John Evans.
Working their copper claim on Birch Creek, Clark County, Idaho. 1937.
The Model-A belonged to my brother Daniel. (See Chapter 8.)

Mary and Dan Thomas. Ronan, Montana. 1972.

Sarah Anne Evans and five of her daughters.
Back: Lettie Gertrude, Mary Elizabeth, and Flora Maye.
Front: Beulah Grace, Sarah, and Mona.
Laura Elsie not present. 1950.

Chapter 2 | School Days at Small, Idaho

"Two school wagons and two rooms."

The Medicine Lodge School

The first year Dan and Mary were married, Mary got a job teaching at the Medicine Lodge School near the ranch. She recalled:

"I started with 45 students, many from dry farm families. By the spring quite a few had moved away, including two large families, the Dingleys with seven children and the Drounds with eight. The Drounds moved when Mr. Drounds was killed tragically in a duel with Bob Bogus."

Mary also had her four sisters and one brother in the school.

"I still believe in country schools. In those days there were no radios or televisions and the students really wanted to learn."

Mary Thomas wanted to continue teaching, but she soon started having children.

"The year my second son (Gerald) was little, I was asked to take a school about seven miles away at a place called Cottonwood. Most of the time I rode by horseback to the school. We needed the money. A payment was due on the ranch."

In 1924, my brother Daniel who had turned six in April packed a lunch and got ready to start first grade. I packed a lunch too and told Mother that I was going to school with Daniel. Mother resisted. She said I was only five and too young for first grade. The school teacher was boarding with us so Mother told me to ask the teacher. Miss Gladys Thomas (no relation) said, *"Let him start. If he can't keep up we can send him home."* This deci-

sion meant that Daniel and I would stay together through high school, junior college and on to the University of Idaho.

When we started to school, the Medicine Lodge School District had been consolidated and was now located a mile and a half from our ranch The new school originally had three rooms, but one room was not needed, so the east end of the building was converted to a gym and basketball arena. The school had a coal-fired furnace in the basement. A large school bell in the center of the building signaled the start of school and the end of the recess.

Since there was no plumbing in the school two out-houses were provided – boys to the east and girls on the west. Water was hauled from the creek for a cistern in back of the building to serve as drinking and wash water. There was a small barn in back for the horses that were used to pull the school wagons or for saddle horses for a few students that might had missed the school wagon. A teachers` cottage was added to help recruit teachers to this remote location in Clark County, Idaho.

Two school wagons were used to transport students to the Medicine Lodge School. One came from the north starting with the Sweifels and Gauchays on Indian Creek and the other collected students from ranches to the south. These school wagons were converted sheep wagons with benches along the sides and a stove near the front. In the winter sleigh runners were substituted for wheels.

The school wagon driver was usually a rancher at the far end of each route. The driver had to start early in order to deliver students to the school by the opening bell at 9 o'clock. Sometimes the driver would leave his team at the school during the day

Medicine Lodge School District No. 24. Fall, 1934.

Medicine Lodge School Wagon ready for the trip home at 4 pm.
The top was transferred to a sleigh in the winter and a stove was added.
Note the teachers cottage in the background. Fall, 1934.

since a barn and hay were available. At other times the driver would return home and come back for the students when school was dismissed at 4 pm. Some drivers were very strict, while others would let us ride the runners and play around. We had a few fist fights on the school wagons and at school.

A big improvement in both wagons occurred when an old car chassis with rubber tires could substitute for the regular wagon wheels. In 1935, the south school wagon was changed to a car since there were only a few students on the south end of the Creek.

School District No. 24 was authorized to teach first through tenth grades. However, the 1934-35 class was the largest in the history of the school, so the County permitted an additional year to accommodate the ranch families. There were six of us in the tenth grade, with the possibility that the teacher's brother could board with him and join our class. Thus, the school now served eleven grades in the two rooms.

The Post Office and Store at Small, Idaho

Small, Idaho was named in honor of one of the oldest pioneer families in Clark County on June 25, 1890. Like many areas in the West, there was no town – just a US Post Office to serve the ranches and farms in the vicinity. John Daniels "JD" Ellis (Jean's Grandfather) was the first postmaster. Ezra Evans, my Uncle, served as postmaster from 1919-1922. The post office and combination store at that time was on Grandfather Evans' dry farm about one-half mile south of the Medicine Lodge Schoolhouse. Walter Finlay took over in 1922, followed by Al Colson. The Small Post Office closed in 1959 under Helen Gauchay (my Cousin Waylette Gauchay's wife). Some of the old buildings remain at the site and the owners have built a new house. The farm land that was a part of Grandfather's homestead has reverted back to sagebrush.

Small, Idaho Mourns a Pioneer

Dennis Small passed away on May 10, 1917. His wife, Sarah, died on the home ranch on November 12, 1933, at the age of 78. The community mourned the passing of Mrs. Small and a large funeral was planned at their ranch. Someone thought it would be appropriate for the Medicine Lodge School to play a role in the Memorial Service. Consequently, our teacher formed a quartet to sing at the funeral. The quartet consisted of Francis Colson, Vivian Gauchay, my brother Daniel and I. The teacher played the piano and we practiced several times at the school house on *Beautiful Isle of Somewhere.*

The time came for the services at the ranch. We were in a large living room. The teacher lined us up facing the open casket. None of us had ever been to a funeral before. We were "just plain scared" and our singing talents were limited. We could not avoid an occasional look at the dead body. Our teacher started playing the piano. After the first few bars Jane Gauchay in the back of the room started crying with a loud, "Boo hoo hoo." My knees started to shake and evidently my quartet partners had the same problem. At any rate, we tapered off and the teacher finished the song on the piano – mostly without the choir. I still believe this was the end of any potential musical career for one of the Thomas boys.

Miss Gladys Thomas with her students at the Medicine Lodge School in 1925. Gerald and Daniel are in the front row (third and fourth from the left). Miss Thomas (no relation) boarded with our parents.

School house abandoned. Marianne and Peggy Thomas standing in doorway.

Small, Idaho Post Office (left) when it was on the John Daniels (JD) Ellis ranch. JD's first wife, Elizabeth Jane (Schopp) Ellis, is standing by PO building. 1890.

JD Ellis and Barney. He was the first postmaster at Small, Idaho.

Gerald, Daniel, and Byron Thomas. Dubois, Idaho. 1924.

Dan and Mary Thomas with Gerald, Byron, and Daniel. Warm Creek, Idaho. 1925.

Chapter 3 | Lidy Hot Springs

"The Thomas-Ellis connection."

Bob Lidy Develops a Major Resort

The most popular resort in Clark County for picnics, swimming and dancing was Lidy Hot Springs. Dances at Lidy's brought the Thomas family from Medicine Lodge and the Ellis family from Crooked Creek together in the 1930s. Jean Ellis noted in her diary on May 5, 1935, *"I became acquainted with the Thomas boys. They sure are nice and full of fun. We went swimming."* In my diary, I noted a few times that I danced with Jean Ellis. For example, on July 4, 1939, *"I took in the rodeo in Dubois and the dance at Lidys. Danced a lot with Gene Lingo and Jean Ellis."*

Robert "Bob" Seamon Lidy, Jean's Grandfather, was born in Ohio in 1865/66. As a young man, he came to Camas, Idaho where he was a freight hauler. *"Bob Lidy could handle a ten-horse team and a sixteen-horse short line team with dexterity. He made many freight trips between the old mining town of Gilmore and Dubois, Idaho."*

Bob Lidy met and married Mary Sullivan, a widow with six children, who owned the property where a natural hot springs was located. Mary's husband Michael Sullivan had obtained the property by trading a team of horses for it. The family that had it originally wanted to sell because they thought the water was making them sick.

Sullivan developed Lidys, then called Sulfur Springs, into a major freight and stage stop on the Dubois/Gilmore line. At that time Gilmore was a booming silver and lead mining center. The ten- and six-horse ore-hauling freight trains would roll into Sulfur Springs, where livery and feed was available for the animals, and meals and boarding for the teamsters.

When Lidy took over, he built the first bath, near the springs, which came out of the ground about a mile from the stage stop. Later he piped the hot water down to a big tub in the yard. Visitors paid 25 cents for a towel and bar of soap.

Business prospered and Lidy built a large, two story house for his family. A few years later, as Gertrude Lidy explained, the house burned down:

"My sister Margaret was going to iron and she had filled the stove with chips. The fire flared out, catching the wallpaper afire. The house burst into flames and burned in a moment, it seemed. We saved only a rocking chair and the sewing machine. No clothes, nothing was left, not even a bed. We cleaned out the shop area and were grateful to move into it."

On March 1, 1917, Lidy leased Lidys and its lands to C. D. Beale and Company. Beale planned to erect a hotel and develop Lidys into a major resort and farming enterprise. On March 8, he published the following notice in the Idaho Falls newspaper:

"Other ground is being secured and management propose to turn the ranch and any additional ground that may be secured into a large diversified farm. Farm buildings will be provided along with a large green house and all kinds of farming and truck gardening will be carried on both in an experimental and permanent way.... The new hotel will be equipped along modern lines, catering to the general public and taking care of those who seek rest, recreation and medicinal baths."

Robert "Bob" Seamon Lidy's freight outfit. Circa 1890s.

Lidy Hot Springs, 1904. At this time Lidys was an important freight and stage stop, providing rooms and meals. Robert Lidy is sixth from the left and Mary Lidy third from the right, behind the corral post. The child in the center in front of the windows is Gertrude Lidy, Jean Ellis' mother. Robert Lidy and Mary Neville Sullivan married in 1897.

Robert and Mary Lidy with children and grandchildren. Sign says "Lidy Hot Springs, The Oasis. Meals, Baths, Rooms." 1926.

Mary Lidy with grandchildren. The small sign is a Coca Cola sign. 1926.

Lidy Hot Springs public swimming pool – photo taken in 1924 before pool was covered. The doors lead to private hot baths. The cement pool and baths were built by C. D. Beale.

Lidy Hot Springs pool showing shade built by Robert Lidy. 1936.

Lidy Hot Springs. 1936.

Lidy Hot Springs swimming pool. 1936.

Robert Seamon Lidy. Unknown date.

Mary Neville (Sullivan) Lidy. Unknown date.

Mary Lidy. Unknown date.

Beale's timing was awful, because the mining at Gilmore was just then giving out. He built private hot baths, a large cement pool, a few buildings – and then went bust.

Lidy took back the property and added a dance hall, which became more popular than the baths. Families from the surrounding area went to many community dances at the resort.

An Overloaded Lumber Wagon

My uncle, Ollie Johnson told me this story about Bob Lidy. Mr. Lidy had decided to build a slatted wooden roof over the swimming pool at the Hot Springs. Since the nearest source of lumber was the Johnson sawmill on Middle Creek, Lidy decided to purchase the lumber from the Johnsons. He drove his four-horse team and lumber wagon up to the mill, about 10 miles away. Ollie said he ordered boards that were narrow at one end to fit the shape of the roof. *"That worked fine for us,"* Ollie said, *"since we could take advantage of the natural shape of the tree."*

Johnsons cut the lumber and Mr. Lidy started loading the wagon.

> *"He just kept piling on boards until he had the entire stack we had cut. I told him that the load was too heavy for that wagon but he said he did not want to make an extra trip. Well, he got about 100 yards and one wagon wheel broke. We had to unload the lumber and pull the wheel. Then Mr. Lidy went to Dubois after a new wheel. He lost a couple of days and had to make two trips with the lumber."*

Dan and Mary Lease Lidy Hot Springs

"The big drought was continuing."

After Mr. Lidy died the surviving family rented the resort to various operators. With Mother's encouragement, our family leased Lidy Hot Springs in 1934. The Depression was in full swing and we needed the additional income. The big drought was continuing and Dad said, *"When we moved to Lidys there wasn't a spear of green grass. We had one milk cow and she nearly starved."* Dad eventually moved most of our cattle from Medicine Lodge and Deep Creek to Lidys and we utilized the hot water to raise as much hay as possible.

One year we cut and stacked tumbleweeds (Russian thistle) for supplemental feed. The dust from the tumbleweeds really irritated our eyes and skin. However, when the tumbleweeds were young and green the cattle selected the plants. We could always tell when the cattle were grazing tumbleweeds. They were a good physic for milk cows and that presented a challenge when milking to try to avoid the swishing tail. We always had a few cows that kicked over the milk bucket. Dad always said *"If a cow fresh off the pasture kicks her foot in the milk bucket we can call that 'pasteurized milk.'"*

The move to Lidys was really exciting for the Thomas boys We met new and interesting people – some old and many our age – at the dances and in the swimming pool. We became good swimmers and my brother Byron followed up by making a letter in swimming at the University of Idaho.

One evening while we were refilling the pool after cleaning, Daniel, Byron and I decided to go swimming. Byron and I were first out of the dressing room and onto the diving board. Since the pool was only partially full we dived off one side of the board into the deeper water. Then Daniel followed us onto the diving board. Evidently he had forgotten the pool was only partially full because he jumped high, formed a jack-knife and landed in about three feet of water. His head hit the concrete bottom. As he came up he shouted *"help"* and sank back down.

Byron and I pulled him up the slope and out of the water. We left him there until we had completed our swim. Then we helped him down to the house. Mother tucked him in bed and he stayed in bed for six weeks. Byron and I thought he was just trying to get out of the farm work but when Mother and Dad finally took him to a doctor in Idaho Falls, the doctor said he had a broken neck and a cracked skull and *"It was a good thing you did not try to move him earlier."*

Daniel, Walter, Mom and Dad. About 1936.
Lidys swimming pool in the background.
Mary and Dan managed Lidys from 1934 to 1946.

Bathing beauties, 1938.
Virginia Laird, Juanita Leonardson, Vivian Gauchay,
Pauline Gauchay, Betty Lou Thomas, and Iva Mae Leonardson.

Rodeos were another big event at the Hot Springs resort. We usually lined up local stock and had local participation in bucking, roping, wild cow milking, etc. At one of these rodeos, Pauline, one of our cousins, teased Daniel into getting on a bareback bucker. I had already taken a turn and been promptly thrown off. Daniel knew the doctor told him not to ride a bucking horse or get a blow to the head because of his broken neck. However, the peer pressure was so great that he climbed the chute and hopped on a bareback bronco. After about three jumps he hit the ground hard. I helped him up. He was barely conscious and he couldn't even remember what happened. Anyway, he survived, but that was the end of his rodeo career.

Mother and Dad worked hard to promote Lidy Hot Springs as a regional resort. The first few years were tough, but the crowds gradually increased. Mother kept a record of the income and expenses for Lidys each year. The rental cost per month was $100 paid to Frank Sullivan, who represented the Lidy heirs. The net profit from swimming dances and confections for 1935 was $174.07. Records of three dances are shown below:

August 17, 1935 – net profit – $54.65

Paid Out:

Music	$25.00
Wax for dance floor	$1.50
Bread	$2.00
Meat & Coffee	$1.50
Ice cream	$2.85

Received:

Tickets	$37.50
Supper	$10.00
Baths	$10.00
Fountain	$30.00

August 24, 1935 – net profit $24.80

August 31, 1935 – net profit $24.98

We supplemented the income from the Hot Springs by renting the Davis Place on Medicine Lodge Creek, selling horses and other livestock from the ranch and in most years Dad contracted to cut and stack hay for Frank Reno on Birch Creek.

We operated Lidy Hot Springs on and off until 1946. The war years took a toll on income for the folks. In addition, Byron and I left for the Navy and Daniel went to Alaska with his new bride, Betty Rider. Nevertheless, experiences at Lidys provided interactions for "us kids" far beyond the routine of farm and ranch chores.

Mormon Crickets

"We gotta do something."

During the 30s, what we called Mormon Crickets (*Anabrus simplex*) were a reoccurring problem. One day when I was riding for cattle, I spotted a huge cloud of crickets that appeared to be heading for Lidys. The infestation must have contained millions of crickets and was about a mile wide and a mile deep.

I rushed home and told Dad. He said, *"We gotta do something to keep them out of the pool. There's nothing we can do about the fields."* We strung old cans on wires and got out brooms and rakes and watched the crickets head straight for the place. Every once in a while the crickets would change their noise and all stop. Then they ate everything down to bare dirt. Suddenly, with a noise change, they would move forward again.

When they began to reach Lidys, we shook the cans, trying to split them around the buildings. At first the noise caused them to jump away from the sound. But as they got thicker and thicker, they just forced themselves forward. We finally gave up.

They covered everything. They climbed up the sides of the buildings into the eaves, they went through the shop and ate the leather, and they plunged into the swimming pool. A rattle snake

Walter and Byron tending bar. Daniel (left) and an unidentified customer.
Lidy Hot Springs, 1936.

Tending bar – detail. The chalk board reads: "Hard Times Dance, Sat
July 20, Cowboy String Band, 8 pm."

we had killed shortly before they arrived, we later found eaten down to the bones. They ate even their dead.

In the pool at first they drowned, but eventually they formed a bridge of dead and live bodies and just marched across the water.

The largest crickets were about 3 inches long.

When they were gone, they left behind millions of dead. We worked like the dickens to clean them up, raking them into huge piles. We drained the swimming pool and had a terrible time cleaning it. The next day, the stink was terrible.

The county responded to the infestations by spraying, and killed several of our cows with their poisoning. Mother wrote numerous times asking the county for compensation, but was refused.

When a wave of crickets crossed a road, they'd get smashed by passing cars, creating a dangerous slick.

By the end of the decade, they were no longer a serious problem. The spraying programs were very successful in killing them before they grew into unstoppable bands.

Jack Rabbits

Jack Rabbits were another scourge. They could devastate a field of alfalfa in no time. They'd eat so much hay around the base of a hay stack that it'd fall over.

To try to keep them down, we'd go out at dusk with a 22 rifle and boxes of shells. As they crept into the field from the open range, we'd shoot them.

Ranchers in the area began to organize rabbit drives. Riding horses, they drove thousands of rabbits into a confined area. Then they would dismount and club them to death. Many people objected to killing them that way, however.

Some people would skin or even eat Jack Rabbits, but we never did, because Mother was scared we'd get rabbit fever (tularemia).

Clark County Loses a Treasured Resort

In addition to the Thomas family, several other families operated Lidy Hot Springs. These included Mr. and Mrs. Claude Bare and Jean's brother and wife, Robert and Maria Ellis. Dennis Sullivan was operating Lidys when he passed away in 1955. Soon after Den's death the Hot Springs was sold to Mr. and Mrs. Ed Wilson of Dubois.

As stated in the clipping from the *Salt Lake Tribune* dated June 20, 1962, Ed Wilson had big plans for the resort, including adding a golf course and a motel. These plans soon evaporated and the Wilsons turned their attention to their expanding mining operations. They covered over the swimming pool, tore down the dance hall, and removed other resort buildings. The Wilsons have utilized the water for power and constructed extensive processing facilities to supplement their mining interests.

Old timers in the region now mourn the loss of one of Clark County's best recreational centers. Fond memories remain of swimming in natural hot water, dancing to the tune of local bands, and socializing at a great recreational resort established by Jean's grandfather, at Lidy Hot Springs.

Lidy's Cemetery

In the field below Lidys is a cemetery, now completely unmarked. I believe the first burial was Arthur Lidy, the second child of Robert and Mary Lidy, who died at 2 years of age in 1901. Two other infants are buried there, a Thomas (no relation) buried in 1918 who was the child of a dry farmer and an Eastman child, whose father was a Gilmore freighter.

In the winter of 1905, John Moran was buried in the cemetery. He was a Congressional Medal of Honor winner. His citation is for "Gallantry in Action" at Seneca Mountain, Arizona on August 25, 1869 in a battle with Indians. Moran was a private in Company F, 8th US Cavalry. The citation was awarded March 3, 1870.

Moran was born in Ireland, date unknown. Pettite reports that Moran lived a mile above what is

Old-Time Celebration at
LIDY HOT SPRINGS
JULY 24th

RACES
STARTING AT 2:00 O'CLOCK

BOYS
6 to 9 years ....50 yd. dash
10 to 13 years ....75 yd. dash
14 to 18 years ......100 yd. dash

Free for all ....100 yd. dash

3-Legged Race .... Prize $1.00 and 50c

FAT MAN'S RACE

GIRLS
6 to 9 years ....50 yd. dash
10 to 13 years ....75 yd. dash
14 to 18 years ......100 yd. dash

Prizes ....50c and 25c

Women's Events

NAIL DRIVING CONTEST   POTATO PEELING CONTEST
EGG RACES   HOBBLE SKIRT RACE
Prizes Given

MILKING CONTEST

GREASED POLE ....Who Gets the $2.00

Catch the Greased Pig. He's Yours, if You Catch Him

Baseball Game
Free Swims to Winners

SWIMMING AND DIVING RACES

"Bring Your Picnic and Spend the Day in the Old Fashioned Way"

DANCE

STARTING AT 9:00 O'CLOCK   GOOD FLOOR! GOOD MUSIC

Lidys handbill for "Old-Time" celebration, July 24, 1936.

David Thomas at remnants of the cemetery at Lidy Hot Springs, 1998.
This is not the original location for the Lidy Hot Springs cemetery.

Lidy Hot Springs in 1998. None of the original structures exist.

The Salt Lake Tribune

Idaho TV
Page 10

Salt Lake City, Utah — Wednesday Morning — June 20, 1962

Page 25

Natural hot water and a twist in air currents give area of Lidy Hot Springs a Florida-like temperature in midst of cold Idaho winter and provide summer swimming facility. Resort is owned by E. J. Wilson, former rancher.

Lidy Hot Springs

Spa Boasts Outdoor Heating

By Carl E. Hayden
Tribune Staff Writer

LIDY HOT SPRINGS, IDAHO—Think cool.

THAT'S THE way to be comfortable in July.

But such small strategy, reversed, doesn't function as effectively in warming the long winters along the ridge of the Bitterroot Mountains that keep Montana from buckling into Idaho.

SO, LONG AS he had to live elevationally upstairs, E. J. (Ed) Wilson silently kept his eye on a haven until he could lay his hands on it.

One miserable winter he bobsledded hay in four-day round trips from Dubois on Highway 91 to the Reno Ranch on Birch Creek.

SNOW WAS four to six feet deep along the 27-mile course (which can now be traveled by oiled highway—State 28) except at the mouth of one canyon, midway, where there was barely enough white stuff to skid a sleigh.

now known as Lone Pine Lodge and died during the winter of 1905.

In 1907, Andrew Jackson Myers was buried in the cemetery. Myers was a good friend of Robert Lidy and had known Mary Lidy's first husband well. He had homesteaded on Myers Creek, which is named after him.

End of the "Free Range" in the West

"The horses were trailed to the cannery in Butte, Montana."

The year 1934 brought another major change to the ranching industry. This was the year the Taylor Grazing Act was passed by Congress and signed by President Franklin Roosevelt. This meant the end of the "Free Range" in the West and the beginning of regulated grazing allotments to reduce widespread "overgrazing."

Members of the Thomas family had several ranch holdings in Clark County, Idaho. My Dad ran cattle and over 100 head of horses. Two uncles were sheep ranchers, and the old home ranch was now run by Uncle Rees, who had large numbers of cattle and horses. All of the Thomas brothers were independent – and bashful. Rees refused to go to the Taylor Grazing office to sign up and claim his long-term rights to open range. Several others were not aggressive enough to compete with the more recent and better educated newcomers in the area, or they refused to cooperate with the new bureaucrats in the Department of Interior. As a result, the Thomas brothers all came up short on Taylor Grazing Rights and Rees was left with only a small piece of property on Lower Medicine Lodge. He later found that he could not graze on "his" traditional range, and since he had livestock with no place to go, he was forced to liquidate when prices were at the lowest point in years. Rees soon went broke and lost the home place.

One of the saddest days I remember on the ranch was when my brothers and I sat on the corral fence with my Dad and Mother, looking at several hundred head of surplus or "trespass" horses. These horses were rounded up by local ranchers, trailed to the cannery in Butte, Montana, and sold for $10 a head – mare with colt at the same price. We held back several good potential saddle horses, but from that day on, we were essentially out of the horse business. Mother said, *"We had to sell back to 25 head."*

Lidy's Hot Spring In Clark County Contains Much Historical Lore

By Wm. Stibal Pettite
(Part of a series on Eastern Idaho by Mr. Pettite, a former county probate judge and author of Memories of Market Lake, who lives in Fair Oaks, Calif.)

One of the many colorful spots in this part of Idaho, is the historic center between Dubois, in Clark County and Gilmore, in Lemhi County —Lidy's.

Lidy's, sometimes called Lidy Hot Springs, has also been named in other days, as The Springs, The Oasis or Sulphur Springs. The number is legend who have taken of the waters, either for pleasure or health.

However, about 70 years ago, Lidy's was known as a stage and freight center, serving the mines of Lemhi country. It was a haven for teamsters, horses and even a few steam engines!

Named for pioneer Robert S. Lidy, who died in 1927, it even had a small cemetery, since forgotten by today's travelers. Mr. Lidy, known in the early days as an excellent hunter and trapper, achieved a later skill as a prominent teamster. He came to Camas in 1890 after many years in the Tetons. In 1897, he wed an attractive widow, Mrs. Mary Neville Sullivan. Their infant son rests in the little cemetery.

Others buried here are John Moran, Andy Myers and two other infants, a Thomas baby and an Eastman baby. The Thomas baby was a child of a 1918 dry farmer, while the Eastman infant was a child of a Gilmore freighter.

Medal Of Honor

John Moran was famous in territorial days as the only person in the region who had been awarded the Congressional Medal of Honor, which is still a rare award in this day and age. He had been an enlisted man with the cavalry in the War between the States and later, with the same force in Arizona Territory. For outstanding service in Arizona's Indian campaigns he had been cited for the coveted honor.

Bearded and of medium size, Moran lived about a mile above what is now called Lone Pine Lodge. He died about the winter of 1905, a highly regarded man.

Andrew Jackson Myers, better known as Andy, rests near Moran. Myers was also part of the pioneer West, having been a government scout during various Indian campaigns. A trapper in his youth, he delighted in recalling how his old buffalo gun had saved him from death. He and a partner were attacked by six Indians in Montana and the partner died almost instantly. However Myers fired his trusty buffalo gun — the blast immediately deceased four of the attackers, leaving their two associates to depart in haste.

Myers, who was small and rather thin, also had a beard. He had a ranch on Crooked Creek and was also associated with Michael F. Sullivan Sr. and Bob Lidy, whom he had known for many years. He died about two years after Moran, having been cared for in his declining years by the later family.

Callison Singer

Another fixture at Lidy's was Callison Free Singer, who purchased the Myers place on Crooked Creek. Before this he had operated the Abshier ranch for many years, selling it to the Shear Brothers. Mr. Singer, a tall, slender man, known for his courtly manner, was noted for his ability to make pets of any living animal. He even had a pet snake. Along in years, Singer often expressed the desire to be buried near his pals Myers and Moran. However, after the sale of his home ranch to the Colson Family, a nephew from Springfield, Missouri arrived and claimed him.

One of the more exciting events of yesteryear took place about 1900 when another character at Lidy's, Antone Scalzo, better known as Tommy Sun, decided to secure a wife, or at least a housekeeper, for bachelors Singer and Myers. Tommy, who had a small place on Grouse Creek above Sullivans, was an interesting chap, less than five feet tall. To make up for a lack of stature, he was always trying to be helpful.

Six Shooter Sal

At this time Six Shooter Sal was living on a small place at Sand Hole, near where Hamer now is. (A noted woman in her own right, Sidionie Emelle, was probably the first advocate of "Woman's Liberation" and was also known as a whiz with a gun.) Tommy Sun made quite a pitch about his bachelor friends near Lidy's and persuaded Sal to ride over to meet the grizzled ranchers. After a two day journey, with Sal trailing her cow in anticipation of finding a large ranch at the end of Tommy Sun's rainbow, she was quickly disappointed to find only a few worn buildings and no welcome at all from her "new husbands" — thus venting her wrath and a number of bullets — at Tommy Sun.

Singer made her stay at Lidy's, where she set up camp under the stars, with her cow for company. Soon she was joined by her adult daughter, Marguerite, who also went gunning for Mr. Sun, who by now had hid out to escape their wrath as well as the wrath of his bachelor friends.

For about a week, Sidonie and Marguerite rode horseback, with their cow trailing along, rifles ready, to assassinate poor little matchmaker Tommy Sun, who safely had departed for greener pastures.

Pioneer Sullivans

Among other prominent settlers and natives of the area were Margaret Sullivan, born in 1890 in a log cabin on a ranch on Warm Creek. Margaret, who knew many of the first pioneers, wed Joe R. Lingo of a well known Camas and Eagle Rock family. Mr. Lingo worked for the Gilmore Mining Co. at one time. Her brothers Warren and Lee were born at Lidy's when it was called Sulphur Springs in 1887 and 1891. Another brother,

Den, was manager of Lidy Hot Springs when he passed away in 1955. Older brother, M.F., was noted as a political sage and historian. Their step-dad was Mr. Lidy, their own father being buried near Warm Spring Creek in 1893. A daughter of Mr. and Mrs. Lidy, Gertrude Ellis, lives not far from the once famous site of Lidy's.

Perhaps the ghosts of Moran, Myers, Singer, Lidy, Sun and Six Shooter Sal still gather there to recall the events of long ago. With so much history, there should be much to talk about.

UPPER LEFT—Note the old wagon wheels and fast stepping horses in this early-day photo showing Bessie Sullivan, Gertrude Lidy, Margaret Sullivan and Charlie Collier at Lidy's. Upper right, a steam engine, used 65 years ago, to haul ore wagons from Gilmore to Dubois. The promotion did not work out because of bad roads, causing a return to old-fashioned horse teams. Bob Lidy, John Peterson and Charlie Collier are among those shown at Lidy's. At bottom, driver Jim Wells, between team changes, on his fast stage from Dubois to Hahn and Birch Creek; changing horses every 20 miles. Shown at the Lidy rest stop are John Weaver, George Webster, Frank Reno, Bob Lidy, Pete Tullgren, Gertrude and Maggie Lidy, Mrs. Henry Kaufman with Mildred and Henry Jr., Rowl Denny, Gene Miller and

Chapter 4 | Mack Ellis and Gertrude Lidy Elope

"Periodic trips by horse and buggy."

Jean's father Mack Stalker Ellis was born May 11, 1897, at Small, Idaho. He was the son of John Daniels "JD" Ellis and Alvira Tolitha Stalker, JD's second wife. He had 3 brothers, 3 sisters, one half-brother and one half-sister. Mack's father had a ranch on the lower end of Medicine Lodge Creek. The Post Office of Small, Idaho was located on the Ellis Ranch for several years.

Mary Gertrude Lidy was born December 29, 1897, at Lidy Hot Springs. On January 1, 1916, when she had just turned 18, she agreed to elope with Mack Ellis. Mack had been courting Gertrude by making periodic team and buggy trips from his Father's ranch to Lidy Hot Springs, about 10 miles to the west. They used that same team and buggy to elope, driving the 64 miles from Lidys to Idaho Falls as fast as they could, where *"Mack's mother, Alvira Ellis, stood up for us,"* Gertrude said.

> *"We were married by the minister of her church. She was a Presbyterian. My Mother was a good Catholic, so when we got home we were married again by the Catholic priest since she thought a Presbyterian wedding may not be valid."*

Early History of the Crooked Creek Ranch

Mack and Gertrude spent much of their life operating a ranch on Crooked Creek in Clark County, Idaho. Their first exposure to the area came when the couple filed for a homestead which was patented in 1919. County records show several other homesteads in the area which carry names familiar to the Ellis/Thomas families:

Claimant	Patent Date
Michael F. (Frank) Sullivan	9-7-16
Michael F. (Frank) Sullivan	5-2-17
M. F. Berryman	5-2-17

Claimant	Patent Date
Lee Sullivan	6-6-17
W. A. Colson	6-6-17
Hiram Speerling	3-26-18
Daniel W. Thomas	5-24-19
Watson A. Turnbull	9-20-19
Dennis R. Sullivan	12-4-19
David A. Reel	12-13-19
John E. Weaver	6-8-20
Irene S. Campbell	10-27-22
Robert S. Lidy	12-14-22
Mary N. Lidy	12-14-23
Otto Bezold	8-7-30

Since most of these homesteads were dry farms without access to water rights they soon had to sell or abandon their places. Mack and Gertrude lived on their homestead for three years. During that time they had a baby girl that died and a son, Weldon. The young couple worked hard but they could not make a living on the dry farm so they moved to Idaho Falls to operate a small dairy farm north of town. During the next nine years, while they lived in Idaho Falls, three more children were born, Jean, Lois and Robert.

Jean's grandmother, Mrs. Mary (Sullivan) Lidy passed away on June 10, 1927, after a lingering illness. The same year Mr. Lidy was killed in an auto accident. The car tipped over on the road from Dubois to Lidy Hot Springs and both occupants were killed.

Two years later, Mack and Gertrude Ellis took over the ranching operations on Crooked Creek. The family now had the water rights for the entire creek as well as grazing permits on the surrounding public lands. But the Depression was in full swing creating hard times for the family. Also, there was no telephone, electricity or plumbing on the ranch.

Crooked Creek Ranch, 1970s. Homesteaded by Michael Sullivan. Owned by Robert and Mary Lidy 1897 -1927 and Mack and Gertrude Ellis 1929 - 1981.

Crooked Creek Ranch, 2004. Now owned and managed by Nature Conservancy.

Home place, Crooked Creek Ranch. Unknown date.

Robert Lidy on his steam tractor, Crooked Creek dry farm. Circa 1915.

Robert Lidy and daughter "Bessie" working Crooked Creek dry farm. About 1915.

Mary Katherine "Bessie" Sullivan (Turnbull), Mary Gertrude "Gertie" Lidy (Ellis)
on Blackie, Margaret "Maggie" Sullivan (Lingo) on Peggy, and
Charles Collier on Bird. Circa 1910.

The Post Office which served the ranches in the Crooked Creek and Lidy Hot Springs area was Winsper, Idaho. This Post Office was opened May 10, 1915 on the Homestead patented by John Winsper in 1913. John's wife served as Postmaster. In addition to the post office, the Winspers had a gas pump and a modest store. In 1939, after Mr. and Mrs. Winsper passed away, the post office was moved to the John Klein Ranch on Blue Creek. John and Gladys Klein operated the service until it was moved to Lidy Hot Springs in 1947. The office at one time served 200 patrons. A one-room school house was located at Winsper from 1915 to 1923. The Winsper Post Office closed after WWII and mail was then delivered from Dubois to a mail box on the dirt road about 10 miles from the Crooked Creek Ranch.

Most families moved out of the Crooked Creek area due to drought and the depression of the 30s. Neighbors who survived were the Bezolds to the north on Myers Creek and the Sullivans on Warm Creek about 5 miles to the east.

Stalker Roots

Mack Stalker Ellis was born at home on JD's ranch at Small, Idaho. He was named Stalker after his mother Alvira's family, who were also early pioneers in Southeastern Idaho. Alvira's mother, Ortencia Howard Smith Stalker, was of Puritan stock, of which one earlier ancestor was a general in the American Revolution. Alvira's father, Alexander Stalker, was born in Scotland, the son of Robert and Jeanette Tanch Stalker.

Lois Ellis Waring, Mack's sister, remembers her Stalker grandparents in a printing of *"Amanda's Journal."*

"The Stalker family were Presbyterians, but Alexander became interested in Mormonism, and decided to leave his homeland and go to Utah. He made the long trip [from Scotland], seven weeks in a sailing vessel, as a ship's carpenter."

Alexander met and married Ortencia in Farmington, Utah. In 1860, they moved to Franklin, Ida-

ho. They had fourteen children. More details on the family are contained in Marianne Shipley's book, *"A View from Here."*

Ellis Roots

Mack's father, JD was a first generation American of Welch decent. JD was born to John Francis and Anne Daniels Ellis on September 29, 1860, in either Salt Lake City or Smithfield, Utah. His parents had arrived in the United States on May 23, 1856 on the *Samuel Curling*. Their crossing from Liverpool, England took 34 days to complete, and it is probable that they met on the ship. Anne Daniels came from Llanpumpsaint, South Wales and John Francis was from Llanbedr, Gwynedd, North Wales, located on the shores of Tremadoc Bay near Harloch Castle. (*Ellis Family History* by Eugene Ellis. Undated.)

JD acquired some schooling in Malad, Idaho where the family had moved around 1871. In 1874, at the age of 14, he went to work hauling mining supplies with wagon teams from Corinne, Utah to Virginia City, Montana, freighting ore with oxen on the return trip. These trips to the Montana silver lode provided JD with the opportunity to observe the lush grass growing in the Medicine Lodge Valley, and in 1881, at 21 years of age, he became one of the first of the pioneers to move into that part of the Idaho Territory.

JD had one of the original filings that in 1883 resulted in the distribution of Medicine Lodge Creek water rights. In addition to JD's 146 inches, the other water right filings in 1883 were Dennis Small, Pyke Brothers, Sam K. Clark, T. A. and R. B. Robson, J. W. Spiers, John and Elizabeth Fayle and Benjamin D. Thomas.

JD married Elizabeth Schopp (1886-1945) in 1886, and before they divorced they had two children, Philip Daniel (1887-1933) and Annie Laurie (1889-1949). Annie Laurie is the first connection by marriage to the Thomas family. She grew up as a neighbor to the Benjamin Thomas's. On September 3, 1907, Annie married Benjamin's son, William Henry Thomas. Annie and Henry had a

JD and Alvira Ellis. Medicine Lodge. Unknown date.

Back Seat: Matilda (Waylett) Thomas, Gertrude Lidy, and
Mary (Sullivan) Lidy. Front Seat: Mabel Thomas, Tish Thomas, and Unidentified.
Standing: George Thomas and Mack Ellis. Lidy Hot Springs, 1915.

Unidentified, Dan Thomas, Gertrude Lidy, and Mack Ellis,
just before Gertrude and Mack's elopement. Lidy Hot Springs, 1915.

Mack and Gertrude Ellis, with Jean and Weldon. 1921.

Mack and Gertrude Ellis, Crooked Creek Ranch. 1951.

The Warm Creek School, established in 1929.
Located between the Sullivan Ranch and the Ranger Station.
Heart Mountain in the background. The school closed in 1947.

daughter named Phyllis Leticia who married Roy Laird.

On August 15, 1893, JD married Alvira Tolitha Stalker at Franklin, Idaho. Alvira was born October 24, 1868, and grew up in a large family at Franklin, where she attended school, and then went to the Presbyterian Academy at Logan, Utah. After finishing her schooling, she taught several terms in the Preston, Idaho area.

JD and Alvira had eight children, Bessie Lisle (Davis), John Howard, Mack Stalker, Elias (who died within a few hours), Leila Anne (Waring), Francis Gordon, Helen (who died within a few hours) and Fremont. After Alvira died on May 17, 1931, JD married his third wife Martha Kent.

In 1906, JD Ellis and Benjamin Thomas were part of a group of stockholders in the Medicine Lodge Telephone Company, which became a line from Dubois to W. A. Colson's ranch and west for 30 miles. Bill Ellis (JD's brother's son) and his wife Mayme operated the telephone system until it was sold to the Government in 1962. Our ring on the ranch was three shorts and a long.

In 1912, JD bought a home in Idaho Falls and in 1916 he built the Ellis Apartments, which were a historic landmark in Idaho Falls until torn down a few years ago.

Lidy and Sullivan Roots

Gertrude Ellis' father, Robert "Bob" Seamon Lidy was born in Ohio in 1865/66. He spent some time in Butte, Montana and later became a teamster in Idaho, hauling freight from Gilmore to Dubois. (For more details on Bob Lidy's origins, see *Appendix C*.) He was working for the Michael (Mike) Sullivan Ranch on Warm Creek when Mike Sullivan died from a gunshot wound he received at Rexburg during a dispute over a foot race (July 23, 1893). Mr. Sullivan was only 35 at the time he died and he left a wife (Mary Catherine Neville Sullivan) and five children. Four years later, February 10, 1897, Bob Lidy married the Sullivan widow and took over the ranching enterprise.

The five children born to Mike and Mary Catherine Sullivan were Mary Catherine (Bessie Turnbull), Warren, Den, Margaret (Lingo) and Lee. Mary Gertrude (Jean's mother) was born after Bob Lidy married the Sullivan widow. They lived most of the remaining years at Lidy Hot Springs.

The Warm Creek Country School

"By horseback, wagon or by sleigh."

A big concern for the Ellis family after they moved to the Crooked Creek Ranch was education for the children. There was no school within 35 miles and no transportation except by horseback or carriage. Consequently, Mack Ellis and Frank Sullivan from the neighboring ranch went to the County seat in Dubois to request that the County open a school on Warm Creek. Some funds were available from railroad land-grants so the County authorized an unorganized school district for the area.

The Warm Creek School opened in the fall of 1929 with six students in a renovated building on an abandoned dry farm between the Ranger Station and the Sullivan Ranch. The six students included the four Ellis children (Weldon, Jean, Lois and Robert) and two Sullivan boys (Franklin and Tom). At one time there were 13 students in the school. The Ellis children usually walked or rode horseback to school and went by sleigh when the snow was deep. School started at eight and was supposed to close at four, but sometimes lasted until dark. Four of the five teachers that taught at Warm Creek boarded with the Ellis family. Jean stated, *"Mom and Dad might not agree with everything the teacher did but they felt parents should always support the teacher."*

The school on Warm Creek closed in 1937 with four students: Robert and Lois Ellis and Franklin and Tom Sullivan. Jean was sent to board with her Aunt Margaret Lingo in Idaho Falls for her junior year in High School. *"When I was a senior, Mother was pregnant with Lamar, so Robert, Lois, Mother and I rented a house in Idaho Falls to continue our education."* Lamar was born on October 26, 1937.

Back: Unidentified, Jean Ellis. Front: Unidentified, Lois Ellis.

Weldon Ellis with the mailbox he built for the Crooked Creek Ranch.

Lamar Ellis (right) with cousin Danny Moore, Lois' first child.

Lamar and Sandy Ellis wedding photo. Lenora Hubbard (Sandy's Mother),
Sandy, Lamar, Gertrude and Mack Ellis. August 27, 1958.

Reunion of some of the Warm Creek students.
Gerald Thomas, Jay and Lois Ellis Hawker, Gene Lingo Harwell,
Jean Ellis Thomas, Dorothy Turnbull Officer, and Bonnie and Guy Lingo.
Laughlin, Nevada. 1999.

Gertrude Ellis with four of her children. Lois, Jean, Weldon, Robert. 1984.

Chapter 5 | Life on Crooked Creek

"We rode to school on the runners of the sleigh."

Diary of a Rancher's Daughter

In 1933, Jean Ellis kept a short diary while the family was living on the Crooked Creek Ranch. Much can be revealed about life at that time from one or two lines in this diary. Times were tough but the diary does not reflect the hardships or the worry of the parents. Jean was 13 on January 27, *"mother and Aunt Margaret made a devils food cake."* Weldon was 15 on July 21. *"Mother made ice cream and Lois made Weldon a birthday cake. Weldon caught a rabbit."* (The cat ate Weldon's rabbit on July 28). Robert was 11 on September 30. *"Mr. Allen came down to help head the grain. Snow and Alma were here for dinner. Steve [Green] is working on his thresher."* *"Lois is 10 years old."* (Dec 29). *"Right now she is making candy."*

The most frequent visitors were the Lingo's (Aunt Margaret and Uncle Rudd) who were living at Lidy Hot Springs. Cousins Gene, Guy and Roy stayed over at the ranch occasionally and came up to the Warm Creek School. Of course, there were many interactions at school and during hay or grain harvest with the Sullivan family on Warm Creek.

School was held in a one-room log cabin which was originally the Reel homestead about 3 miles from the ranch. The Ellis children usually go by sleigh in the winter and wagon in the summer – or they walk. Mr. Lougee is the school teacher.

Jan 12 -- *"Gene and I rode to school on the runners of the sleigh."*

Jan 19 -- *"Uncle Frank brought Tom and Franklin to school today."*

Jan 30 -- *"We got our report cards. We almost froze coming home. We couldn't see the road."*

Feb 3 -- *"I wrote my story for the Salt Lake Tribune. Gene wrote hers too."* (Note: both Jean Ellis and Gene Lingo succeeded in getting several articles published in the **Salt Lake Tribune Junior Edition**. (This was quite an accomplishment for country students.)

Feb 6 -- *"We had a terrible blizzard. We did not go to school."*

Feb 12 -- *"Gene, Lois and I rode 3 miles up to the Lunds."*

Feb Memo -- *"Roy and Weldon froze their feet. Uncle Den froze his nose."*

Mar 8 -- *"Gene got her story printed in the Tribune."*

Mar 24 -- *"Gene and I rode down to the Springs (10 miles)."*

Apr 11 -- *"We went over to see Mrs. Lougee and the baby."*

Apr 17 -- *"Lougee's car broke down and he didn't get to school."*

Apr 25 -- *"Gene and I took our State Exams in Physiology."*

May 1 -- *"Mr. Lougee and all us school kids went on a hike."*

May 17 -- *"Gene and I went down to Aunt Marian's to practice our duet."*

May 18 -- *"We went to Dubois with Uncle Rudd to the Commencement. Gene and I played our duet."*

Jean, High School. 1935.

Jean with Lamar (brother). Howard Ellis Ranch. 1938.

Gene Lingo with Lois and Jean Ellis. Crooked Creek Ranch. 1938.

Bessie Sullivan, Jean, Gene Lingo, Lois. Idaho Falls, Idaho. 1938.

Jean. San Jose, California, while attending summer school at San Jose State. 1940.

Jean with her 2nd Grade Class at Preston, Idaho, 1942.
Young David Fitson, on Jean's left, next to his favorite teacher.

Sept 18 -- *"First day of school. Mr. Lougee let us out at recess."*

Sept 22 -- *"Weldon got through raking and took my place in haying so I could go to school."*

Oct 5 -- *"Gene and I sent a story into the Tribune Junior."*

Oct 12 -- *"Started to thresh here at noon. I stayed out of school to help Mom."*

Oct 26 -- *"We got our stories published in the Salt Lake Tribune."*

Nov 1 -- *"Mrs. Clark (County Supt) and Connie came to visit the school."*

Nov 15 -- *"Mr. Lougee took us to see the cave northwest of Dubois. We visited the Dubois school."*

Nov 29 -- *"My story was published in the Tribune"*

Dec 2 -- *"We went to a show in Dubois. Marlene Dietrich in **Song of Songs**."*

Dec 9-11 -- *"Staying at Aunt Bessie's in Idaho Falls."*

Dec 18 -- *"A foot of snow. We went to school in the sleigh."*

Dec 21 -- *"Tommie and Franklin gave the whole school an Eversharp."*

There was lots of static on the radio and sometimes it faded out. Radio programs mentioned include:

Death Valley Days
Cecil and Sally
Myrt and Marge
The Utah Buckaroos
Arizona Wranglers

Many of the farm animals and pets had names:

Jan 28 -- *"Winnie had a little calf. It was red."*

Feb 19 -- *"Jersey had a white calf with brown ears."*

Mar 1 -- *"June got down in a snowdrift and couldn't get out. Weldon and Roy had to help her out."*

Mar 30 -- *"Dad's pet pig Nose took sick."*

Apr 20 -- *"Lois' cat caught a mouse."*

Apr 30 -- *"Muley is raising Spot and Bally's calves."*

May 27 -- *"Derrel went by riding Blue Rocket."*

May 28 -- *"Old Bob Tail had eleven little pigs."*

May 29 -- *"I named my little pig Clarabell."*

May 31 -- *"Clarabell is sick. She had Black Teeth. Den was here. He cut Clarabell's teeth off."*

June 1 -- *"Clarabell died last night."*

June 5 -- *"Lois caught a squirrel."*

June 8 -- *"One of the old sows pigs wasn't getting enough to eat so we brought it in and fed it. I call it Sarah."*

June 17 -- *"Lois named her colt Midge."*

June 19 -- *"Lois lost her squirrel."*

June 29 -- *"Lois buried Sarah."*

July 24 -- *"Nose's sister has 3 little pigs."*

July 28 -- *"The cat ate Weldon's rabbit."*

Sept 8 -- *"The hawk tried to get one of Longtail's pigs."*

Dec 7 -- *"Our pullets are laying."*

Ranch work and miscellaneous comments (Crooked Creek froze solid in the winter so no water reached the ranch):

Jean. School Teacher, Pocatello, Idaho. 1943.

Jean. Pocatello, Idaho. 1943.

Jan 14 -- *"Dad went after water."* (At Warm Creek.)

Feb 7 -- *"Dad had to go to the middle ranch after water."*

Feb 16 -- *"Mr. Campbell came down to help Dad kill a pig."*

Feb 25 -- *"Dad cut all the boys' hair. The sheepherder came to get his hair cut."*

Mar 29 -- *"Campbells and Dad dehorned the cattle."*

Apr 17 -- *"Dad went to work on the ditch."*

Apr 22 -- *"Dad started to harrow. Weldon fixed fence."*

Apr 23 -- *"We haven't got a drop of water."*

Apr 29 -- *"Frank and Den went up to Campbells to see the horse buyers that are there. Dad cleaned the ditch and started to plow."*

May 6 -- *"We got word today that Uncle Phil died."*

May 22 -- *"Weldon went riding [for cattle] with Glen, Ed, Bezolds and Darrel."*

May 24 -- *"Weldon and Mother fixed fence."*

June 9 -- *"Dad and Weldon went up the canyon to work on the ditch."*

July 1 -- *"Dad turned the water on the lower field."*

July 19 -- *"The wind blew all day so we stopped haying."*

Aug 14 -- *"Mother washed. We canned berries."*

Aug 31 -- *"Robert and Lois herded the cows."*

Sept 3 -- *"Mr. Allen wanted Dad to bind his grain."*

Sept 12 -- *"Weldon started to mow."*

Sept 20 -- *"Robert and I stayed out of school to help hay."*

Sept 29 -- *"Mr. Marlow [Game Warden] is here to keep the antelope out of the field."*

Oct 12 -- *"They started to thresh here at noon."*

Oct 15 -- *"Dad and the boys are digging spuds."*

Oct 21 -- *"The ditch froze dry."*

Nov 5 -- *"Hop and George [Thomas] were here to measure the hay. Gene and I went down to the Springs with them and were we teased."*

Nov 19 -- *"Weldon and Roy got a load of stumps."*

Dec 4 -- *"Mother and Dad went down to vote. The water is still froze."*

Dec 5 -- *"Mother took the cows and horses to Warm Creek [for water]."*

Dec 12 -- *"We have been hauling water for 10 days."*

An interesting notation was made by Jean on May 5, 1935:

> *"I became acquainted with the Thomas boys. They sure are nice and full of fun. We went swimming."*

He Remembered His Favorite Teacher.

> *"Miss Calamity Jane at the bombardier dance."*

After graduating from High School in Idaho Falls, Jean Ellis entered the Southern Branch of the University of Idaho (now Idaho State Univer-

The Salt Lake Tribune

Salt Lake City, Utah, Thursday Morning, July 15, 1943

Stampede Queen Boosts Ticket Sale

Riding right up to the city hall steps, Jean Ellis, queen of the Victory Stampede rodeo next Friday, Saturday and Sunday at North Bannock fairgrounds, sells tickets to Pocatello Mayor C. D. (Dinty) Moore. Receipts will provide recreation for Pocatello army air base personnel. (U S A A F photo.)

Jean. Victory Stampede Rodeo Queen. *The Salt Lake Tribune*, July 15, 1943.

sity). Lois and Robert stayed with her in a rented apartment. Jean cooked the meals and supervised the household. After graduating with a teacher's certificate in 1940 and summer school in California, she signed on to teach first and second grades at Preston, Idaho. This teaching contract, as was common at the time for single females, carried the stipulation that, *"The marriage of a woman teacher during the school year shall be regarded both as a violation and a termination of this contract."*

Jean enjoyed her first teaching experiences at Preston, Idaho. Many years later, one of her second graders (David Fiston) finally located Jean by tracing down Jean's Mother at the Crooked Creek Ranch. He eventually reached Jean by telephone in 1977, 36 years after he was a student at Preston. *"I wanted to talk to my favorite teacher and arrange a visit if possible."* He said he lived in Orem, Utah. Jean informed him that we would be going through that area in the summer. On July 2, 1977 Jean had a reunion with David Fiston – now grown into manhood with a prosperous business and holding the title of former "Mr. Utah." He still remembered his favorite teacher.

After 2 years at Preston, Jean accepted a contract to return to Pocatello as World War II was raging in Europe and the Pacific. There was an active Air Force Base at Pocatello and Jean signed up for part-time work after school hours at the Base. She also served as an USO Hostess at the Base.

The Pocatello newspaper reported, *"In March [1943], Miss Ellis was titled Miss Calamity Jane at a bombardier dance at Pocatello army base for her comely appearance in western togs."* The fighter group at the Air Base also painted the name "Jean" on a P-47 in her honor and later that year another news release announced that, *"Jean Ellis, Pocatello elementary school teacher has been named rodeo queen by the fair board."*

In addition to all of her other activities, Jean signed up for flying lessons and, caught up in the spirit of the times, she decided to get directly involved in the war effort by joining the Navy Waves. The orders read:

"You have this date enlisted in the U.S. Naval Reserve, Class V-10, for a period during the present war and for six months thereafter, or until such earlier time as the Congress by concurrent resolution or the President by proclamation may designate. You are hereby assigned to the Director of Naval Reserve Officer Procurement, 117 Marion Street, Settle, Washington where your service and health records are being retained."

This was the busy and popular young lady I called on for a date when I returned from the Pacific in May 1945.

Nature Conservancy Buys Crooked Creek Ranch

"A visit after the house was torn down."

The Mack Ellis family lived on the Crooked Creek Ranch for many years. Mack passed away on August 10, 1967, and Mrs. Ellis stayed on the ranch with Lamar assisting with the management until 1981. Mrs. Ellis then moved to Monteview, Idaho where she stayed wit her son Robert and his wife Maria. Later, with the help of her daughter Lois she was moved to the Good Samaritan Village in Idaho Falls. Mary Gertrude Ellis passed away on August 19, 1994. Mack and Gertrude were honest, hard-working pioneer ranchers. They raised a good family and left an important imprint on the history of Clark County, Idaho.

The Crooked Creek Ranch and the associated BLM, Forest and State grazing allotments were sold by the Ellis family in 1980. The sale involved Mary Gertrude Ellis, James Lamar Ellis and his wife Sandra, and the children of Mack and Gertrude (Weldon, Jean, Robert, Lois and Lamar). Lamar retained some dry land south of the main ranch. Eugene and Mary Place made the initial purchase. The property was later sold to Reed Ricks.

The money from the original sale was largely used by Mrs. Ellis to support her move to the rest home in Idaho Falls. She maintained her independence until she passed away.

Jean. Victory Stampede Rodeo Queen. Pocatello, Idaho. 1943.

Jean. Victory Stampede Rodeo Queen. Pocatello, Idaho. 1943

The Nature Conservancy bought the home ranch consisting of 2,600 acres of deeded land and 35,000 acres of grazing allotments on State and Federal Lands in 2001. The Conservancy plans to *"Run the ground as a cattle ranch... with a great opportunity to protect open space and help wildlife in the region."* (News Release dated August 23, 2001.)

As the attached photos show, our family visited the Crooked Creek Ranch each time we returned to Idaho. It was very sad to see the Ranch house gradually deteriorate and to visit the site after the house was burned down. Many exciting and nostalgic memories of Crooked Creek will always remain with us.

Thomas family visit to the Crooked Creek Ranch house, summer, 1958.
Jean, Marianne, Peggy, and David.

The abandoned Crooked Creek Ranch house after sale to Nature Conservancy.
Jean, Marianne (Thomas) Shipley, Ethan Vickery, Amy O'Neal, David, and
Gary Shipley. June 28, 1991.

Jean examines burnt remains of Crooked Creek Ranch house.
August 28, 2007.

Chapter 6 | Old-Timers, Pioneers, and Tales

"I'm going to go up and kill him!"

Duel to the Death

"Bob Bogus and Ed Drounds, men in the employ of the Clark and Denning Co. of Dubois, fought a duel to the death on the Clark and Denning ranch Sunday afternoon. Drounds was killed instantly and Bogus was brought to Idaho Falls and died in the General Hospital Monday morning."

"From word that was received from Dubois, Drounds was the aggressor and shot Bogus as he was climbing through a wire fence, using a heavy rifle and sending the bullet through the body of Bogus, wounding the man so that he was unable to lift himself from the ground, but managed to roll over, pull his gun and shoot Drounds between the eyes, blowing out his brains."

"The men fought over a remark that Bogus is alleged to have made to the effect that Drounds was the man guilty of stealing sheep from Clark and Denning Co. Drounds is said to have stated that he would make Bogus pay for his words. Bogus left Dubois Sunday about noon in a car with Chas. McCabe for the ranch intending to look after some trapping. He left the car when he reached the ranch and started on foot across the country toward a group of men and while crawling through the fence, Drounds rode up to him, shooting and inflecting the would that proved fatal."

"A number of men were standing near and one of them, Den Sullivan, rode to the home of Jim Denning to give the alarm. J. K. Clark of the Ranch Company of Clark and Denning hurried to the scene of the shooting and found the body of Drounds lying in the sagebrush, and with Bogus desperately wounded lying by the fence where he had fallen. The men who had witnessed the shooting had for some reason made no effort to assist the wounded man."

"Bogus had been with the Clark and Denning Co. a number of years, first as a herder, and was employed as a foreman when shot." (From **Idaho Register,** October 23, 1917.)

I asked Dad to tell me about this shooting:

"Hop and I were bringing these calves down to the corral after the roundup. We left the other cowboys up by the Stringham place. Bogus came by in his old car without a top. He had a pint of liquor on his car seat. He asked where Drounds was. I told him we just left him with the other cowboys. He says, 'I'm going up and kill him!' We never thought much about it. Then somebody came by in a car and scared Hop's horse. He broke loose and ran up the canyon. He was caught later with the saddle turned under his belly – big long-legged sorrel."

"Jim Denning said that Bogus and Drounds had stole some sheep from him and took them over into Montana. Bogus got drunk and claimed Drounds had squealed on him."

Mother added, *"Oh, that was awful. Mrs. Drounds with those 8 kids. They lived in that one-room house on Indian Creek and they were very poor. The kids would all come to my school the year Dan and I*

Byron welcomes Art Briggs to Lidy Hot Springs, July, 1936.
He stopped for a hot bath.

Weldon and Lamar Ellis. Feb, 1940.

were married. And, you know, those little kids had never been taught to wash. Their hands were just scaly. Dan made a bench at the school to hold a bucket of water and a wash basin. I had all the kids wash. And, when one of the Drounds boys washed his hands, he showed them to me, 'Look, Mrs. Thomas, I never knew my hands looked like that.'"

An Old Safety Pin

On February 8, 1946, Jean and I started toward Lidy Hot Springs in our 1939 Nash when the weather turned bad – snow and a blizzard. Our only hope for reaching Lidys was to stay overnight in Dubois and catch a ride the next morning with Bill Ellis as he carried the mail in his old WWII command car. I made the following notes in my journal:

"The ride to Lidys was really rough. Bill's old command car dug through the snow in low and compound most of the day. Took out through the sage whenever the road was drifted bad. Bill told us about going up and getting Art Briggs out of the hills. It seems the old fellow had frozen his feet and ran out of food and fuel. He had not eaten for about 30 days. Bill says he was not out of his mind at all, even though he was wasted away to practically nothing. Briggs gave bill and Hop an old safety pin, 'To remember him by,' and told them to present their bill to 'the Briggs Estate.' The old fellow lived a few days in the hospital in Idaho Falls before he died."

Goat's Milk and Mountain Water

"All I ever saw him drink was whiskey and coffee."

C. J. Rumbar, known as "Shamrock," was a colorful character in Clark County. Several version of his life circulated among old timers in the area. Here's an account my brother Daniel gave:

"In 1938, my wife Betty was cooking for my folks at Lidys. It was the year before we were married. We had gone to Idaho Falls for supplies. Betty was left alone to take care of anyone who might come by and want a swim. She heard a noise. She opened the front door and there stood old Shamrock. You can imagine her surprise and fear, never having seen him before. What a character! He had one leg cut off just below the hip; he used a homemade crutch; his hair was long and braided, wadded in a ball, with a big red handkerchief tied around his head, and an old cowboy hat on top of that. He had a Van Dyke beard and mustache and an old leather vest. He was driving a team with an old beat up wagon."

"Later that year there was a forest fire in Blue Canyon. I went to help fight the fire. The Forest Service had hired Art Briggs and Shamrock to cook for the firefighters."

"Boy, Sham and Briggs were sure good cooks. Served mostly beans and potatoes and argued with each other all the time. Shamrock would tell us stories by the hour – about all the men he had killed by beating them to the draw. He rode a mule to herd his sheep. He would just hop up to the mule, grab the saddle horn, and a little jump and he was in the saddle. He always carried an old 45-70 civil war rifle, the single shot with the big hammer. All in all he was a tough character. One day he slapped me on the back and said, 'Young man, if you want to live forever, drink goat's milk and mountain water.' All I ever saw him drink was whiskey and coffee."

My brother-in-law Weldon Ellis told me:

"Sham was colorful – different. He had lost a leg riding a freight train in Texas. He had a crutch and a leather sling. He had long hair tied up in a red bandana. He claimed he was half-Cherokee and half-Irish."

Main Street, Dubois, Idaho. 1940.

Palm Cafe and Fremont Cash Store, Dubois, Idaho. 1940.

"Shamrock's son Billy used to visit him once in a while. One day when Sham came back from Rigby, his son was missing. Sham hired Ed Campbell to search in his car but they could not find Billy. He came to the ranch and offered me $2.00 to help look for Billy by horseback. I searched, but expected to find Billy dead. As it turned out, I came very close to where they eventually found him. I don't know who found the body, but the dog was still with him. Everybody got the impression that Sham had got mad at Billy and killed him with his crutch. Billy was retarded. The Forest crew dug the grave. He was buried by a Juniper tree in very rocky ground so they couldn't dig a very deep grave. Sham was later buried in the same place. However, there is a grave marker for C. J. Rumbar in the Dubois Cemetery."

Jean recorded in her Diary:

Apr 3 (1933) -- *"Billy and the sheep are lost. Sham hired Weldon to help look for him. They think poor Billy might be dead."*

Apr 4 -- *"Billy Shamrock was found dead this morning. Heart failure I guess. It certainly is a shame."*

Apr 6 -- *"Billy was buried on Shamrock's land in a beautiful spot under a tree. Mother and Dad went to the funeral."*

The Land of Opportunity

"Then I could get the rest of the hides real cheap!"

The old man walked up to me. He seemed to want to talk. I was working for the Soil Conservation District, preparing a topog map. It was 1946.

"I just paid my taxes here in the courthouse. They told me I paid more taxes than any one else in Fremont County. America is truly the land of opportunity. I migrated to America from the old county when I was

16. I worked at various jobs before I found out about the Homestead Act. I filed for a homestead on Warm River.

"Before long, I found a wife. Times were hard. My wife got pregnant and she needed a belt to hold up her stomach. I had no money for a belt, but I got to thinking. 'America is the land of opportunity. We have made it so far so there must be a way.'"

"So I got in my old Model-T Ford, left the wife home, and drove to Ashton. I pulled into the service station and told the owner I needed some gas. 'Go ahead and fill her,' he said. I pumped up the gas server and drained the contents into my tank. When I went to pay the man, I reached into my hip pocket and said, "Gosh darn it! I must have left my wallet home.' 'Oh, that's OK,' he said, 'you can pay me the next time you come to town.'"

"Then I drove to the bank in St. Anthony. I walked in, picked up a book of blank counter checks, and walked out. I drove over to Medicine Lodge and started buying sheep and cow hides from ranchers up and down the creek. I wrote checks even though I had no account. I loaded the Model-T to the top and headed for Idaho Falls. There I sold the hides."

"Next day I went to the bank in 'Anthony, deposited the money, bought a belt for my pregnant wife, and returned to the ranch. That's how I got my start. America is the land of opportunity."

The old hide buyer continued:

"I leaned a lot about people buying hides. One time I was negotiating a purchase of sheep hides from a rancher. He had a big stack in one place and a single hide hanging over the fence nearby. He

wanted to know what I'd give him for the stack. I looked them over and made him an offer, and he seemed satisfied."

"Then he asked me what I'd give for the hide on the fence. It was an average hide, so I gave him a price. He got mad as heck! 'You mean to tell me that hide ain't worth more than those in the stack? That was a registered ram! I had him shipped from New Jersey.' And he refused to sell me any of his hides."

"I learned from that experience. After that, when I spotted a hide out by itself, I always offered a little bit more for it, and then I could get the rest of the hides real cheap!"

I asked Dad about the old hide buyer. He said:

"He came by our ranch several times to buy hides. He usually talked me into selling, but he never did pay me what the hides were worth."

Dubois, Idaho. August, 2005.

Chapter 7 | To Keep Her Boys In School

"We hooked the trailer on the Model-A Ford."

After graduating from Medicine Lodge in the spring of 1935 our 11th grade class with Daniel and Gerald faced a real dilemma – how to finish high school. Mother was determined to "keep her boys in school." With much worry and prayer, Mother contacted an aunt in California who suggested she rent a house in Pasadena, take in boarders and enroll Daniel and Gerald in John Muir Technical High School.

My Dad had some reservations about the whole idea, but Mother had made up her mind so plans were made for the move. Dad built a 4-wheel trailer out of our old Model-T Ford and we loaded potatoes, apples, chickens, canned fruit and other living supplies in the trailer. We hooked the trailer onto our Model-A Ford that we had purchased from Mr. Walter Finlay, Postmaster of Small, Idaho. Before we left Medicine Lodge, Mrs. Bob Chastain came by to ask Mother if she would please take Robert with her so he could finish high school with his Thomas classmates. Mother agreed with the stipulation that Robert was not to have any more spending money than her boys. Mrs. Chastain was to pay Mother $30 a month for room and board.

Dad had to stay home to run the ranch, so Mother was in charge of the trip. The safe speed for the rig was about 25 miles per hour. It took several days to get to Pasadena. We camped out at night. Mother kept track of the expenses. The total cost was $25.23.

California: "No cows to milk – no pigs to swill."

Mother's new baby arrived on November 23, 1935. Since all of the other boys had been born in the log house on the ranch at Medicine Lodge, Mother refused to go to the hospital for the 5th. With Aunt Mary's help she finally located an old family doctor that agreed to come to the house for the delivery. The baby was named William Henry, a big name for a little guy. We took turns helping with the baby. Mother was soon convinced that he would become a movie star so she started writing to Hollywood agents to brag about his talents. Breaking into the Hollywood scene proved to be beyond the reach of the proud Mother.

Every day in California was filled with exciting new adventures for the Idaho farm boys. We had lots of time after school and on weekends – no cows to milk, no pigs to swill, no horses to harness or other farm chores. We were only a few blocks from the high school with unbelievable sports facilities so that we could play tennis, shoot baskets and practice baseball. We could ride the streetcar and go to the movies for 10 cents. We saw our first Tournament of Roses on New Years of 1936 and Robert, Daniel and I graduated in the Rose Bowl in June. I kept a small diary and Mother saved most of our letters home.

Mother insisted that Robert and her boys go to church. The Baptist Preacher offered a number of extra prayers and songs hoping we would come forward and confess our sins, but we were too bashful to respond.

April 14: "I got a job at the circus selling candy and fresh roasted peanuts and a free pass to the circus. On April 18, "We saw Sally Rand, the Fan Dancer, at the San Diego Exposition."

We celebrated Daniel's 18th birthday on April 21st and Byron's 14th on April 22nd. Daniel, Robert and I took dancing lessons. They cost $10 for 10 lessons.

Packing for California. Dad made this trailer out of our old Model-T Ford. We loaded
it with food and supplies, hooked it on the Model-A, and Mother drove. 1935.

Car trouble. 1935.

Dad and Mother with William Henry. Pasadena, California. 1935.

William Henry Thomas.

Daniel Thomas. Pasadena. 1935

Byron Thomas. Pasadena. 1935

The Dan Thomas family in Pasadena, Winter, 1935.
Daniel, Dad, Gerald, Mother with William, Byron, Robert Chastain, and Walter.

The streetcar fare was 10 cents and we could go into downtown Pasadena,
South Pasadena, Cal Tech, and around the area. Pasadena. 1935.

Rose Parade, Pasadena. 1935.

The house we rented in Pasadena in 1935.
The Jackie Robinson family lived nearby. After school, we often played
tennis and shot baskets with Jackie and his older brother.

The school was built in 1913 and was a vocational school until 1926.
The 1937 yearbook with pictures of Jackie, Daniel and me is now a
valuable collector's item - because of Jackie's photo.

Later in April Mother left for Idaho with Walter, William and Uncle Henry, leaving the boys to batch. Daniel was left in charge and he took the job seriously.

In a letter home dated May 13, 1936, I informed Mother that:

"I'm getting short on change so tell Walter to send me that 30 cents he owes me from the Exposition in San Diego.... Uncle Seymour goes to about every Townsend (Old Age) meeting that is held within riding distance.... Our swimming coach asked me to come out for swimming next year.... Daniel and I were down to the fashionable Vista Del Rio Hotel tonight and last night putting on a skit for the Pasadena Chamber of Commerce. We had a lot of fun and went through the hotel. Boy, they had a big ball room."

On May 19, Daniel wrote a short letter to Mother stating:

"We received a card from Robert's Mother saying she would start down the 6th of June to pick up Robert.... The Music and Drama Department is putting on a festival. Gerald's in the play. I'm selling tickets. Been working hard on our life-saving tests."

On May 29, Byron wrote:

"Dear Mother and Daddy: We were glad to receive your letter with the money in it. We got it just in time too, for Uncle Seymour had just returned from the store with twelve cents left. Pretty close I call it. I would have wrote (sic) sooner but I have been typing Daniel's term paper. Love, Byron."

Mother drove back to Pasadena in early June and on June 19th *"Daniel, Robert and I graduated from John Muir Tech in the Rose Bowl and went to the Junior-Senior Prom (without dates)."*

We left for Idaho on June 21 in the Model-A and trailer and arrived home at Lidy Hot Springs on June 24.

Baseball with Jackie Robinson

"He broke the color barrier in major sports."

The 1934-35 baseball team at Medicine Lodge was the best in the history of the school. We beat Dubois once, Spencer twice and tied Hamer. We had very little time to practice. The school wagons dropped us off in time to start school at 9 am, and then we had two 15-minute recesses, an hour off for lunch and a few minutes to practice before the wagons picked us up at 4 pm for the trip home.

When Mother left Small, Idaho for California in the fall of 1935 she had four members of the Medicine Lodge baseball team in the Model-A (Robert Chastain, Daniel, Byron and Gerald Thomas). Soon after we enrolled at John Muir Technical High School we all went out for baseball. As it turned out none of the Idaho boys made the team. However, Robert became manager of the varsity team and Byron and I became managers for the Junior Varsity. Jackie Robinson was a short stop for the Muir Tech varsity.

Mother had rented a house in the same neighborhood as the Robinson family. Daniel, Robert and I frequently played tennis and shot baskets with the Robinson boys. Jackie and his older brother, Mack, were good athletes. We enjoyed the interaction with them.

After graduation from high school at Muir Tech, Daniel and I went on to Pasadena Junior College. Jackie Robinson also enrolled at PJC and was now recognized as an outstanding baseball player. Daniel and I continued to play an occasional game of tennis with the Robinson boys but eventually we lost touch. We had no idea that Jackie would later attain baseball fame and become the first black to break the color barrier in major professional sports.

Medicine Lodge Baseball Team. Back: Leland Small, Francis Colson, Daniel Thomas,
John Clark, Gerald Thomas. Middle: Byron Thomas and Lynn Thomas
Front: Charles Livesay, Robert Chastain, and Virgil Burnsides.

Varsity Baseball Team, John Muir Technical High School. 1936.

Chapter 8 | Back To The Ranch In Idaho

"Daniel bought the Model-T for $25."

It was good to get back to Idaho for the summer. Since Dad and Mother were still renting the resort at Lidy Hot Springs we had an exciting life, splitting our time between Lidy Hot Springs and the Medicine Lodge Ranch. Selected notes from my 1936 diary helps to recall some of our activities during this time. Byron also started a diary when we reached the ranch from California.

Jun 25 -- *"Daniel and Gerald brought in the cows. Milked first time in 10 months."* (Byron)

Jun 26 -- *"Rode over in the Lavas looking for the workhorses. Never found them. Branded calves today."*

Jul 7 -- *"Haying for Fayles. The boom pole broke on the derrick. Had quite a time replacing it. Went fishing with Mother tonight."*

Jul 31 -- *"Rode the bench and Rocky Hollow for horses. Found 35 head. Branded 8 colts."*

Aug 3 -- *"Got up our first crop of hay. I stacked and fell off 6 times."*

Aug 7 -- *"We cleaned the chicken house."* (Byron)

Sep 4 -- *"Went up Gallagher Canyon to help mark and cut posts & poles. Daniel hauled them back to Lidys."*

Sep 7 -- *"Labor Day. Gerald, Daniel and Daddy went to the timber."* (Byron)

Mother took the car and trailer from Idaho to Pasadena for three years to *"keep her boys in school."* Daniel and I finished high school and two years of Junior College in California. Daniel majored in Geology, I chose Forestry.

On New Years Day in 1937, *"The Thomas family watched the 48th Tournament of Roses on Colorado Street in Pasadena."* We were living in a rented house at 1929 Summit Ave. We had one boarder, a Mr. Jeffers that stayed with us for two years while he worked at the Santa Anita Racetrack.

Daniel and I were in school at Pasadena JC. We were both enrolled in ROTC and I joined the "Red Crown" Unit – a special group that put on fancy drills and marched in the Memorial Day Parade. Byron was at John Muir Technical High School and Walter was going to Jackson Elementary.

William became very sick in February. Mother finally took him to the doctor. We could not seem to find out what was wrong with him. On Feb 25, I noted that, *"William is awfully sick today."* Then on March 8, *"William was operated on for an abscess."* March 9, *"Mother brought the baby home as he was given up by the doctors."* March 17, *"William was operated on again today."* (William started to improve later in March.)

Chester Woods (Uncle Seymour's son-in-law) was working in the grocery distribution center at the Nash grocery store in Pasadena. He helped Daniel and I get jobs delivering groceries to wealthy families in Pasadena, Beverly Hills and parts of Los Angeles. We learned the hard way that you never deliver to the front door of wealthy homes. We were paid $2 to $3 for a hard days work. This provided us with spending money.

On March 17, 1937, Daniel bought a Model-T Ford in Monrovia for $25. Our classmate, Leo Wachtel, helped us tow it to Pasadena so we could start the repair work. After we got the T going we

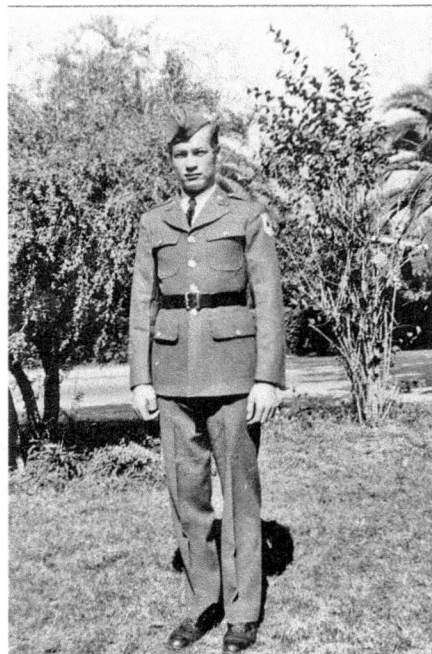

R.O.T.C. Private Cadet Thomas. 1937.

"Red Crown" R.O.T.C. Unit drilling. Pasadena. 1937.

Model-T Ford bought by Daniel for $25 to return to Idaho. 1937.

Even after throwing a rod, we still made it home to Idaho in 4 days. 1937.

Camping out on the way home to Idaho. 1937.

could go to new sights around California. Also, since Mother had left for Idaho before school was out we needed the Model-T for transportation home in June. Just out of Barstow the Ford threw a rod but we made it home in 4 days. Daniel later sold the Model-T to Weldon Ellis and recovered his cost of $25.

The next year Daniel and I graduated from Pasadena Junior College in the Rose Bowl on June 17, 1938. Byron joined us the next day as we started for home in a used 26 Chevy. On the 19th we had two blowouts and a wheel came off. On the 20th we had a flat tire, ran out of gas twice and the generator broke. We visited relations in Salt Lake City on the 21st, lost a wheel leaving town, fixed several flats and traveled all night without brakes. We arrived home on the June 22nd and, *"I went for a ride on old Dime."*

After the July 4th celebration at Lidy Hot Springs we started haying again for Frank Reno. We were milking 6 cows and trying to run the Medicine Lodge Ranch as well as the Hot Springs. We converted the old Chevy to a 4-wheel trailer and my adventurous Mother decided to run for State Senator on the Republican ticket. (She lost).

On July 26, Daniel and I joined Grandpa and Grandma Evans on an exciting camp out on Birch Creek to stake out copper mining claims.

Prospecting with Grandpa and Grandma Evans

"Grandpa had trouble learning to drive the car."

Rumors spread rapidly in Clark County when Jack O'Brian reported a new copper discovery in the foothills near the head of Birch Creek. My Grandfather and Grandmother were visiting our ranch at the time. My brother, Daniel and I were excited as we listened to the family discussions about the possibility of filing a claim next to the O'Brian discovery.

Mother always carried the spirit of adventure for our family. She said:

"Dan, we have worked our fingers to the bone on this old ranch and still can't make a decent living. Why don't we go over to Birch Creek and stake out a claim?"

When Mother could not get a positive response from Dad she turned her attention to Grandpa. After all, it was Mother who had convinced Grandpa to sell the farm in Kansas and move to Idaho in 1915. Mother prevailed, and sure enough, Grandpa and Grandma Evans decided that they would represent the family in this latest adventure providing Daniel and I could go along to help make camp and dig the required assessment holes.

Papers were filed in the County Seat at Dubois, Idaho on July 16, 1937, concerning "Notice of Quartz Locations." Grandpa filed on the "Treasure Mining Claim." Mother named hers the "Prosperity Copper Lode" and I can't remember the names of the other two claims.

Since Grandpa couldn't seem to learn to drive, we took Daniel's old Model-A and a homemade trailer. Daniel said:

"I tried to teach Grandpa to drive but when he got into trouble he would pull on the steering wheel and yell Whoa! Whoa! He ran into the ditch several times and almost wrecked my car."

We loaded a tent and camping supplies and drove over to Birch Creek on Sunday, July 26, 1937. There was an old road that left Birch Creek near the Kaufman Ranger Station that took us up on the east bench and over to O'Brian's mine. Since the camp was dry we hauled our water from Birch Creek.

Jack O'Brian had dug several holes in the gravel on his claim. He showed us what kind of rocks to look for and he helped us locate our corners.

"We staked four claims," Daniel said:

"Then came the hard work of digging the assessment holes. That was the hardest digging I have ever seen. The ground

George Waters digging a 4x4x8 foot hole at his copper claim at Birch Creek. 1937.

Grandpa and Grandma Evans with Daniel at Birch Creek claim. 1937.

was like cement. We were supposed to dig a hole 4x4x8 for the $100 assessment. My granddad said he didn't think he would live to get any money out of those claims. He died about 6 months later."

On July 27, I recorded in my diary, *"Worked out the assessment hole on the 'Prosperity Copper Lode' which was Mother's. Found a little good ore."* The next day I wrote, *"Started work on the 'Treasure' lode but struck hard cement. Got 4 feet dug. Rainy night. Tent about blew over."* Then on July 29 I stated, *"Dug most of the day on Grandpa's 'Treasure' lode Real hard digging."* I should have added that Daniel and I really enjoyed the campout with Grandpa and Grandma-our last good visit before Grandpa died. (Grandpa Evans died January 14, 1938, and Grandma passed away on May 5, 1961, in Ronan, Montana.)

As we turned over the dirt and gravel with a pick and shovel we kept our eyes peeled for copper sign – anything greenish would be welcome. We found very little indication of mineral content. However, we completed the holes on the 4 claims to the dimensions specified. That would keep someone else from jumping our important mineral discovery.

We never returned to the copper claim the next year or the next. In a few years even Jack O'Brian had moved to another location – still searching. However, prospecting was now in my brother's blood. In the following years, Daniel prospected with Johnny Peterson near the Scott Mine on Birch Creek and Ren Green on Indian Creek. He also searched for buried treasure on Deep Creek with Dave Esbie. With the discovery of uranium in Utah, Daniel worked a dangerous uranium mine near Moab. He finally settled for a career in salmon fishing in Alaska, but prospecting always remained in his blood.

I started breaking a new 3-year old sorrel horse that I called "Kinky" on August 11. For the next several weeks I rode him nearly every evening. He bucked a lot but I stayed in the saddle. On September 9 I noted: *"Rode down to Uncle Rees' ranch for dinner and took the bull and two cows over to Lidys. Kinky is well broke by now."*

Grandpa Evans staking one corner of the "Treasure" claim. Birch Creek. 1937.

Feeding my horses. Medicine Lodge Ranch. 1938.

Stacking hay. Medicine Lodge Ranch. 1938.

Chapter 9 | At the University and in the Forest

"Hitler's speech on the radio."

Daniel, Byron and I enrolled at the University of Idaho for the 1938-39 school year. The shortest route to the U of I in Moscow was through Montana in Daniel's Model-A. At the university Byron decided to follow Daniel's lead with a major in geology. My advisor, Professor Vernon A. Young, noting my ranch background, insisted that I take the Range Management option in the College of Forestry. We found a boarding house downtown that was less costly than the school dorms.

Daniel dropped out of the university after the fall semester. He fell in love with Betty Rider, a young girl back home in Clark County. They married on June 23, 1939, in Roberts, Idaho and then moved to Montana.

I was still keeping a small diary. A few comments were included on the European situation but most notes were rather routine.

Sep 26 -- *"Listened to Hitler's speech on the radio and exchanged viewpoints with the fellows."*

Sep 27 -- *"Heard Chamberlain's speech over the radio and some discussion of European issues."*

Dec 7 -- *"Talked over some of my poor grades with some of my teachers and got set back to where I belong. Studied until the library closed."*

Jan 6 -- *"Byron and I came down with the German measles and checked into the university infirmary."*

Jan 15 -- *"Got out of the infirmary with tons of schoolwork and exams coming up."*

Mar 12 -- *"Discussed politics and Hitler's policy over a cup of tea tonight with the other boarders."*

Mar 14 -- *"Interesting argument on Herr Hitler at the supper table."*

Mar 31 -- Spring vacation. Byron and I loaded the Model-A, picked up the Taylor boys, traveled all night and reached home on April 1, *"in time to milk the cows and help with the chores."* Then on April 5, *"Byron and I rode the desert for horses. Run in about 40 head, cut 3 two-year old studs. Didn't find 4 head of yearlings."*

The Salmon National Forest

"You will need a saddle horse and a team and wagon."

Each year after the close of school we returned to Idaho to help Dad with the ranch and farm work. Our ranch was always a marginal operation due to the shortage of water for alfalfa and grain in the dry years. To supplement our income, Dad contracted to stack hay in Idaho and in the Big Hole Valley of Montana. His boys were a part of the crew. With Mother's leadership, we were still leasing the Resort of Lidy Hot Springs where swimming, dancing and amateur rodeos kept us entertained.

On July 4, 1939, I recorded that, *"I took in the Rodeo in Dubois and the dance and celebration at Lidys. Danced a lot with Gene Lingo and **Jean Ellis.**"* (Although this is the first mention of my future wife in my diary, we had met a number of times at Lidy Hot Springs or at community events.)

I was down in the corral milking cows on July 11, 1939, when I was surprised by a visit from

Gerald, Charlie Howe, unidentified. Charlie was the Camp Tender
for the Reno Ranch. 1939.

Gerald hauling water troughs to Spring Canyon. 1939.

Larry Garner, the Forest Ranger for the Lemhi District of the Salmon National Forest. Garner came by to offer me a job with the US Forest Service. He knew that I was studying forestry at the University. He said he had a job opening but I would need a saddle and packhorse and the occasional use of a team and wagon. The work involved livestock water development on sheep and cattle allotments, fire prevention, trail construction and timber stand improvement. I took the job with enthusiasm and went to work the next day at $25 per month. Good jobs were scarce during the thirties.

For the next 3 years I worked summers for the Salmon National Forest. We covered the rugged high country by wagon and horseback. The work provided an opportunity for me to supplement my studies of vegetation and geology at the University and I received credit for summer camp by reporting on my forest work. To illustrate the nature of the work, I cite examples from my field notes.

Summer, 1939. *"We were welcomed at the Fritz Creek camp by Charlie Howe, Camp Tender for Wright, owner of the Reno Ranch and the sheep in the area. While we were preparing supper, Charlie kept us entertained with his discussion of everything in general and sheep in particular. Like most men who are constantly associated with sheep, he is quite a talker. Sometimes he never sees anyone for weeks yet he is always well up on the news of the day. His sourdough biscuits are tops in any man's language."*

"After we finished the construction at Cole Springs we loaded our equipment in the wagon and started down the steep mountain toward Fritz Creek. Using two log chains we double rough-locked the hind wheels. Charlie drove the team while Buster and I each rode a hind wheel. We plowed two furrows down the slope as the chains dug in. In the rocky places the wheels jumped about a great deal making it difficult for the team to hold back the load

and keep the wagon from turning over."

"On Monday July 24, I left the Dry Creek camp to take in the Amateur Rodeo and Old Time Celebration at Lidy Hot Springs."

"We salvaged an old 'Go-Devil' to haul our equipment into Shorty's Springs on the Divide between Birch Creek and Little Lost River. On the steep inclines it pulled easier than a wagon. Regardless of the frequent stops that were necessary to rest the team, we completed the trip before dark. Here among the few rugged Limber Pines we began our water development work."

"We stopped at Bob Stewart's ranch at the old town of Nicholia to borrow a 4-horse team and wagon for our work on Sliderock Springs. As we were moving toward the camp, Bob Stewart gave us a brief history of the old mining town of Nicholia, Idaho. It seems that over thirty years ago an old prospector struck it rich on this mountainside north of Reno, Idaho. His discovery leads to a rush of mining claims. A town sprang up reaching a population of over one thousand. Several large mines such as the Viola Lode and the Nicholia Lode became famous. However, as time went on the rich veins petered out. Today the town has taken its place among the other ghost towns of the west with only one family left who make their living, not from mining, but from farming and ranching."

After the summer work on the Salmon National Forest I returned to UI to continue studies in the College of Forestry. Byron and I boarded with Pete and Margaret Taylor from Spencer, Idaho. Pete was also majoring in Range Management, so we studied together. Alan, Pete's brother, was in the same class with Byron. Margaret cooked for us and we hunted deer and elk to supplement our rations. In a letter to Mother in November, I wrote, *"Pete and Margaret have decided that they cannot*

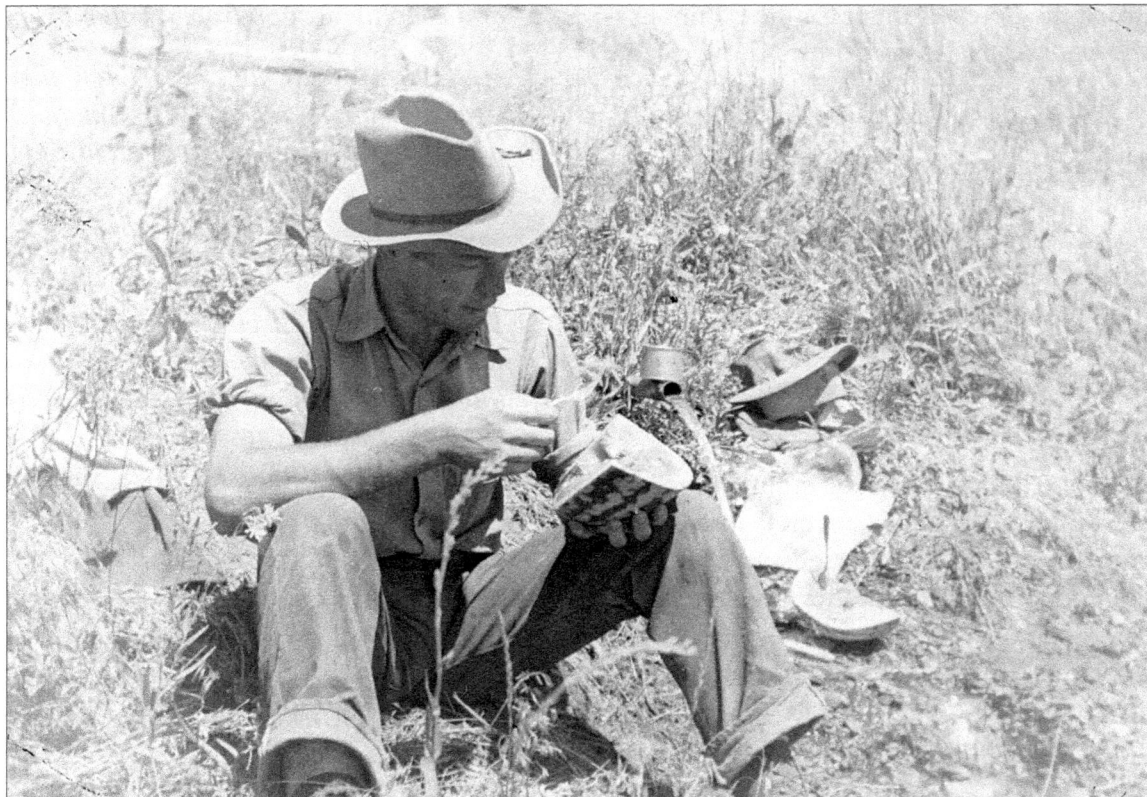

Gerald at camp at Spring Canyon. 1939.

Gerald setting rocks for camp fire cooking. Spring Canyon. 1939.

keep Byron and me for less than $46 a month – that includes board and room. I think this is plenty reasonable because food is high this year. Margaret is doing all of our washing (she also patches our socks, etc.) for $2.50 a month. So the total is $48.50."

On September 18, 1939, a news release stated that *"German and Russian troops joined up in Poland and the two governments quickly implemented plans to divide the country."* We did not realize that this was the beginning of World War II. The headlines read:

UNDECLARED WAR BREAKS OUT IN EUROPE

HITLER INVADES POLAND

ENGLISH ENTER WAR

A Wave of Isolationism

"The major opinion is that we will not be drawn into the controversy."

A wave of isolationism was sweeping the nation as many people still remembered World War I. In my letter to Mother on November 11 from 426 West 3rd in Moscow, I expressed the prevailing sentiment about the European problem:

"Dear Mother:

Today is Armistice Day. Just 21 years ago today the World War ended, and a treaty was signed by all the major countries of the world, a treaty which supposedly would end all conflicts to come. Yet we find Europe now engaged in another war. We can only hope that the United States will not foolishly become involved. Here at the university, the major opinion seems to be that we will not be drawn into the conflict. As long as we can keep the propaganda machine in check, I am certain that we can remain a sane country. History has proven that war can accomplish nothing. I sincerely hope

that the people will realize this and not be influenced by those who profit by war." – Love, Gerald

As Byron and I continued our studies at the University of Idaho in the spring semester in 1940, the war was heating up in Europe. In spite of Britain's continuing requests for help, we, like most Americans, still believed we would not be drawn into the conflict. In a letter to Mother dated October 14, I noted, *"We register for conscription day after tomorrow. I will not be in the first draft."*

The semester ended in late May and I went back to work for the Forest Service. Some notes from my journal in 1940 indicate the nature of the work.

In June, Ranger Garner assigned me to:

"Take a saddle and pack horse and rebuild the trails up the Webber Creek Canyon into the head of Crooked Creek and then on down to the Cow Camp on Dry Creek. Should take about a week or ten days. Clear and blaze a trail through the timber areas, dig out around the slide rock and make sure the trail is wide enough for a fully-loaded pack horse."

This should have been relatively easy, but I was breaking a new bronc that I called "Buster" and he did not want to cooperate. Shortly after I left the ranch on Medicine Lodge Buster bucked the pack off, *"strewing food and equipment all over. While he was bucking the box of matches in the pack caught on fire adding to the excitement."* Fred Small came along and helped me repack and Buster again unloaded the pack. I had to return to the ranch and start again the next day. Dad decided to send my brother, Walter, with me for the first night out. This time I rode Buster and packed Dime. Buster was still giving me trouble when Walter had to go back to the ranch.

Then I encountered another problem. When I reached the top of the divide between Idaho and

Like "Old Faithful," the Model-A overheated on me regularly. Nicholia Canyon, 1940.

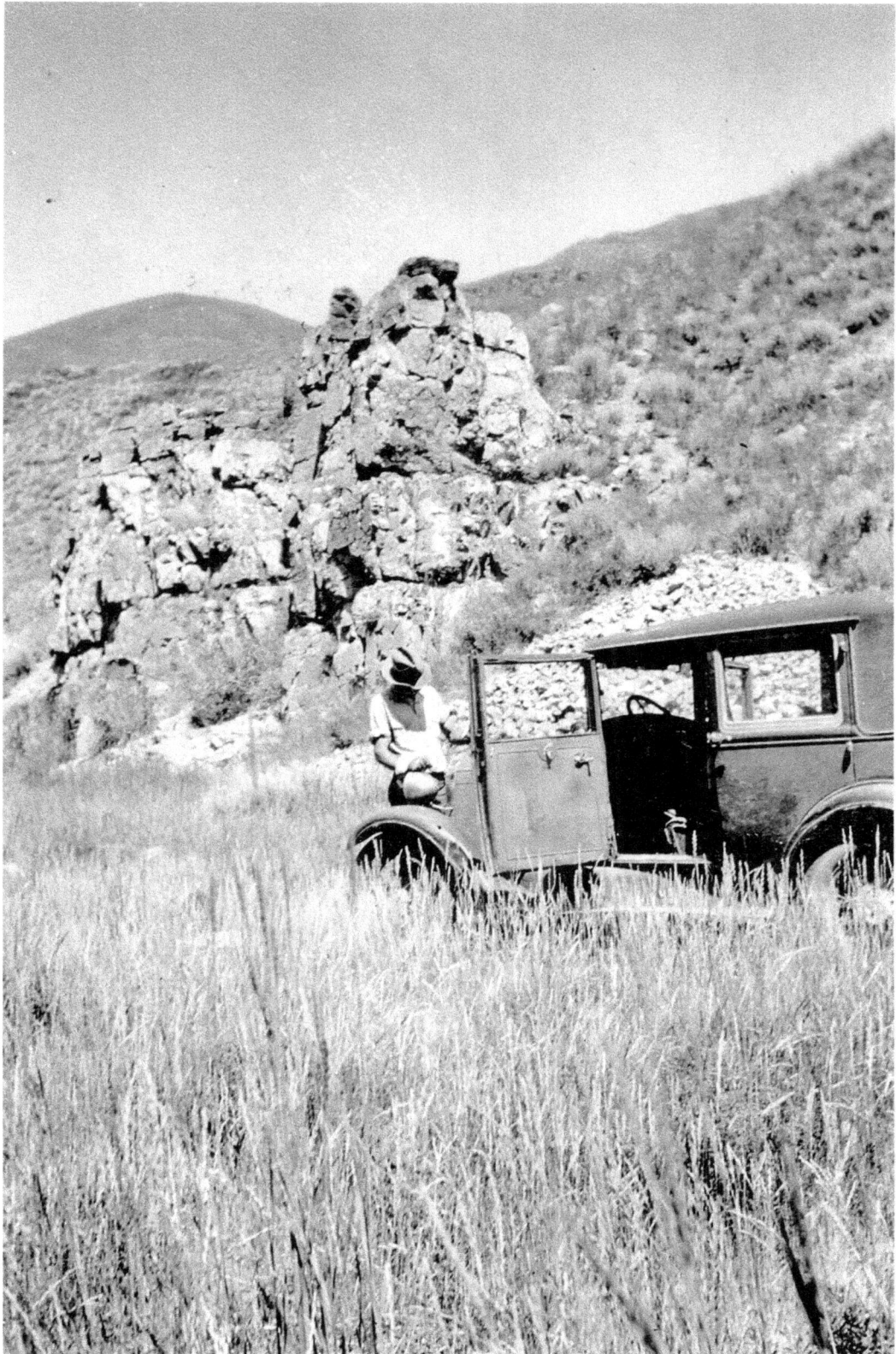

Gerald putting water in the radiator. Nicholia Canyon, 1940.

Camp in Nicholia Canyon while working on Boulder Springs. 1940.

Water development. Nicholia Canyon. 1940.

Montana, I took out the hand-drawn Forest map to locate Divide Creek. I misread the map and spent two days clearing trail down the wrong canyon. When I ran across a sign that said *"Dead Man's Canyon, Beaverhead National Forest"* I knew I was in trouble. I was in the wrong State and on the wrong Forest. I headed back over the mountain to the Idaho side, worked fast on the weekend to build a passable trail up Divide Creek and into McNary gulch. I was overdue when I met the Forest Ranger at the Cow Camp. He said my folks were worried because of my new bronc.

I never told the Ranger that I had been lost and worked on a trail for two days in Montana because I was afraid he would fire me. I wondered later if the Ranger from the Beaverhead Forest in Montana noticed a new trail of unknown origin in his forest.

Blue Canyon Fire. August 10-30. This was my first experience with a forest fire. The Salmon F. S. Office called out 250 men, mostly CCC boys from Dubois to fight the fire. I was in charge of some of the men, but I took orders from the Forest Ranger. Our biggest problem was trying to keep inexperienced CCC boys safe from the advancing flames. (Jean's brother, Weldon Ellis, brought in food and water by horseback for the firefighters.) This fire was confined to 950 acres.

At Pete Springs, July 18, 1941. Buck, my new bronc, and I:

"disagreed again tonight. I rode him up to Nicholia and he sure bucked at the Reservoir. Rode him 8 or 10 jumps but he swapped ends and I went off. My shoe caught in the stirrup and he drug me around in a circle about four times. My sole broke loose and I escaped with a broken tooth and sore muscles. Rode him back to camp without further trouble."

Sliderock Development, Sept 6-13, 1941:

"Ranger McDonald, J. B. Throckmorton and I started to the Sliderock Water Development amidst a snowstorm. The Ranger had 4 horses and I packed Buster. Got about ½ mile along trail when Buster went nuts and ran away bucking with pack. I got on Pegasus and followed him. Trailed him until dark but never found him. He lost the pack just before he hit sliderock. I rode clear down into Crooked Creek but no luck so returned in total darkness and a snowstorm to Nicholia troughs where J. B. was sleeping under a makeshift tent. The Ranger had gone in to the Station after having trouble with one of his horses. J. B. and I spent Saturday and Sunday riding for Buster. Found him down in Crooked Creek Sunday afternoon."

I enjoyed my 3 years of work with the Lemhi District of the Salmon National Forest. I had enough flexibility to spend many weekends at our Medicine Lodge Ranch or at Lidy Hot Springs.

I graduated from the University of Idaho in February 1941 with a degree in Forestry with the Range Science option.

After the work on the Salmon Forest terminated in the fall of 1941, I found a job with the Targhee National Forest, headquartered in Spencer, Idaho. **I was working on a Timber Stand Improvement project near Yellowstone National Park when the Japanese bombed Pearl Harbor on December 7, 1941.** We were living in tent houses and working in about two foot of snow – mostly piling brush after a timber harvest or girdling "bug" trees. The work was hard and the crew came into camp every night wet, cold and tired. Some of my notes in early December follow:

"Another miserable day of ax swinging. The picture of the day shows the four major articles of our household. The alarm clock which wakes us up at 5 am. The coffee pot on which our very existence depends has more rings than we have miseries. The complicated philosophical remarks found in Shakespeare's works keeps out tongues and minds active. The remaining article in the picture is a role of tissue paper. It de-

Buffalo skull found in upper Crooked Creek Canyon. 1940.

Heading up Scott Canyon. 1940.

serves special mention because it is a very important item in our backwoods life. With the end of this roll near, our one remaining luxury passes on. The defense program has *brought about this major tragedy. It is with the deepest regret that we again return to catalogues because, my friends, toilet tissue has gone up to six cents a roll."*

Water development, Edelman Canyon. 1939.

Gerald looking down Scott Canyon. 1940.

Detour to Torpedo Squadron Four

"I hitchhiked to California."

I learned about the declaration of war two days later when I went to Island Park for groceries. I soon turned in my time with the Forest Service, parked my Model-A at Medicine Lodge, hitchhiked to California and tried to enlist in the Navy as an Aviation Cadet. I met the first criteria, a college degree, but I ran into trouble with the Navy doctor. He said he would not consider me unless I had my tonsils pulled and a tooth filled at my own expense. The doctor also had reservations about the shape of my nose. I followed the doctor's orders and finally completed the enlistment procedure for Aviation Cadets on February 5, 1942. The story of my service for 42 months during WWII is in my book entitled, ***"Torpedo Squadron Four: A Cockpit View of World War II"*** and the web site AirGroup4.com. Selected notes from my journal follow.

Jan 1, 1942 -- My cousin, Delbert Rice joined the Army and decided to get married before he was called to Active Duty. My journal version of the marriage follows:

> *"At 1:30 this morning Delbert and Irene were married in the Abbot home in Las Vegas, Nevada with Loeva Jean as Bridesmaid and me as Best Man. After the very interesting ceremony we climbed into Delbert's car and drove out on the desert... camped under a bridge. Del and Irene spent their wedding night in my sleeping bag (it was larger), I slept in Delbert's and Loeva Jean slept in the car.... We were back in Pasadena by 3:30 p.m. for a big wedding fiest at Aunt Flora's."*

The movie star, Wayne Morris, swore me into the Navy on February 5 while he was on the phone with someone in Hollywood. (Morris was in the Naval Reserves and later became a member of "McCampbell's Heroes" in Air Group 15. He was credited with shooting down 6 Japanese planes.)

Pilot Training in the US Navy

For my first Active Duty I was assigned to the "Elimination Base" at Los Alamitos, California. The concept of the E-Base was to prescreen prior to regular aviation cadet training. Elimination was the key word and the instructors set about this task with a vengeance. Everyone feared the "down-checks" which would lead to a "wash-out." I wrote many letters home during E-Base and later flight training. Most contained details that I thought would be of special interest to my teen age brother, Walter. Some samples:

> **Jun 21, 1942, Los Alamitos** -- *"We have been busy with flying and ground school. Some of the navigation problems are very difficult. Another fellow washed out of my class yesterday."*

> **Jul 2** -- *"The B-check is the most important flight in this preliminary training. I passed it OK. We call these planes 'Yellow Perils' but they are technically known as N3Ns.... We are practicing Circle Shots, Precision Spins, Emergency landings... I made many mistakes and deserved a down-check. However, the instructor was a swell guy, and, after telling me how to remedy my errors, he gave me an up-check. He said, 'Thomas, I guess you know you gave me a lousy ride,' then he wished me good luck at Corpus Christi."*

The Naval Air Station, Corpus Christi, Texas was commissioned March 12, 1941.
The first flight training started May 5, 1941.

To Corpus Christi as an Aviation Cadet

I completed "Elimination Base" aviation training in July 1942 and was ordered to Aviation Cadet training at Corpus Christi, Texas.

Jul 19, Cabaniss Field -- *"This letter will be somewhat short since it is about time for taps. Today is Sunday but instructors pile on so much work we never see any relaxation. I have been working all day on navigation problems. Yesterday I passed the final check in N3N planes. The next training stage is aerobatics. Boy it will be fun doing loops, snap rolls, split S`s, etc. About half of my class from Long Beach got at least one down-check since they arrived here."*

Jul 23 -- *"Almost wound up in an inverted spin as I fell out of an Immelmann. Also one cadet couldn't get his wheels down [flying a Curtiss SNC] so he was forced to fly out to the Bay where he made a crash landing by the rescue boat, 'Mary Ann.'"*

Aug 2 -- *"Last week I passed the two toughest checks in this stage of flying, the C and D checks. They had me worried but I slipped through."*

Sep 24 -- *"Don't trade my sorrel mare off. I want to keep her. I should have a good start in the horse business by the time I get out of the Navy. I bought my uniforms downtown last weekend. They are expensive. The Government gives us a uniform allowance of $150 upon graduation but I will have to pay $90-100 out of my own pocket."*

Oct 12 -- *"Busy flying. Finished up with the Curtiss SNCs Saturday. Got a check and soloed the SNJ today. Last week we flew formation mostly. Then the fun begins. We dive from about 4000 feet and zoom the farms. Sure fun to watch chickens and dogs and cows scatter. I don't imagine the farmers like being dived on very much but they always wave at us as we zoom by.... By the way, just because I am going through the dive bombing squadron, that's no sign what duty I will get after I am commissioned."*

Oct 23 -- *"Ground looped and scraped a wing. Penalty: 2 weeks hold up on graduation."* (This penalty was never imposed. ground loops were common in the N2S.)

Nov 12 -- Kingsville, Texas. *"By the way, I was complimented today by several officers. It seems that my gunnery record is abnormally good for a student pilot. We fire a fixed gun forward at a towed sleeve. Anyway, I had 114 hits in five runs. The next closest student had about 25."* Some officers wanted me to consider going into fighters rather than dive bombers, but I wanted to stay with my buddies.

A Navy Ensign with Wings of Gold

I received my Navy Wings and Ensign Commission November 27, 1942.

"Graduation exercises at Corpus Christi were comparatively simple. We received our diplomas from Admiral Montgomery, saluted and were dismissed as officers. The government gave us $150 plus $30 back Cadet pay which covered part of the cost of our new uniforms."

We were then sent by train to Opa Loca, Florida for dive-bomber training. Operational training in dive-bombers lasted 6 weeks, mostly flying over the Everglades in the Curtiss by-plane (SBC), the Northrop (BT) and the SNJ. Brief encounters with "Vertigo" were common-particularly during night flying. I wrote home to say,

"I'm still with about the same bunch of fellows that were at Corpus. Of course they all have wings and officer's stripes now, which makes them seem somewhat older. Otherwise we are the same carefree lot.

Naval Air Station, Corpus Christi, Texas. July 20, 1942.

Officer's Club, Naval Air Station, Corpus Christi, Texas. August 17, 1942.

Naval Air Training Center

United States Naval Air Station
Corpus Christi, Texas

Know all men by these presents that

Ensign Gerald Waglett Thomas, A-V(N), USNR

has completed the prescribed course of training and having met successfully the requirements of the course has been designated a

Naval Aviator

In Witness Whereof, this certificate has been signed on this 27th day of November 1942 and the Seal of the Naval Air Station hereunto affixed

Navy Wings Graduation Photo.
November 27, 1942.

GERALD W. THOMAS RECEIVES WINGS

Gerald W. Thomas, son of Mr. and Mrs. D. W. Thomas of Small, Idaho, has been awarded the coveted "Navy Wings of Gold" and commissioned an ensign in the U. S. Naval Reserve at the Naval Air Training Center, Corpus Christi, Texas.

Ensign Thomas received his wings with the designation of a Naval Aviator from Admiral A. E. Montgomery, USN, Commandant of the training center, at class graduating ceremonies today.

Thomas volunteered for flight training last February and received preliminary instruction at the Los Almaitos, Calif., reserve aviation base. Upon completion there he was transferred to Corpus Christi for intermediate training at the world's largest naval air station.

In addition to flight instruction Thomas completed a thorough ground school course, including navigation, gunnery and bombing theory, communications and allied aeronautical subjects at the "University of the Air."

Thomas attended Pasadena Junior College and the University of Idaho where he was a member of the Forestry Club prior to his enlistment.

Clark County Enterprise-Banner,
December 4, 1942.

Wilbur "Will" S. Souza.

Felix E. Ward.

We fly long hours and are treated nearly the same as aviation cadets, liberty being limited to one day in eight. A few of the fellows took advantage of the new regulations which allow marriage."

On December 26, I wrote:

"Although I admit that I was homesick yesterday I am highly thankful that I am alive and well and not in some of the hell holes many of the fellows are in Asia, Europe and Africa."

Jan 3, 1943:

"Dear Mother and Dad: Another year has gone by... if man could put idle moments to good use he could accomplish great things.... Suffice to say, I believe so long as there are human beings there will be idleness and discontent and wars. Human nature has remained unchanged throughout history... Finished up night flying here at midnight. Should complete the remainder of the syllabus in about two weeks. Tell Walter to write."

After completing dive-bomber training in Florida in January I was one of four new Ensigns ordered to Torpedo Squadron Four. Bob Ruth, Will Souza, Felix Ward and I had been together since cadet training. <u>We four served together during the entire war, stayed in touch after the war, and as I write, age 91, three of us are still alive and kicking!</u>

Carrying a torpedo or going in for a glide bombing attack did not have the glamour of a dog fight. The fighters had the opportunity to engage in plane-to-plane combat and maybe become an "Ace." No "torpeckers" were ever classified as Aces.

The only famous torpedo pilots that I know of were Ensign George Gay and Lt(jg) George H. W. Bush. Gay became famous as the sole survivor of Torpedo 8. Bush became famous as President of the US – not because he was a torpedo pilot who bailed out after he was shot down over Chichi Jima.

Robert "Bob" F. Ruth.

A formation of TBF torpedo bombers. Bob, Will, Felix, and I were surprised to be shifted
to a torpedo squadron, although we were aware of the shortage of torpedo pilots.

Chapter 11 | Torpedo Four in the Atlantic Theater

"Rough seas and hazardous flying conditions."

In January, 1943, I was assigned to Torpedo Squadron Four attached to the **USS RANGER** (CV-4). VT-4 was a 9-plane unit with 12 pilots and 2 non-flying officers. We were a part of Air Group 4 along with a 16-plane fighter squadron and a 16-plane dive bomber squadron. Our primary mission was Convoy Escort Duty and Anti-Sub Patrol in the North Atlantic as well as strike capability.

Carrier Qualifications

Since the **RANGER** was out of the area, several of the Air Group 4 pilots were ordered to conduct the necessary 8 qualification landings on a British carrier, the **HMS ATTACKER**, which was lying off the East Coast.

We had been practicing "Field Carrier Landings" on a marked part of the airfield at Quonset Point, Rhode Island, for several days and were supposed to be ready for the actual test of our landing ability. An experienced Navy Landing Signal Officer from our Air Group was on the British carrier to bring us aboard.

On my eighth and last landing, after I cut the throttle and hit the deck, I felt a sharp jerk but the plane never slowed down. I crashed into the barrier and stopped with my Avenger facing toward the fantail of the carrier. I did not know what had happened. Then I heard a load speaker, *"Taxi back down! Taxi back down!"* My engine was running and the bent prop was turning. I could not understand the order, but I added throttle and got even further tangled in the cable barrier. Then I spotted a deck hand giving me the "Cut Gun" signal, which I understood. As soon as the engine stopped, I heard the order, *"Send that pilot up to the Bridge!"*

I went to the Bridge and the English Officer said, *"What the hell were you doing?"* I said I was following orders to "taxi back down." He said I did not say that, but *"Cut Your Gun."* The English accent had confused me.

By this time, the deck reported that I had caught a tie-down iron instead of a wire and the tail hook had snapped off. The officer said, *"Since it was not your fault, we'll count this as a qualified landing."*

On the RANGER

On April 25, German newspapers announced that Adolph Hitler had decorated U-Boat Commander Otto Von Bulow for sinking the **USS RANGER**. This report turned out to be false.

About 200 German submarines were operating in the Atlantic in the first months of 1943. Twelve merchantmen fell victim to sub torpedoes in February and in one March battle, 14,000 tons of Allied shipping was sunk in 6 days. Winston Churchill admitted in his history of World War II that, *"The U-Boat attack was our worst evil. It would have been wise for the Germans to stake all on it."*

> **Apr 28, 1943** -- *"Sure would like to be home to break that two-year old of my sorrel mare's.... I checked out in another plane last week -- a Grumman J2F seaplane. I was picked to fly it up to Newfoundland in a few days."*

Carrier Air Group 4 attained another first when we were ordered to qualify for night operations. Because of the presence of German subs it was important to keep the lights on the Carrier to a minimum. Thus, problems were inevitable. The first night, June 20th, there were 3 barrier crashes; second night: 3 barrier crashes; third night: a TBF spun in on approach and an F4F barrier-crashed and flipped on its back, injuring the pilot.

Insignia for Torpedo Squadron 4
(VT-4) designed by Walt Disney.

Our nickname was the
"Torpeckers."

USS RANGER. Note the 6 stacks aft. These were folded down during air operations.
It was the first American carrier built as a carrier. It was launched in 1934.
It carried the designation CV-4. The pilots assigned to it were Air Group 4.

Night qualification landings on the **RANGER**. June 20, 1943.
Light track shows a wave-off. Light on horizon is the mask light of a destroyer.

Barrage balloon, Scapa Flow, Scotland. In the foreground is a submarine net.
Taken from the **RANGER**. Sept 8, 1943.

Torpedo Squadron 4 aboard the **RANGER**. September, 1943.
Back row (left to right): Lt(jg) John H. Palmer, Lt(jg) Lawrence L. Hamrick,
Lt(jg) R. R. Anderson, Lt(jg) Robert E. Trexler, Ens Gerald W. Thomas.
Middle row: Lt(jg) Louis G. Gardemal, Lt J. Welch Harriss, Lt Richard Claytor,
Lt Cdr D. Woot Taylor, Lt Cdr Homer H. Hutcheson, Lt(jg) George W. Bolt.
Front row: Ens George D. Walker, Ens Robert "Bob" F. Ruth, Lt(jg) Page P. Stephens,
Ens Felix E. Ward, Ens Wilbur S. Souza, Ens Gerald M. "Buck" Barnett.

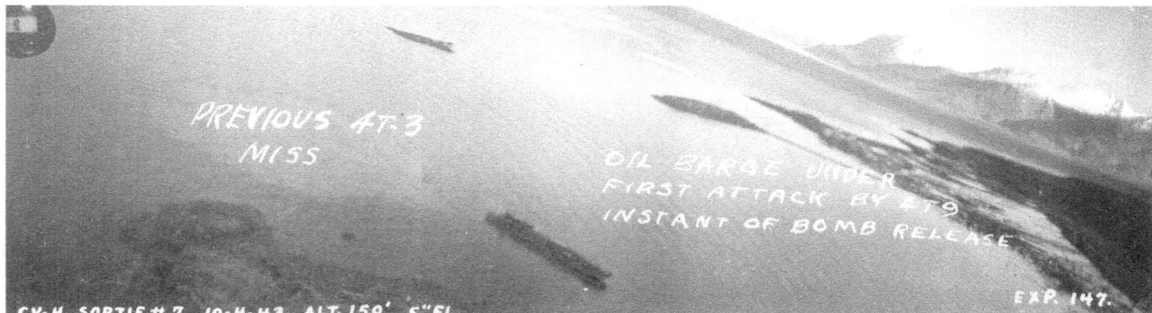

Gun camera photo taken by Gerald's TBM Avenger (4-T-9) at the instant
his first 500 lb. bomb was released by his plane in the attack on MFS 231,
a freight barge. This bomb missed the target, but his second bomb struck the ship.
OPERATION LEADER. Bodø, Norway. October 4, 1943.

On June 24th, Otto Klinsmann, the skipper of VB-4 plunged into the drink on take-off. Since I was not scheduled to fly that night, I watched his plane crash in the water. He was rescued by the trailing destroyer. (Otto became our Air Group Commander in the Pacific and was later killed during a strike on Japanese shipping. After the war I helped identify the wreckage of his SBD in Placentia Bay after it was recovered by the Canadians.)

Most of the following material on our squadron activities in the Atlantic is quoted directly from my journal records. Quotations from letters home are so marked.

Aug 19 -- *"FM2 crashed through two barriers and caught fire. Pilot not injured."*

Aug 20 -- Letter home. *"Received two newspapers in about four months. One of them included an article on Jean Ellis as Rodeo Queen."*

Aug 31 -- *"British Commander in Chief on board to watch operations. One FM2 crashed in the starboard catwalk. Another FM2 broke tail hook and crashed into the barriers. Pilot cut on head. TBM crashed into barrier without injuring pilot."*

Sep 8 -- *"Left Scapa Flow to join **HMS RENOWN** bringing Churchill back to England."*

Sep 20 -- Letter home. *"Well, your letters finally got thru -- six of them at once. First mail I have received for a month and a half. When mail call was sounded you should have seen the stampede. Just like Christmas to see everyone's smiling faces when the mail was handed out. One of the fellows just discovered his wife had twins -- several others became fathers since the last word from home... we have been at sea almost continuously for the past six months. Gosh, I would like to get home for hunting season.... Hope you made a good investment in that place in Montana.*

$5000 is a lot of money. It will take a long time to pay it off at $10 a month."

Operation Leader: Attacks on German Shipping

"Crash landing on a wave-off."

The **USS RANGER** was assigned to the British Home Fleet under Admiral Sir Bruce Fraser during some operations in the North Atlantic. We fought rain, snow or sleet much of the time – and the sea was almost always rough.

My first combat was October 4, 1943, during OPERATION LEADER while the **RANGER** was attached to the British Home Fleet. This operation involved strafing and bombing attacks against German shipping along the Norwegian Coast. I made two low-level runs on a German ship scoring with at least one 500-pound bomb. My plane was hit by AA fire and I ordered the crew to bail out of the smoking plane. My belly gunner accidentally popped his parachute in the plane and could not get through the escape hatch. We stayed with the damaged plane as it made the 100-mile flight back to the carrier over the cold waters of the North Atlantic.

When I reached the carrier, my cockpit canopy was covered with oil and I couldn't see the landing signal officer. I crash landed the smoking plane on a "Wave Off" and received a verbal reprimand for fouling up the flight deck. Several of us were later awarded Air Medals for these strikes. According to my flight log, this was Carrier Landing No 13.

This was our first experience with combat, and our losses cut deeply:

Killed were Lt(jg) Clyde A. Tucker and his crewman ARM2c Stephen D. Bakran when their SBD (#19) was hit and crashed in the water with no survivors.

Taken prisoner were Lt(jg) Sumner R. Davis and crewman ARM2c D. W. McCarley. Their SBD (#15) was shot down by AA fire. The men were picked up by Norwegian fishermen but could not be kept from the Germans.

CV-4 SORTIE #7. 10-4-43. ALT. ? 6-3/8" FL.
4-B-19 AT INSTANT OF STRIKING WATER.
1-1/2 MI. OFF "BODO". FORCED DOWN BY AA FIRE.
PILOT: LT(JG) C.A. TUCKER, USNR. PASS. S.D. BAKRAN

Lt(jg) Clyde A. Tucker's SBD striking the water after being hit by AA fire.
Tucker and crewman ARM2c Stephen D. Bakran were killed.
OPERATION LEADER. October 4, 1943.

GERMAN MERCHANT VESSEL
8056 G.T.
S.W. RODO, SOUTHERLY COURSE
WHEN ATTACKED BY SOUTHERN GROUP.
"LAPLATA"
2ND ATTACK
SW →
CV-4 SORTIE #7. 10-4-43. ALT. ? 5" FL.
EXP. 141

German merchant ship *La Plata* under strafing attack. Gun camera photo.
OPERATION LEADER. October 4, 1943.

Personnel presented medals and citations for actions under fire during
OPERATION LEADER, October 4, 1943.
(Left to right) Cmdr Joseph A. Ruddy, Distinguished Flying Cross;
Lt Cmdr G. O. Klinsmann, Air Medal; Lt Cyrus F. Weeks, Air Medal;
Lt(jg) Gerald W. Thomas, Air Medal; Lt(jg) Robert F. Ruth, Air Medal;
ARM1c R. F. Gray, Purple Heart.

OPERATION LEADER Strike Results

- Steamship *Rabat* hit by bomb and sunk.
- Steamship *Cap Quir* damaged by bomb under the waterline.
- Steamship *Malaga* lightly damaged by a dud bomb.
- Steamship *Ibis* lightly damaged.
- Freight barge *MFS 231*, with 40 tons of ammunition, hit by bomb and beached.
- Troop Transport *Skramstad* hit by bomb. Burning and beached. Ship had 834 soldiers aboard. 200 killed, 15 seriously wounded, 1 Norwegian crewman killed.
- Steamship *Wolsum* damaged by heavy strafing.
- Steamship *La Plata* hit by 3 bombs. Burned and beached.
- Tanker *Schleswig* hit by 3 bombs, disabled.
- Steamship *Kerkplein* hit by 2 bombs, burned. Ship had 1,551 Russian prisoners on board. The bombing kills 14 prisoners, seriously wounds 29, and leaves 9 missing. No one on the American side knew the ship was carrying prisoners, nor was it marked as such.
- Navy *365*, an Norwegian Sleipner-class destroyer, heavily strafed.
- Steamship *Vaagen* sunk after being hit by bomb.
- Steamship *Topeka* burned after being hit by 3 bombs.

TBF Avenger receives the signal to land on **RANGER**. 1942.

TBF Avenger drops a practice torpedo. 1943.

TBF Avenger lying on port stacks of ***RANGER*** after rolling over on side upon landing.
A munitions specialist is removing undropped depth charges from the bomb bay. 1943.

Snow laden deck of *RANGER*. Placentia Sound, Newfoundland. April 1943.

My "bluenose" certificate for crossing the Arctic Circle. October 3, 1943.

Also taken prisoner was Lt(jg) John H. Palmer when his TBM was hit by AA fire. His crewmen ART1c Joseph L. Zalom and AMM1c Reginald H. Miller went down with the plane and were killed. Palmer was in Stalag Luft 3 until the end of the war.

Back to Carrier Operations

"Scuttlebutt and Anti-sub patrol."

The **RANGER** continued operations in the North Atlantic after the Norway strike. Much of the scuttlebutt was about further attacks on the Germans, with an emphasis on how to "sink the **TURPITZ**."

Oct 22 -- *"A TBM ran over a man who fell in path of plane and was killed."*

Nov 5 -- *"Operating out of Scapa Flow. FM2 rolled over on the stacks. FM2 crashed in water. Pilot recovered but died of pneumonia."*

Each time the **RANGER** moved toward anchor in Scapa Flow all planes from the Air Group were flown ashore to Hatston Air Base. We scheduled as many flights as possible from the narrow airstrip at Hatston. At first we tried 3 flights a day but we soon found out that the third flight was in conflict with "tay time." So we abandoned the third flight and joined the Limeys for "tea and crumpets," followed by warm beer and gin and orange.

Nov 12 -- *"Ens Hawkins went in the drink coming aboard. He was picked up by a can but had drowned."*

Nov 21 -- *"The C in C, British Home Fleet came aboard to thank the **RANGER** for its work in the European Theater."*

Nov 23 -- *"Enroute to Iceland. This is the roughest sea I have ever seen. Sure wish I was back on the farm."*

Nov 26 -- *"Leaving Reykjavik, Iceland. High wind blew a fighter off the flight deck with man in plane."* No rescue possible.

On December 5, I wrote to my parents summarizing some of my experiences in the Atlantic:

*"I'm back in God's Country again – the good old USA. Arrived Boston yesterday, was granted two days leave, so came to New York to be best man at Will Souza's wedding. I've been almost a partner of his since we joined the Navy. He has been trying to get married every time the ship came in but never quite made the grade until now. His girl came all the way from California for the occasion. They both have wealthy families so expect the wedding will be quite fancy. Since this letter won't be censored I can tell you of my activities for the past four months. I've been attached to the flattop **USS RANGER** as a torpedo pilot. I joined the ship after ferrying a dive bomber up to Newfoundland in May. We spent 3 months operating out of Argentia. Then we escorted the Queen Mary from England with Churchill on it, made several convoy escort jobs, and headed for Scapa Flow which is in the Orkney Islands north of Scotland. We spent some time in Edinburgh and London. Also visited Iceland twice and got within sight of Greenland. Made a raid on German shipping in Norway and finally returned to the US as of yesterday. Crossed the Arctic Circle three times and got practically to the North Pole once. My part in the raid amounted to the sinking of a tanker and flying the Avenger back to the carrier 100 miles off shore with two anti-aircraft hits in the engine and one in the wing. Made a crash landing aboard with no oil left except that over the windshield obstructing my view. We got 10 ships that morning at the crack of dawn and didn't lose too heavily. I consider myself darned lucky. It wasn't any more exciting than riding a bronc out of the chute. That brings me up to date. Just finished a two-dollar meal in a ritzy restaurant. Enjoyed the things we could not get at sea."*

Gerald (Best Man), Bernice "Bunny" Kershner (Maid of Honor), Lyn and Will Souza.
Wedding photo. Stanton Island, New York. December 6, 1943.

Gerald. Boston, Massachusetts. March 3, 1943.

Dec 6 -- *"Lyn and Will Souza were married on Stanton Island, NY. Bunny was maid of honor and I was best man."*

Dec 15 -- *"The squadron officially changed command this afternoon. Lt. Cdr. D. W. Taylor was replaced by Lt. H. H. Hutcheson. Torpedo Four regrets the loss of a Skipper that led us in flights all over the Atlantic and an engagement with the enemy on the Norwegian Coast."* (Taylor was later killed in a plane crash.)

Jan 1, 1944 -- Letter home. *"Dear Mother, Dad and Walter: Happy New Year! I'm still in the U.S. Had the duty last night so slept the old year out and the new year in.... I was supposed to have Christmas day off but we had an alert on the East Coast so was confined to the base. Several old letters have caught up with me recently. Some of them 2 months old. New Years Day is just another day for us. I think we have a flight coming up so will close. Love, Gerald."*

Jan 4 -- From: Commanding Officer, *USS RANGER.* *"All stipulated conditions having been fulfilled, your appointment to the rank of Lieutenant (jg) is delivered. Your BuPers file number is 158053. Signed Gordon Rowe."*

Jan 22 -- *"I led four fighters on a 200-mile navigation hop from the ship. Missed the RANGER about 115 miles. No YE or Radar so the Maru sent a vector.... Landed at Floyd Bennett, NY with nothing to spare on gas or daylight."*

Jan 24 -- *"Lugged a real live torpedo up to Bar Harbor, Maine and dropped it on an Island."*

Jan 28 -- Letter home. *"Dear Walter -- Say Bud, isn't it about time you were turning out one of those typing masterpieces? Golly, all the fellows are won-*

dering, 'Have you heard from worthless Walter lately?'. I told them that Daddy calls you worthless because you only do enough work for two men. Even some of the aviator's wives ask about you – they all know you from hearsay. Since there is not much else to talk about I'll tell you about my stay in London. I rode down from Edinburgh, Scotland by train. The British trains are all equipped with black-out curtains so you can't see much of the somewhat dreary countryside. As you enter London you note that all the homes have small air raid shelters in the back yard. Kings Cross, where the train stops, is a mass of people – practically all in uniform – men and women alike. One of the boys and I caught an old style cab to Piccadilly Circus, which is a section in the center of town, where we got a room in a hotel taken over by the Red Cross. We went out to a ritzy restaurant for lunch which cost us about 12 shillings ($2.40). A mass of French waiters stood around and annoyed us. A lot of classy people around the place made the atmosphere stuck-upity. No one hardly talked above a whisper. We were glad to get back into the streets where there was plenty of noise and activity. Shortly after dark sirens started wailing and we stopped a pedestrian to ask what was going on. 'Oh, just and air raid,' he said and went on about his business. No one seemed worried or made any effort to get into shelter so we figured it didn't amount to much. Pretty soon search lights started popping up here and there and we spotted a plane way up over the city. Anti-aircraft guns opened up here and there. Don't know whether any of the planes were shot down or not. Only a few bombs were dropped on the outskirts of town. We got a big kick out of watching the affair. Someone told us these nuisance raids went on every few nights. Not much damage was done but it kept the people on their

Flight Reconnaissance Training. Harrisburg, Pennsylvania. May, 1944.
Front: Lt(jg) G. D. "Mak" Makibbin and Gerald. Others unidentified.

Two Navy brothers meet in Harrisburg, Pennsylvania. Byron from the
USS KASAAN BAY and Gerald from the **RANGER.** May 20, 1944.

toes. The next day, we visited the bombed out regions of London and were amazed at the damage done during the first part of the war. We also looked over the Palaces of the English Kings, Westminster Abbey, St. Paul's Cathedral, and other places of interest. I am enclosing my Blue Nose Certificate which I obtained for crossing the Arctic Circle. Write soon, Gerald."

Feb 21 -- *"Two day hops and two night carrier landings. Lt(jg) Edwards was killed last night during carrier landings. Eddie was a good kid. Just married. Memorial Services today."*

Feb 26 -- Letter from Dad. *"I am sure proud of you boys. I think you are the best in the world. I want you to give Mother all the credit for your schooling -- you have got the best mother in the world. Tell her something nice every time you write to her. She has got the blues most of the time since you went to war."*

Feb 28 -- *"The Airgroup was launched for a (practice) attack at 0730. Solid cloud layer. Started up through it with 40 planes. Two dive bombers collided due to poor visibility. Hovey chewed Phillips tail off and he and his radioman bailed out. They were picked up OK."*

Mar 2 -- *"Candyman and I had the day off (the second for me this year) so we went to Boston and got skunk drunk. Hit every night club in town."*

Mar 4 -- *"Taxied planes aboard ship for more sea duty this afternoon. Started to bounce tonight but the signal officer's wands burned out so we packed up and went aboard ship."*

Mar 5 -- *"Don Henry landed an Avenger on a Dauntless in the gear -- tore both planes up. No one hurt seriously."*

Mar 11 -- *"Visited my cousin, Betty Lou,*

at the Naval Training Station, Hunter College. She is in the Waves. Met a couple of girls I knew from Boston so passed the time away with them."

Mar 15 -- *"0230 Reveille. Take off and land aboard. Weather foul. Night black as hell. Thirty planes took off in the stuff. What a mess! Henry crashed into the Island. Plane burned but no casualties. Wreckage fouled up the flight deck so all remaining planes vectored to land. I started frantically conserving gas as we headed for the beach. Arrived Quonset OK."*

Mar 16 -- *"Harriss, Mak, Trex, Candyman and I went to Boston tonight -- Dinty Moors, The Latin Quarter, Shangri-La, Ruby Foos Den, etc. Stayed in Boston tonight.... Saw Martha Ray in person."*

Mar 20 -- *"Received a long distance phone call from Byron (my brother). Hope to arrange a meeting while we are both in the Atlantic."*

Mar 25 -- *"Taxied the planes to the dock where they were loaded aboard ship in preparation for a short cruise."*

Mar 28 -- *"Ens. Allander got vertigo in a cloud and was last seen spiraling down in his plane. The Avengers and Dauntless dive bombers spent the remainder of the day searching for survivors. No luck. Allander, a new man in VB-4 was only 19, married with a child on the way. Candyman, Mak and I went to Providence tonight. Had a rip-roaring time."*

Apr 2 -- *"Gunnery hop this afternoon. Night flying tonight. Black night but no mishaps."*

Apr 3 -- *"It was Jack Fulnecky's turn tonight. Bad wave-off. Caught a wire and over the side. Happy-go-lucky 'Ful' -- just married -- well liked -- good aviator. He*

*"In one of Jean's letters she enclosed a photo which I was
proud to show to some of my squadron buddies."*

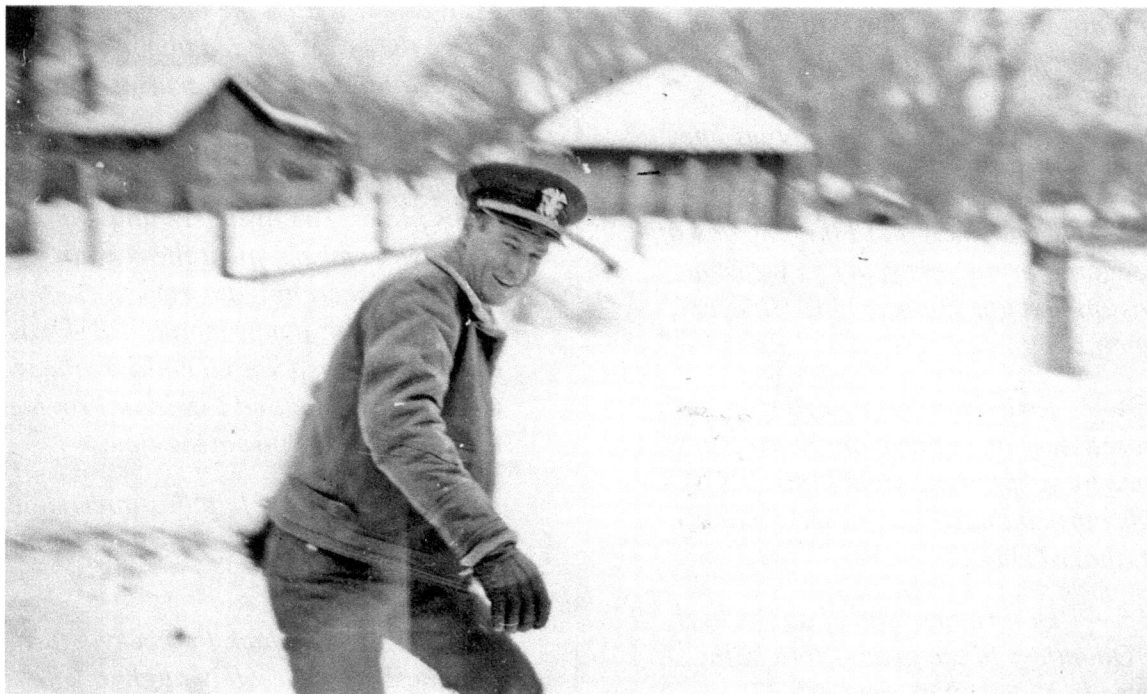

Gerald home at Medicine Lodge Ranch on an 8-day leave. April 24, 1944.

has been on this tub 14 months and never had any trouble."

Apr 16 -- *"Sunday: Rainy day. Flying secured. Spent the time packing and moving off the* **RANGER**. *Airgroup 4 has been detached from the* **RANGER** *and is to move to Fort Devens, Mass to be enlarged to a 90-plane outfit. A 7-day leave is coming up soon but we can't get more than 24-hour away so I'm stuck again. Bad Luck."*

Apr 17 -- Letter home. *"Dear Mother and Dad: Just a note to let you know there is a strong possibility of me getting home soon. Expect about seven days leave starting around the 20th. Will travel both ways by air to lengthen the stay at home.... Byron is in Norfolk again. He expects to get into Quonset about the time I leave.... Surprised to hear Daniel and Betty have another baby -- a baby girl again.... I will fly to Missoula and catch a bus to Ronan.... Don't spread this around until it actually happens but I'm to be decorated with the Air Medal about tomorrow for my part in the Norway attack. I read the citation. Someone sure gave me a terrific write-up. Sure surprised me."*

On April 20th I was authorized an 8-day leave to go home. I flew into Missoula, Montana, and back to Idaho. While I was on leave in Idaho, I learned that Jean Ellis was now teaching school in Pocatello. I took a chance and called her up for a dinner date. To my surprise, Jean accepted and she brought along her sister Lois for the evening meal. This meeting resulted in periodic correspondence while I was in the Pacific. In one of Jean's letters she enclosed a photo which I was proud to show to some of my squadron buddies. Most everyone had a photo of their wives or sweethearts in their locker.

On May 9th, my buddy Makibbin and I were assigned to a special aerial photography training program at Harrisburg, Pennsylvania. On May 20, Byron came to the base for a visit. I took him on a hop in my TBM but he did not appreciate the ride in the belly of the Avenger. We went to a night club in the evening and I introduced him to Mary Barbara Neidig, a girl I had dated several times. That was the end of my relationship with Mary. Byron and Mary fell in love and were married August 3, 1945. I completed photo-recon training on June 2 and rejoined Torpedo Four at Devens Field.

While I was attached to the **RANGER** in the Atlantic, I wrote the letter reproduced on the next page to my father in recognition of his 48th birthday. This letter expressed my feelings at the time and still seems appropriate. Dad and Mother set high standards for honesty, integrity and hard work as they raised their six boys.

Gerald getting on the bus in Dubois, Idaho at the end of his leave. April 27, 1944.

TORPEDO SQUADRON 4
****

August 28, 1943

Dear Dad,

I suppose that you are wondering why this letter is written and addressed specifically to you. Well, the occassion is your approaching birthday. I have taken the privelege to deviate from the customary "Dear Folks" to pay my respects to you alone. This is only an inadequate effort to show you that I am thankful for the many things you have done for me. I know that I speak for not one, but six boys, when I say that we are honored to have you as a father.

You know, every so often, during periods of inactivity, I get terifically homesick--for you, and mother, and the ranch--and I began remeniscing. Certain instances become outstanding, and always you are present as a part of the picture.

I can see you leaning against the Round Corral fence while the herd of horses that Daniel and I had just brought off Deep Creek restlessly mill around. You calmly chew on a stem of alfalfa as Daniel and I, all het up inside, talk profusely about the possibilities of making a good saddlehorse out of Dixies' new colt. You say we aught to halter-break Babe's yearlin', or advertise that stray black mare because she has been with this bunch since last fall. In the excitement I drop Dime's reins and he walks sidewards as he drags them over to the manger. You cuss as one of the geldons kicks with both hind feet at a young stud and William gets too close. Then there is lots of confusion as Daniel and I try to rope the colts we have to brand. After we just about run them down and maybe accidentally catch one or two you take the lasso rope and finish up. Then there is the smell of burning hair and possibly warm blood if a two year old stud happens along. Finally we start the remainder of the herd back to Deep Creek on a high lope so the bay mare won't lead them out in the lavies. Then we unsaddle and go to the house where we finish the discussion of horses with Mother and Henry.

That night we are pretty darned tired and we dread the thought of milking those few cows. But with your iniatitive we all chip in and it really wasn't so bad after all.

When haying season comes around you again lead the way. Stelzer was right when he said you raised yourself a hay crew. We make short work of that Reno contract despite that old broken down derrick and the wind, and that roan stud that no one could bridle but you. You let Frank gyp you on the hay measurement, but then you always gave the other ranchers the best deal because you were easy to get along with.

There were numerous times following a long night at Lidy's when you let us boys sleep in while you milked and done the chores all alone. You went out and harnessed up and fed the stock during those winter blizzards when we were in school. You did all the hard work on the Fourth and 24th and at those little rodeos we put on while the rest of us had fun. These are only a few of the things that make us indebted to you as the best father in the world.

Well, Dad, I guess you know that all this adds up to me wishing you a happy birthday this year and many years to come.

Your Son,

Gerald

P.S. I am enclosing a little check and you can buy your own birthday present. Give my regards to the rest of the family.

Ens. G. W. Thomas
Torpedo Squadron Four

Gerald's letter to his Dad. August 28, 1943.

Chapter 12 | Air Group 4 to the Pacific Theater

"Three planes collided in a thunderstorm."

Tragedy Strikes Night Operations

On June 26, 1944, our entire Air Group (fighters, dive-bombers and torpedo bombers) received orders to travel to the West Coast for an assignment in the Pacific. We were expecting this move as we were now an experienced Air Group. Most of us took the train to the point of departure, the Naval Air Station, San Diego. I wrote to Mother about the move and asked about the new horse Walter was breaking. He named the horse "Ranger" after my aircraft carrier. He named another saddle horse, "Kasaan Bay" for Byron's carrier. However, my folks did not realize that all Navy ships are referred to as female. Walter's saddle horses were geldings.

July 13: We were loaded on the **USS BARNES** for transportation to Hawaii. We arrived Pearl Harbor on July 21 and were immediately sent to the Air Base at Hilo for further training. We flew in and out of Hilo in all kinds of weather for both day and night operations.

On September 21, during night training operations, three of our Avengers ran together in a severe rain squall, and the squadron lost our skipper and 8 other airmen. I was not on this flight but I helped in the 3-day search for survivors after the crash – without success. There was great sadness in our squadron, not only on the loss of our skipper, but several of us were very close to Bill Canty (Candyman) who had joined us from the famous Torpedo 8.

Memorial Services were held in St. Joseph's Church at Hilo for:

Homer Hamby Hutcheson, Lt. Cdr.
William H. Canty, Lt(jg).
Merrill Silver Stocker, Ens.

Henry N. Karsemeyer, ACRM.
Edward James Dooner, ACOM.
Thomas Charles Bradley, AOM2c.
William Laverne Finkenbinder, ARM3c.
Harry Lester Johnston, AOM3c.
Raymond N. Glew, ARM3c.

We say, *"God reward you and well done."*

Lt. Paul J. "PJ" Davis, with no combat experience, took over as skipper of Torpedo Four. He had not asked for the command, but happened to have he lowest serial number. None of us had the confidence in PJ that we had under Woot Taylor or Hutch.

Tour of Duty on the BUNKER HILL

"Ferried to Saipan."

The Air Group was loaded on the **USS LONG ISLAND** on October 22 and ferried to Saipan in the Marianas. At this time Saipan was largely secured, but Tinian remained in Japanese hands. Our Air Group, while on shore, was subjected to periodic sniper fire and one bombing raid by Japanese planes. As the air raid sounded I took refuge under a canvas cot in the tent. While on Saipan I traded a bottle of Schenley's Whisky to a Marine for an M-l jungle gun with the words "Mary" carved on the stock. Evidently the Marine received a "Dear John" letter from Mary and no longer cherished the weapon.

We were surprised when the **BUNKER HILL** pulled into Saipan and our Air Group was ordered aboard. We took over the Avengers, Hellcats, and Helldivers that were on board from the previous Air Group.

Strike on Manila Bay, Philippines. November 13, 1944.

Strike on Manila Bay, Philippines. November 13, 1944.

This was our first experience on an Essex class carrier. The **BUNKER HILL** had a flight deck that was 103 feet longer and nearly 40 feet wider than the old **RANGER**. I was thrilled to be on the **BUNKER HILL** – a great ship carrying a name important to American history.

On November 5, 1944, the **BUNKER HILL** log states that she was "under way for the Philippines" and a very brief shake-down cruise for Air Group 4.

Six days later (Nov 11) we had our first combat assignment. Since this was the first action against the Japanese, there was a high level of excitement during the briefing in the Ready Room. We were informed that there would be two strikes during the day. Both strikes would be designed as coordinated attacks involving Hellcats, Helldivers and Avengers. My plane was loaded with four 500 lb SAP bombs. We were launched just after daybreak. The target was a Japanese convoy entering Ormoc Bay with troops and supplies. Although there were enemy Oscars and Zekes in the area, our formation was not attacked.

We dived on two destroyers and an AK which took evasive action. Even though the fighters and dive bombers had made their run, our Avengers came under intense AA fire. My plane was not hit and evasive action saved the ship I selected as a target.

On November 13, we made strikes on Luzon, Manila Bay and Cavite. I received a DFC on November 13 for *"Making a glide bombing attack on two enemy destroyers in the face of intense antiaircraft fire, he scored four direct hits on the destroyers contributing to their destruction."* Clipped to the citation signed by Admiral M. A. Mitscher was a statement which read, *"Medals are at present unavailable in the combat area."*

The following day we hit ships in South Harbor, Manila. The combat reports states, *"VT-4 pushed over from 9500 feet under heavy AA Fire. Five bombs bracketed the AO, three credited to Ens Landre and one each to Lt Trexler and Lt(jg) Thomas. The ship was set afire as VT-4 departed."*

As the Air Group proceeded back to the **BUNKER HILL**, we counted our losses:

"Ens W. N. Ostlund was not seen after the dive."

"Ens K. W. Watkins was hit by AA fire and crashed in flames."

"Lt(jg) Don Dondero's plane was hit and two persons were seen to bail out."

Dondero was a close friend. He and his crewman survived after a harrowing escape and months hiding from the Japanese.

During our tour on the **BUNKER HILL**, Air Group 4 lost 7 pilots and 4 crewmen. In a summary report Air Group Commander Otto Klinsmann stated that: (1) We had attacked too many targets rather than concentrating on a few; (2) We must accept losses from the accuracy and intensity of Japanese antiaircraft fire and; (3) Radio discipline must be improved so that Mayday or rescue calls can be acknowledged.

Air Group 4 transferred off the **BUNKER HILL** at Ulithi on November 17, 1944. The carrier went home for repairs and was back in the Pacific by February, 1945. On May 11, the ship was put out of action by a Kamikaze attack.

Planting Spuds and Milking Cows

"Walter's letters gave us a home front perspective on the War."

In our family during the war, Byron and I had joined the Navy, Daniel was married and working in Alaska, and John and Bill were too young to do much farm work. So that meant my teenage brother Walter was left to help Dad and Mother with the farm and ranch chores. Walter, therefore, became my primary source of back-home information and, without his knowledge, a sort of counselor. His letters on the farm problems were greatly appre-

After Air Group 4 was transferred off the Bunker Hill, the ship was hit by two kamikaze planes only 30 seconds apart. The date of this attack was May 11, 1945. The ship suffered the loss of 346 men killed, 43 missing, and 264 wounded.

Burned planes, flight deck, *BUNKER HILL,* after Kamikazes. In spite of the damage, the ship was able to return to port under her own power.

ciated and widely circulated among my squadron buddies. Walter was learning to type on the school typewriter and he did not know the location of the periods, commas, etc. Here are some quotes from Walter's letters:

May 21, 1943 -- *"School is out thank goodness I passed isn't that surprising. The old ford is still running good having a little trouble getting gas though since gas rationing... Lynn was home last week he was asking about all you kids. You know you guys never was home long enough for me to find out the wrong side of you you sure have a good reputation... helps the reputation of the rest of the family too...."*

May 22 -- *"Well today Daddy and I went over to the Lodge he harrowed and I cut spuds... Milk nine cows about $28.00 a week of cream. Sold two pigs the other day got $35.00 a peace for them."*

May 23 -- *"Daddy finished harrowing and sold Buster for $60 I cut spuds... The saddle horse got out and run off I left the gate open when I got the cows."*

May 24 -- *"What a day I and Daddy planted spuds till Im sick of them came home and milked then caught old Dime and learned him to jump."*

May 25 -- *"I hazed cows today up Blue Creek had a duce of a time I dednt have no saddle to ride... got my foot in a sagebrush and got sent a rolling... my horse run off and left me afoot with a cow to drive from the upper spring."*

May 26 -- *"Same old thing today milked cows and planted spuds me and paw are on the lift today the spud planter keeps breaking down... John Foster fell of the bed just now he done about everything today ate the chickens clabored milk drank the pigs swill waded in the ditch pulled fethers out of the gobbler dumped ashes in my bed broke his dish at the table and what not ??? well no excitement today so I guess I'll quite."* (Note: My youngest brother, John Foster was born Nov 2, 1941.)

May 29 -- *"Today we planted spuds. Bought 3 new parts for the spud planter and it wont plant. It went on the bum today so we planted by hand."*

Sep 2 -- *"Mother bought a place in Montana around $5000... school starts up there the 7th. I wanted to start but Daddy said I had to stay home and help thresh, pick spuds, fix fence and a million other things... a feller never gets to do anything he wants to anyway so I shouldn't have figured on it... I'm going to get in the Navy when I get old enough so I can help get this war over with...."*

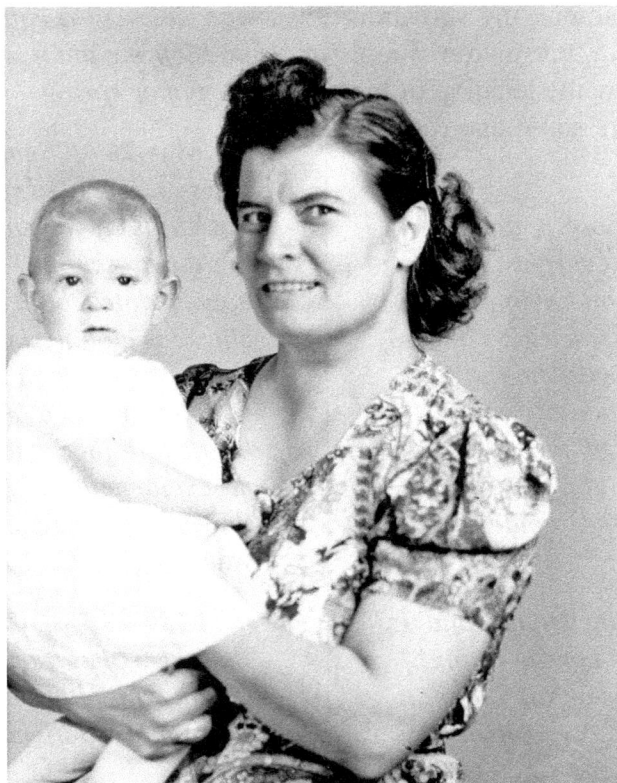

My Mother with John Foster. John was born November 2, 1941.

Walter Thomas on Dime. Lidy Hot Springs. 1943.

Chapter 13 | Air Group 4 on the USS ESSEX

"A kamikaze flew through heavy flak and crashed on the ESSEX."

Transfer to the ESSEX

On November 18, 1944, our Air Group was transferred to the **USS ESSEX** for continued attacks on the Japanese. Air Group 4 replaced Air Group 15, under whose action the **ESSEX** had been named the "fightenist ship" in the Navy. We felt the burden of keeping up that reputation. Some of the action we were involved in is shown here.

Japanese Subs Penetrate Ulithi: While the **ESSEX** was anchored in Ulithi Lagoon and Air Group 4 was getting bunk assignments, two Japanese mini-subs got through the nets and torpedoed the **USS MINNISSINEWA**, a tanker anchored near us. It exploded and burned, killing 63 sailors and the Japanese sub pilot. I was on the flight deck at the time and took photos of the explosion. However, as it turned out, the camera was not loaded with film. Luckily, other photos of the explosion are available. The date was November 20, 1944.

Strikes on Japanese Convoy at Santa Cruz

Early in the morning of November 25, the **ESSEX** launched the usual Combat Air Patrol and a morning fighter sweep against Clark Field on Luzon. I was with the main strike group for attacks on shipping at Santa Cruz.

Two Helldivers went in the drink while our torpedo planes were warming up on the fantail (the VB-4 Skipper Lt. Cdr. Cecil V. Johnson and Lt(jg) Russell L. Deputy). Our torpedo planes carried four 500 lb bombs for glide bombing attacks. We sank or damaged several ships. Buck Barnett's plane was hit by AA fire and his crewman was wounded. However, all Torpedo 4 planes returned to base.

ESSEX Takes a Kamikaze

We were launching a second strike group on November 25 when the Kamikaze hit. I had just returned from the morning strike and was in the Ward Room eating my noon meal when the Japanese Judy flew through heavy flak and crashed on the **ESSEX**. There was a huge explosion and the room filled up with smoke. The official record shows that 16 men were killed and 44 were wounded in the attack.

Don Gress, my gunner, was standing in the catwalk when the kamikaze hit. He stated:

"I saw all of the 20-mm and 40-mm guns shooting at it.... It was smoking but no one could shoot it down. I jumped back into the Ready Room when it hit. After the explosion, I ventured out – and I wish I hadn't – all those people killed – most burned to death."

Post-war research reveals that the Japanese pilot's name was Yoshinori Yamaguchi with the Special Attack Corps stationed at Malabacat Field in the Philippines.

A swarm of Kamikazes attacked that day, hitting 3 other carriers too. One post-war report states that over 7400 Kamikazes flew to their deaths during WWII. 474 ships were hit with the loss of 3,253 officers and men and over 6,000 wounded.

After the smoke cleared from the Kamikaze attack the **ESSEX** deck was repaired and the afternoon strike group took off. I made a note that:

"VT carried torpedoes and hit two ships off San Bernardino Point. Scored

USS ESSEX (CV-9). Air Group 4 transferred to the *ESSEX* November 18, 1944.

Kaiten suicide torpedo recovered in Ulithi Harbor following Kamikaze attack
on November 20, 1944. The front part of the Kaiten is destroyed.

Kamikaze flown by Yoshinori Yamaguchi dives through intense gun fire toward the **ESSEX**.
The plane was identified as a "Judy" (Yokosuba D4Y3 dive bomber), tail number 17.
The pilot was aiming at the flight deck, but the ship's defensive fire deflected him forward
and to the left. The streaks are tracer fire. November 25, 1944.

The Kamikaze hits the **ESSEX** and explodes.

Another view of the Kamikaze strike, taken from **USS SOUTH DAKOTA**.

ESSEX crew responds to the fire caused by the Kamikaze strike.

The fire is brought rapidly under control.

The Kamikaze struck along the port side gun mounts. The 16 men killed were manning these guns. 44 men were wounded. If the Kamikaze had hit the flight deck with its munitions-loaded planes, the damage would have been much worse.

Funeral service for the men killed in the Kamikaze attack on the *ESSEX*.
November 25, 1944.

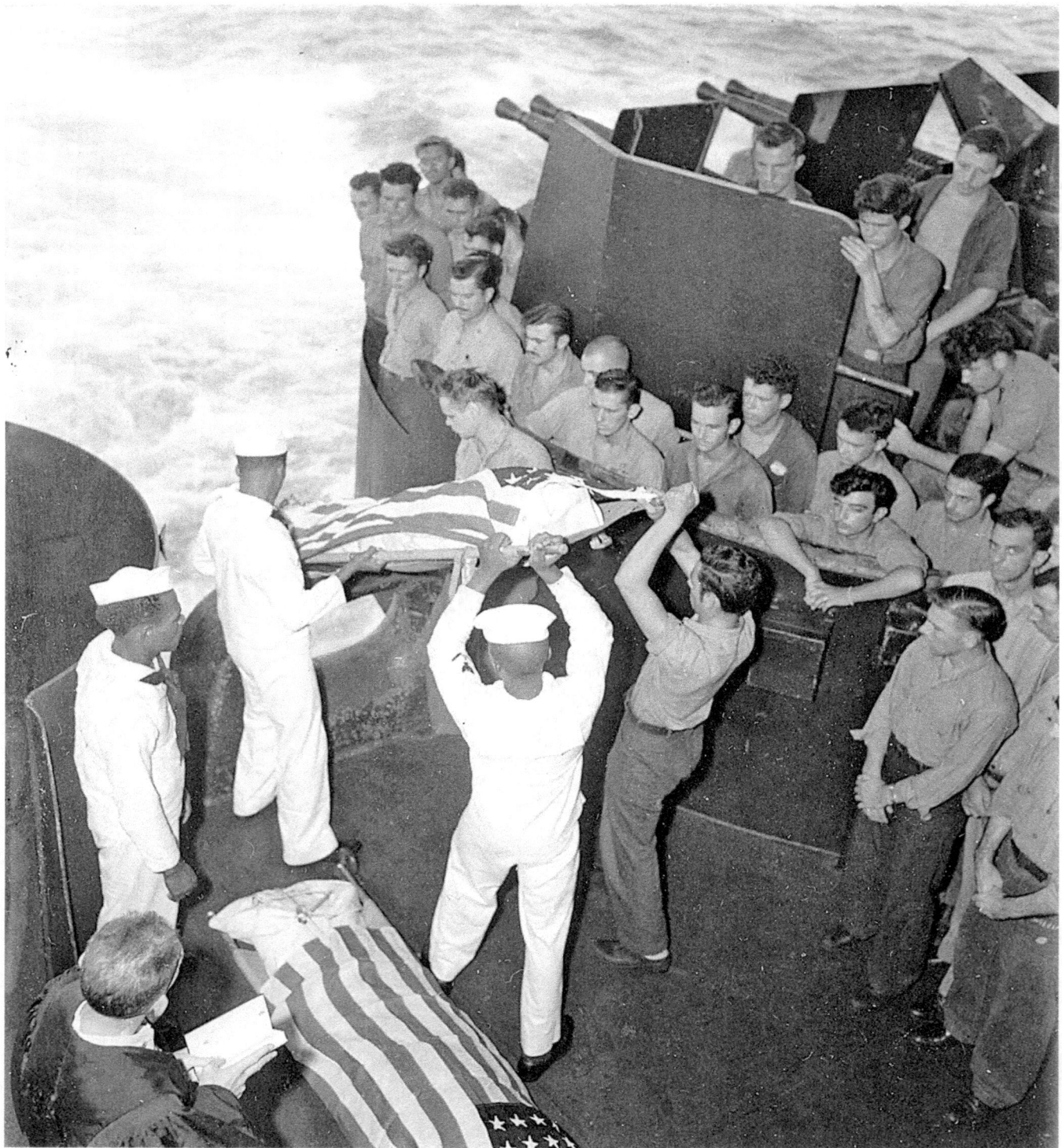

Burial at sea for the men killed in the Kamikaze attack on the **ESSEX**.
Combat made it impossible to return the bodies for land burial.
November 25, 1944.

four torpedo hits out of nine. VB lost Lt(jg) Kinder, another photo pilot, leaving six out of nine of us that went to Harrisburg to photo school."

Marines Replace Dive-Bombers

Combat operations continued out of Ulithi into December. Then on December 28th two Marine Squadrons (VMF-124 and VMF-213) replaced our dive-bombers (VB-4) on the ***ESSEX***. These were the first two Marine squadrons to be carrier-based during WWII. We now had 36 Corsairs, 55 Hellcats and 15 Avengers. When we lost our Air Group Commander (see later report), Marine Col Millington took over command – the first Marine to command a Navy Squadron during WWII.

The Marine pilots soon learned that carrier operations were more difficult than land-based operations. During the period December 30 to March 1 we lost 12 corsairs – mostly in routine operations.

We made our first strikes on Formosa in the soup on January 3. This was our first exposure to radar-controlled anti-aircraft fire. Back to the Philippines on January 6 we lost our Fighter Skipper in an attack on Lauag, Luzon. This was a sad day for our "Red Rippers." The combat report states:

"Lt. Cdr. Hammond's plane was mortally damaged by heavy AA. He made a water landing without dropping his belly tank and the plane exploded. Aircraft circled for 20 minutes but nothing was observed on the surface in the area."

"KG" Hammond had been with us on the ***RANGER*** and was well-respected by all in the Air Group.

On January 7, five Marine corsairs from Air Group 4 were "lost at sea." Then on January 9 we supported the D-Day invasion of Luzon. That day three of our torpedo planes were hit by AA fire.

On January 12th the Task Force moved into the South China Sea. Robert Sherrod, *Time Magazine*

correspondent stated, *"The venture into the South China Sea was as audacious as it was unlikely. Who ever heard of taking 11 carriers, 6 battleships, 13 cruisers and 48 destroyers into an area surrounded by kamikazes?"* Tokyo Rose reported that the *"American fleet was bottled up in the China Sea and will be destroyed!"*

Our planes attacked Hong Kong, Singapore and Saigon. Don Henry, the only other VT-4 pilot from Idaho, was shot down over Saigon. He was wounded but rescued by the Free French. Later, he joined other Americans and, in an attempt to reach friendly territory, the group was attacked by the Japanese. Don was shot during the skirmish and most of the other Americans were captured and beheaded.

On January 15, we lost Air Group Commander Otto Klinsmann. He was shot down in a rocket attack in the Pescadores Islands. There was great sadness aboard the ***ESSEX*** over the loss of our friend and Commander. Lt. Col. William Millington from Marine Squadron 124 then took over Command of Air Group 4.

Splash Down in the South China Sea

On January 16, 1945, after a strike on Hainan, 3 torpedo planes ran out of gas and went in the drink. I was the pilot of one of these planes. Willie Walker went down first. I circled his crash site and tried to call in a position report but the radio was cluttered and the call was not acknowledged. Later, about 30 miles from Willie, I ran out of gas. Fortunately, my "May Day" call went through. I turned into the wind and made a full-stall water landing. My photographer Robert B. Montague and I got in a one-man rubber boat and my crewman Don Gress floated off in the larger raft. Just before dark we were rescued by the destroyer the ***USS SULLIVANS***. I gave the DD the approximate location for Willie and his crewman and we found them in their rubber boats. After a day of seasickness and dry heaves on the DD, we were finally transferred back to the ***ESSEX***.

A Marine F4U Corsair gets the take-off signal. Note the Air Group 4
tail marking (horizontal bar). *ESSEX*. January 25, 1945.

A Torpedo 4 Avenger drops a torpedo on a ship seeking shore cover.
The ideal drop was at 250 knots from an altitude of 250 feet.
Luzon, Philippines. January 9, 1945.

Torpedo Four strike on shipping and shore installations along the Saigon River,
French Indo-China. January 12, 1945.

The tail of my TBM Avenger just as it sinks into the South China Sea.
Photo by PhoM3c Robert B. Montague. January 25, 1945.

Gerald being prepared for transfer from *USS SULLIVANS* to *ESSEX* by
breeches buoy after being rescued at sea. January 27, 1945.

In a letter to my folks on January 31, 1945 I stated:

> *"Yesterday I received a letter from you implying that Byron may now be in the Pacific. A few hours later I saw a Baby Flat Top pull up and anchor beside us. Sure enough it was the KASAAN BAY. I bummed a ride on a guard mail boat over to her and went aboard. Golly it was good to see Byron again. We talked for hours... and finally ended up talking about ranches, horses and future plans."*

Our Air Group continued in the Pacific during the invasion of the Philippines, D-Day coverage of Iwo Jima, and on to strikes on Okinawa, Formosa and Saigon, French Indo-China. I received a second DFC for a torpedo hit on a 10,000-ton tanker near Saigon on January 12, 1945: *"Torpedoes were dropped at 250 feet altitude; average speed of aircraft being 250 knots indicated.... The torpedoes of Lt(jg) Thomas and Ens Hopfinger struck the Sugar Able."*

Credit for bomb hits on a Japanese Destroyer in a Formosa harbor on January 21 brought a third DFC and another Air Medal came from later combat action.

Flying Conditions "Average"

"Typhoon: the other enemy."

One thing that never seemed to change during our service on three aircraft carriers – the weather summary. The teletype in the Pilot's Ready Room may have given details about the heavy overcast, freezing rain, and high winds, but invariably the concluding statement was *"flying conditions average."*

We finally learned to send a pilot out to the flight deck to check. Buck Barnett was a likely candidate since he was our "night flying expert." He would report back, *"Can't see the other end of the flight deck for the fog. Wind nearly blew me into the catwalk, but the teletype is correct, flying conditions are average."*

Torpedo Four, like most of the Navy squadrons in the war, lost more men in so-called "operations" than in combat and weather was the big contributor. In addition to routine bad weather, our carriers were in and out of several typhoons.

As one historian stated Typhoons were "the other enemy." One of these that received exceptional notoriety was "Haley's Typhoon," December 16-18, 1944. Three destroyers, the **HULL**, **MONAGHAN** and **SPENCE** were sunk in this storm with 778 men killed. Virtually all ships in the Task Force sustained damage – and many planes on the carriers were torn loose from their tie-down lines and sent crashing across the flight and hanger decks. The final count was 146 aircraft lost or damaged by this typhoon.

Air Group Four supported the D-Day landings on Iwo Jima on February 19 and made the first carrier-based strikes on Tokyo and the Japanese mainland since Doolittle. The following quote is from my book concerning an attack on Tokyo:

> *"When all planes were back aboard the ESSEX, and we had secured flight quarters for the night, there were many exciting stories of dogfights, close calls, and first impressions of the snow-covered Mt. Fujiyama. On February 17, 1945, the Fighting Four Red Rippers reported 8 confirmed kills, and the Marine Corsairs were credited with seven. Cozy Cole sort of summarized many of our feelings: 'One of my most satisfying moments of the war was that first strike on Tokyo! I had saved up for the occasion, and when we flew over Japan, I used the 'relief tube' with pleasure.'"*

My last combat in the Pacific involved a glide bombing strike on Naha Airfield on Okinawa on March 1, 1945. We lost Scott Vogt (VT-4) and Doug Cahoon (VF-4) to AA fire on this attack.

Our Air Group was then transferred to the **USS LONG ISLAND** during a Kamikaze attack at Ulithi. Makibbin and I were on the flight deck when we heard two planes overhead. We com-

"Flying conditions average." Note the breakers crashing over the 80-foot flight deck. ***ESSEX***. February 22, 1945.

VT-4 ready for first strike on Japan. Gerald at right. February 17, 1945.

mented on the sound that was different from that of our own planes. We were shocked when we heard a huge explosion next to us as one of the Kamikazes hit the carrier *USS RANDOLPH*. 25 seamen were killed and 105 wounded in this attack. A second plane mistook the airstrip on the island for a ship and crashed without significant damage.

The *LONG ISLAND* took us to Pearl Harbor where we boarded the *USS ALTAMAHA* for the final leg to stateside. We arrived San Diego on April 1. My new orders directed me to the Naval Air Station, Corpus Christi, Texas, as a flight instructor. We were authorized a 30-day leave before reporting for this new duty.

Gerald receives the Distinguished Flying Cross with two Gold Stars from
Capt. John G. Crommelin, Jr. Others unidentified.
NAS, Corpus Christi, Texas. May 1945.

Torpedo Four aboard the "Essex" – Ulithi Lagoon – December 1944

front row: J.E.Ganley, J.W.Frost, A.J.Tankard, R.R.Pittman, C.L.Ely, J.W.Aldrich, J.F.Ballard, S.A.Hastings, T.R.Sims, H.L.Blalock, G.J.Rauch, R.A.Trembley, E.A.Shirley, D.L.King, R.E.Simindinger, N.J.Schmolke, D.H.Gress, W.T.Lundry, W.S.Lace, H.R.Green.

second row: G.D.Makibbin, L.A.Cole, R.B.Cline, G.M.Barnett, B.R.Trexler, E.S.Binder, Scott Vogt, P.J.Davis, L.L.Hamrick, J.W.Harriss, G.W.Thomas, L.C.Gay, R.M.Hopfinger, J.E. Hewitt, L.G.Gardemal, P.P.Stephens.

third row: A.Beard, D.E.Venderville, L.S.Leach, J.J.Pinkney, L.E.Halverson, E.A.Newell, V.A.Landre, W.H.Gannady, D.A.Henry, J.D.Clemenson, H.J.Deimel, R.F.Ruth, W.F.Walker, F.E. Ward, W.J.Hopkins, G.M.Bell, W.S.Souza, C.Christopher, W.D.Jenkins, A.P.Robistow, C.J.Galeano, J.S.Serafin, N.L.Shiverdecker.

back row: M.A.Clark, F.W.Wilson, S.W.Coller, A.DeGenza, J.C.Gerke, C.J.Warrington, G.F. Zeimer, R.E.Kelly, J.E.Holloman, D.L.Huston, N.H.Knox, A.Macsary, C.L.McConnell, D.M. Applegate, R.C.Campbell, C.C.Slatter, L.P.Shuman, A.G.Schiesz.

The men of Torpedo Four (VT-4). These men have been called *"the Greatest Generation."*
It was the most honored privilege of my life to serve with them.
ESSEX. December, 1944.

Chapter 14 | Stateside: Sweeping Changes as the War Ends

"Flying high but not in the cockpit of my trusty Avenger."

Home – And Engaged

The 30-day leave – the longest I had received since joining the Navy – was filled with exciting events. The war was obviously winding down. This gave everyone a feeling of immense elation – a sense of buoyancy. In addition, as returning service men, we were welcomed everywhere almost like heroes.

I was anxious to get back to Idaho and Montana to see my parents and relatives. But, of much more importance, I wanted to follow-up on the occasional correspondence I had received in the Pacific from a beautiful young school teacher named Jean Ellis. She was now teaching school in Pocatello, Idaho. So I called her up as soon as I reached home. We dated in Pocatello and went on horseback rides in the hills above Lidy Hot Springs. Before my 30-day leave was up, we were engaged to be married. I was now flying high – and not even in the cockpit of my trusty Avenger.

We encountered one serious problem with our marriage plans. Jean had joined the WAVES and was awaiting orders. I couldn't stand a forced separation, so we contacted everyone we could think of in the Navy with an outline of the situation. The higher echelons of the Navy knew that the war was about over and, unbelievably, they authorized an Honorable Discharge for Jean, *"without a call to active duty."*

I was still on leave when President Roosevelt died on April 12, 1945. This announcement sent shock waves through the military. For nearly four years I had felt secure in knowing that America was in the good hands of a knowledgeable Commander-in-Chief. The deep sense of loss was not mitigated as a relative unknown, Vice-President Harry S. Truman, took over supreme command. Fortunately, American military momentum did not falter. Truman faced some difficult decisions, and his performance was soon lauded by those of us in the service. His decision to drop the atomic bomb no doubt saved hundreds of thousands of Allied and Japanese lives.

I reported for duty at the Naval Air Station at Corpus Christi on schedule and was back in the cockpit of an SNJ on May 17. I was preoccupied with my upcoming marriage, but I still tried to keep abreast of the blur of changes sweeping through both theaters of war.

April 28, 1945: Benito Mussolini was shot by Italian partisans while attempting to flee Italy.

April 30, 1945: Adolph Hitler shot himself and his new bride, Eva Braun, committing suicide with cyanide capsules.

The German High Command surrendered unconditionally several days after Hitler's death. Churchill and Truman proclaimed May 8, 1945, as V-E Day. There was a great celebration all over the Allied world. Those of us fresh from the Pacific knew that the world was still not at peace.

Wedding and a One-Day Honeymoon

"Mother and Jean drove my 39 Nash to Corpus Christi."

Another important event took place in June – Jean and I set June 2 as our wedding date. I was so excited I could hardly keep track of the "Flight" of French cadets assigned to my care at the airbase. These "frogs", as they were called, were carefree but dangerous flyers. I worried about getting my wings or tail chewed up by their props as I taught

Pilot's license obtained by Jean while teaching school in Pocatello, Idaho.

Jean and I standing in front of my old 1939 Nash, which I had purchased before the war. My Mother volunteered to help Jean drive it to Corpus Christi so we could get married. The trip took five, very difficult days.

them formation flying. And the inverted spin checkouts for the cadets left me in a daze several hours after the ride. The only plane we had on the base that could take the rigors of an inverted spin was the old N2S biplane. This Stearman, with the open cockpit, was really a joy to fly – particularly for aerobatics.

Between flights I made arrangements for our wedding ceremony at the Naval Air Station Chapel. My worst problem was finding a place to live. The housing situation in Corpus Christi was critical and most of the empty apartments were filthy and roach infested. I rented one, found another a little better, and finally rented a third. No money back on the first two rentals. I became so well acquainted with the real estate lady that she set up a reception for us following the wedding ceremony.

In a letter home dated May 20, I stated my frustration with the Navy because they would not allow time off for my wedding:

> *"Here is the sad news. I've been to see every big shot on the Base with this result. It is impossible for me to get over one day off to get married regardless of the circumstances. I have checked every possibility. That settles that matter."*

It was obvious that the Naval aviation program was still under pressure from the Pacific War.

My mother and Jean drove my 1938 Nash from Idaho to Corpus Christi for the wedding. The tires on the car were retreads, because rationing prevented the purchase of new ones. Consequently, it was not long before the tires started throwing rubber and more old retreads had to be located. Add a few mechanical problems and the trip to Corpus took 5 days. Jean called periodically to report the circumstances slowing progress toward our reunion. The wedding date was still firm for June 2nd.

Jean's sister, Lois, came over from Louisiana for the ceremony. My Navy buddies filled in the other slots to complete the wedding party. Jean asked Felix Ward, a fellow pilot, to go down the

isle with her to "give her away." Bob Ruth, another pilot served as Best Man and other pilots provided moral support.

With so much help from the Navy at the wedding, I knew it would be wise to leave town after the reception. We decided to go to Beeville, not far from Corpus Christi, for our one-day Honeymoon. I found the only hotel in downtown Beeville – small, old, rundown, no bridal suite, and without air conditioning. The Texas heat – and the overhead fan really made an impression on my new bride.

I reported back to the flight line on schedule a day after our exciting honeymoon in Beeville. Only now, I was a married man, and consequently, a more cautious pilot.

My logbook shows 2 to 4 hops every day except Sunday through June, July and August. We heard nothing about the experimental explosion of the first atomic bomb at the Trinity Site near Alamogordo, New Mexico on July 16, 1945.

The big news came on August 6! A 9000-pound atomic bomb with destructive power previously unimagined was dropped by the B-29 Enola Gay on Hiroshima at 8:15 am.

Official US estimates placed the dead as high as 78,000.

The second atomic bomb was dropped on Nagasaki on August 9. Casualties from this explosion were estimated at 35,000.

Those of us fresh from the Pacific and those lined up for the invasion of the Japanese mainland, applauded President Truman's decision to release these two bombs. We wanted the war to end without a costly invasion of the Japan where estimates were that; *"There will be more than a million casualties if an invasion becomes necessary."*

V-J Day was proclaimed by the Allied Powers on August 15, 1945. While there had been wild celebrations as the European war ended, this was the big day for those of us who had experienced a touch of the Pacific. Corpus Christi was jubilant.

Jean and Gerald, wedding photo. June 2, 1945.

Bob Ruth was my "Best Man."

Felix Ward "gave Jean away."

Church bells rang, horns blared, and people took to the streets. I was at the Navy Base, and Jean was taking a course at the beauty school when we heard the news. All duty was cancelled. We joined our friends in a big celebration – unconditional surrender by the Japanese! The world was again at Peace!

Slow Rolls as We Celebrate V-J Day

"Released from active duty."

Three days after V-J Day I was back to my flight instructor duties. My flight of French cadets had finally graduated. I was now trying desperately to get a new flight of English cadets through the final aerobatic, navigation and ground training. These "Limeys" were also wild flyers, but they, too, fought hard to keep from washing out.

With the announcement that the war had ended, my Limey cadets came to see me with very sad news. They were ordered to report back to England "immediately." With only two weeks to go before receiving their "Wings of Gold," they were ordered home! I could not believe that their government would not let me finish their training. I solicited the help of our CO and others to try to get an extension of their time but of no avail. Their country was economically drained. There was no time for an orderly phase down.

On August 26, a major hurricane hit Corpus Christi with winds up to 135 miles an hour. Pilots were ordered to the base and we flew all of the flyable planes out of the Air Station to Del Rio, Texas. Wives and families were left behind to fend for themselves. Returning pilots heard many interesting stories later.

Our life was changing rapidly. The schedule for discharge from the military was set up on the basis of earned "points," giving credit for length of service, overseas assignments, and so on. However, there was a simpler way to qualify for release. Any person with a DFC or better was eligible for immediate discharge regardless of accumulated points.

Several of us took advantage of this regulation based on citations and applied for inactive duty. Of course, we had to stay in the Reserves and become "Weekend Warriors," just in case the vision of a peaceful world might fade.

The last view I had from the cockpit of my SNJ was of Corpus Christi, Texas on September 6, 1945. I flew solo for 2.5 hours – with a happy but nostalgic feeling. I slow-rolled a couple of times just for fun. The world was at peace, I was happily married, and Idaho was a logical destination to start a new professional career.

UNITED STATES NAVAL ★ AIR STATION ★ CORPUS CHRISTI, TEXAS

Jean and Gerald celebrate the end of WWII. Riviera Dinner Club,
Corpus Christi, Texas. August 15, 1945.

Chapel, U. S. Naval Air Station

We were married in this Chapel at the Naval Air Station, Corpus Christi, Texas.

Chapter 15 | Return to Civilian Life in Idaho

"We loaded the 39 Nash and headed for Idaho."

Civilian Life

I was released from Active Duty on the 18 of September 1945 with orders to:

"Proceed to your home. You are granted 2 months and one day leave, upon the expiration of which, at midnight on 19 November 1945, you will regard yourself released from all active duty. During the period of leave, you may wear civilian clothes and are authorized to engage in any occupation not contrary to law... you're entitled to a Certificate of Satisfactory Service."

I was now in the Organized Reserve – subject to recall – but it was good to know that I could "engage in any occupation not contrary to law."

Jean and I bid goodbye to our Navy buddies in Corpus Christi, Texas, loaded the 1939 Nash with all our worldly goods and headed for Idaho. The world was at peace and we enjoyed a leisurely trip back home. We placed an old mattress in the trunk of the Nash for sleeping and stopped enroute to visit the Painted Desert, Bryce Canyon and Zion National Parks. Our destination was the Mack Ellis Ranch on Crooked Creek.

An inventory of our assets revealed that we had about $1000 in the bank, maybe 2 or 3 horses and no other livestock that we could identify as ours. My saddle was worn out and I owed 3 years of back income taxes. (Most of us had deferred our taxes since there was a possibility that we might not survive the war.) We had no firm plans for our future but, during the war, I had sometimes dreamed of returning to Idaho and going into the ranching business. For example in a letter I wrote to Mother and Dad on January 31, 1945, I stated:

"Byron and I together, by selling our war bonds and using my bank account, rustle up close to $2000 cash. We want to invest in land... maybe make some kind of a deal to purchase Lidys... or Blue Creek."

Back home, it was obvious that Lidy Hot Springs and the Blue Creek Ranch were beyond our reach. However, as a World War II Veteran, I was invited to participate in a random drawing for sagebrush land in southern Idaho. The size of these blocks ranged from 40-60 acres – supposedly with surface or underground water for irrigation. Later, I also applied for a land drawing in the Toolee Lake area of Oregon. I was lucky. My name was not drawn. These parcels of land that seemed to promise immediate wealth for the lucky vets after the war provided only hard work and poverty-level living a few years later.

We made another attempt to obtain land in December 1945. Byron and I learned that Clark County was holding an auction to sell sagebrush land turned back for taxes. The price was expected to be one to three dollars an acre. We did not realize that the auction was rigged with predetermined decisions on who would bid on each parcel and how high to go without opposition. As a result, no one would let our bids stand and we upset a lot of people. However, as I told my folks in a letter, *"We made a few dollars for Clark County by running up the bids."* Reality had now set in. Farming or ranching was not in our immediate future.

A Wedding Dance

"Never try to break up a fight at Lidy Hot Springs."

My brother Byron married Mary Barbara Neidig on August 3, 1945, and mustered out of the Navy

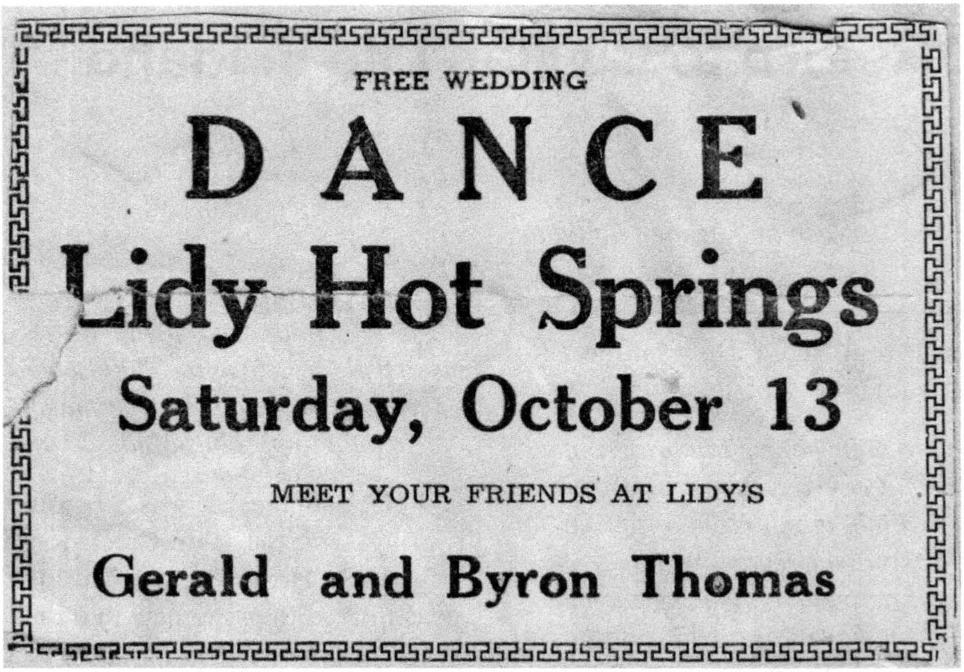

FREE WEDDING

D A N C E
Lidy Hot Springs
Saturday, October 13

MEET YOUR FRIENDS AT LIDY'S

Gerald and Byron Thomas

The advertisement that Mother ran in the local paper for the free wedding dance at Lidys for Byron and me. October 13, 1945.

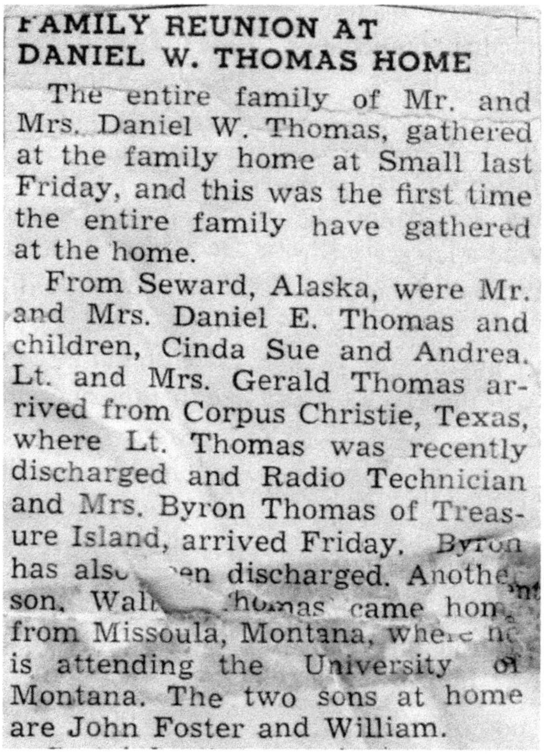

FAMILY REUNION AT DANIEL W. THOMAS HOME

The entire family of Mr. and Mrs. Daniel W. Thomas, gathered at the family home at Small last Friday, and this was the first time the entire family have gathered at the home.

From Seward, Alaska, were Mr. and Mrs. Daniel E. Thomas and children, Cinda Sue and Andrea. Lt. and Mrs. Gerald Thomas arrived from Corpus Christie, Texas, where Lt. Thomas was recently discharged and Radio Technician and Mrs. Byron Thomas of Treasure Island, arrived Friday. Byron has also been discharged. Another son, Walt Thomas came home from Missoula, Montana, where he is attending the University of Montana. The two sons at home are John Foster and William.

Everyone gathered at home for the first time since before the war.

at the end of the war. To celebrate the marriage of two of her six sons mother decided to hold a community wedding dance at Lidys. The date was set for October 13, 1945. Friends of the Thomas and Ellis families came from all over Clark County and the surrounding area. Some strangers also came to celebrate a "Free Wedding Dance."

In the middle of the festivities a fight started on the dance floor. I did not want a fight to ruin a great evening celebration. Consequently, I moved forward in an attempt to separate the combatants and ask them to move outside. I pushed them apart and, as I was facing one man the other surprised me with a hard blow to the nose. I then started fighting him. I was bleeding profusely. Friends soon separated the three of us and started moving the two fighters outside.

As they dragged the man that hit me past Jean she gave him a good hard kick. He looked surprised but could not identify the source of the kick. With the exception of this altercation, the dance was a great success. Two things were now clear. One, Jean will defend me at all costs and two, never try to break up a fight at a dance at Lidy Hot Springs.

Post-War Employment with the SCS

"Jean went to work at the seed house sorting beans and peas."

While we were resting at the Ellis Ranch (and helping out with the chores, which included salvaging the pigs when Crooked Creek flooded the pens), Mr. McBirney, Soil Conservation District Supervisor from Idaho Falls came by the ranch to offer me a job with the SCS. He said there was an opening for a Soil Conservationist in the Yellowstone District at St. Anthony, Idaho. Since I had a degree in Range Management and a veteran's preference, he could put me to work right away. I decided to take the job. We needed the money and it seemed obvious that since I could not get into farming or ranching perhaps a job servicing agriculture would be a good choice. Besides I could get Civil Service credit for my former work with

the Forest Service. The SCS appointment was effective January 7, 1946, at a salary of $3,220.

We located a small used trailer house while visiting my folks in Montana in October and towed it to St. Anthony. We lived in this small trailer for the first cold winter. Since it was not self-contained we used the central facilities of the trailer park.

Jean and I developed an annual budget and kept an account of all of our expenses. This helped us live within our limited resources. I was able to wear most of my Navy clothes: we raised a garden, hunted Elk and Deer, and otherwise watched our pennies. Jean was a great household manager. We kept a journal in our early years. This record shows that:

Jan 15, 1946 -- *"Jean scouted around town for a job. Turned down an offer at the Drug Store to work at the Seed House sorting peas, beans and corn."* (She also signed on as a substitute teacher for the St. Anthony schools).

Jan 19 -- Jean got some plain buttons for my Navy blue suit -- finished altering my suit from Lt. US Navy to Civilian 1st Class and we *"traipsed off to the Armory for the Ball. Home by 3 AM."*

Jan 20 -- We went to the Community Church served by a Presbyterian Minister. (There was a small Catholic Church in St. Anthony and a large contingent of Mormons.)

In a letter to Mother, Daddy, Daniel, Betty, Walter, John Foster and Cinda Sue dated Jan 24, I wrote that:

"Our trailer house is almost snowed under. I really like my work [as a SCS Conservationist] and the farmers appreciate what we are doing... all the people are friendly... one family at Ashton, Mr. and Mrs. Larsen, who used to live between Medicine Lodge and Dubois offered to buy

Jean beside the trailer that was our first home. Also shown are the Army surplus Jeep we obtained at the Mt. Rainer Ordnance Depot Veteran's drawing in Seattle. 1946.

The house near Parker, Idaho, that we purchased for $2,854.50.
A barn on the property enabled us to keep a milk cow.
There was no indoor plumbing. The outhouse was located near the garage, shown on the left. 1946.

me a farm... that just shows how friendly this country is."

Jan 26 -- We met Byron and Mary downtown and talked about life in our respective trailer houses. (With our encouragement, Byron and Mary had bought a small home-made trailer built like a sheep wagon. Byron was working as a geologist at the Palisades Dam on the Snake River and there was no place to live nearby.)

Feb 17 -- *"Mr. Hirche, Superintendent of Schools came by to ask Jean to serve as a substitute teacher for a few days [$5 a day]."*

An Army Surplus Jeep

"Our primary mode of travel in St. Anthony."

Mar 14-25 -- We traveled to the Mt. Rainer Ordnance Depot in Seattle for a Veteran's drawing and the purchase of two Jeeps and an old Army truck. Daniel and Betty and Walter and Betsy went with us to help pick out the vehicles. We had to swipe parts from other surplus vehicles in order to get the truck and one jeep started. We kept one of the jeeps and sold the truck and the other one to Daniel and Walter. (My two brothers were now operating the Medicine Lodge Ranch). The Jeep became our primary mode of travel for the next several years.

Apr 16 -- We sold our 1939 Nash for $698.78 -- the OPA ceiling. Many retail prices were controlled at the time by the Office of Price Administration.

Apr 18-28 -- Jean had an appendectomy and was confined to the Sacred Heart Hospital in Idaho Falls for 10 days.

In the summer of 1946 we pulled our trailer with the Army Jeep up to Henry's Lake, Idaho for my conservation work on ranches in the area. Jean noted in our Journal, *"We were parked near Chet*

Elliott's Ranch. Jane Russell, the Movie Star was staying at the Ranch. There, by a rippling stream in the green, fresh outdoors, we ended our first year of married life." (Note: On June 2, 2010, Jean and I celebrated our 65th Wedding Anniversary. It is now safe to say, that for more than 6 decades, "Flying conditions have been Above Average.")

We started looking for an alternative to the restricted living of the small trailer house in 1946. We were really excited when we located a small house on a one-acre piece of land between St. Anthony and Parker for $2,854.50. A white picket fence outlined the property. The house had two rooms and a porch. Water was piped from the well to a tank on the porch and we could draw water to the kitchen sink. The two-hole outhouse was out by the garage. By this time it was obvious that I was lucky to have married a country girl who understood the hardships of living on a limited budget.

To pay for our new home we sold the trailer house for $1,250, the 39 Nash for $700, two horses for $116 and War Bonds for $986. Mother loaned us $150 to round out the purchase price. There was a good barn on the property, which made it possible for us to supplement our income with a milk cow and some chickens.

Sep 2 -- We went over to Medicine Lodge to pick choke-cherries with Dad and Mother and then on to the Crooked Creek Ranch. We hooked on our trailer, loaded a stove and some chickens and returned to Parker. Lamar came to live with us while he attended school in St. Anthony.

Deer and Elk season started in October so some of the SCS crew took time off to join in the hunt. I shot a 7-point bull elk with my 30-30. (The elk hunt cost $5, but I made $1.70 playing poker with the hunters.)

Our first baby was born on November 19, 1946, at the hospital in Idaho Falls. We named the baby David Gerald Thomas. Jean spent 8 days in the hospital and some time recuperating in Idaho Falls before coming back to Parker on December

The runt pig nursing our cow. 1946.

Visiting Yellowstone National Park with Mother and my brother's family.
Gerald, Mary, Jean, Betty, Cinda, and Daniel. Winter, 1946.

David, the day we brought him home from the hospital.
November 28, 1946.

Walter married Betsy Willes November 16, 1947, in Dubois, Idaho.

My VT-4 buddy Will Souza and wife Lynn visiting us at Parker. They were shocked to see us living in a house with no indoor plumbing. Summer, 1948.

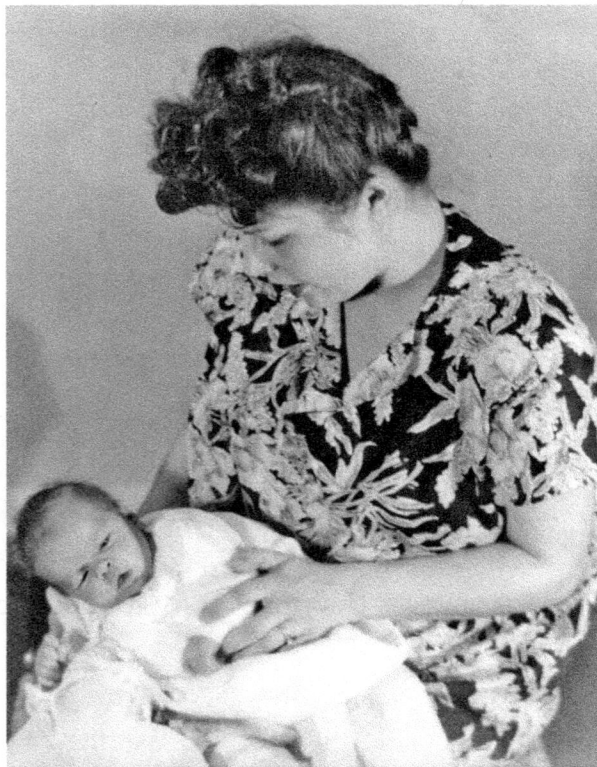

Peggy, born March 20, 1949, at St. Anthony, Idaho.

8. She bought a Good Housekeeping Baby book and recorded pertinent information about our new addition to the family.

We started remodeling our little house at Parker in 1947 by raising the roof and adding two rooms and an inside bathroom. In our spare time we also built some furniture and Jean painted everything in sight. Lamar, Jean's brother, stayed with us for the school term since there was no way for him to get to Dubois from the Crooked Creek ranch. I taught ground school for the new pilots at the airport for several months. I could not afford to fly on my own, but I took the required two weeks of flight duty at the Naval Air Stations in Seattle and Spokane.

On Sunday, December 22, I borrowed a horse trailer, drove up to Crooked Creek for some chopped barley then to the Medicine Lodge Ranch to pick up a cow that Mother had given to us on my birthday. I noted that, *"The cow looks like she may have a calf on the way."* We made it back to Parker at 5 pm and at 7:30, *"A new little black heifer calf was born who we Christened 'Chrissie' because it is so close to Christmas.... We rubbed the new calf down and got settled for the night."*

We now had a milk cow, calf, and a few chickens on our Parker farm. Jean's folks gave us a small cream separator so we could sell cream and yet have milk for the new baby. On Feb 1, 1947, we weaned the calf and I hauled it back to Lidy Hot Springs. Jean noted that our first cream check was $2.46 for 2 days.

A Milk Cow and a Runt Pig

"A Special Relationship."

Shortly after we weaned the calf, Jean's Dad gave us a little runt pig that had been neglected by the already heavily burdened sow. We added the little pig to our daily bottle-feeding routine and turned him loose in the corral with our lonely milk cow. That's when the "special relationship" developed.

Sometime later, when I returned from work, I went out to milk the cow. The little pig let out an urgent squeal and to my surprise the cow laid down and the pig began nursing. I guess he had found the source of milk with his sensitive nose some days earlier and the cow responded since she no longer had a calf to support. Jean and I though this was an interesting phenomenon and we let things rest for a while, since the little pig was not too competitive for the milk supply.

As time went on the pig grew. He could now rise up on his hind legs, place his front legs on the cow's hind legs and nurse in the manner shown in the photo. Soon the pig's teeth caused problems with the cow's teats and we had to discontinue this special relationship. Life is tough down on the farm, especially if you are a runt pig.

Daily Life

There was a heavy snow in the winter of 1947. Mother and Dad had a herd of horses on the Deep Creek Range that were "snowed in." Daniel and I tried to reach the herd with our saddle horses but failed. I then contacted Jenks, a pilot at the Rexburg airport to see if we could spot the horses by air. We hit a bad storm over the Medicine Lodge Bench and had to turn back. Some of the horses never made it through that winter – "winter kill" was common in those days.

My brother Walter who gave our Squadron so much enjoyment with his letters from home got married on November 16, 1947, in the LDS Chapel in Dubois, Idaho to Betsy Willes. Mother made her usual comment, *"Oh, Son! Do you really want to get married? And you are so young!"*

We summarized our expenses for 1947 as follows: Groceries averaged $26.60 per month. We spent $10.50 for pigs, but we made $157.55 on cows and $30.46 on chickens. Our net was on the plus side and our bank balance was slightly over $100. In 1948, groceries jumped to $37.00 per month and we spent over $1,250.00 on materials to remodel our house.

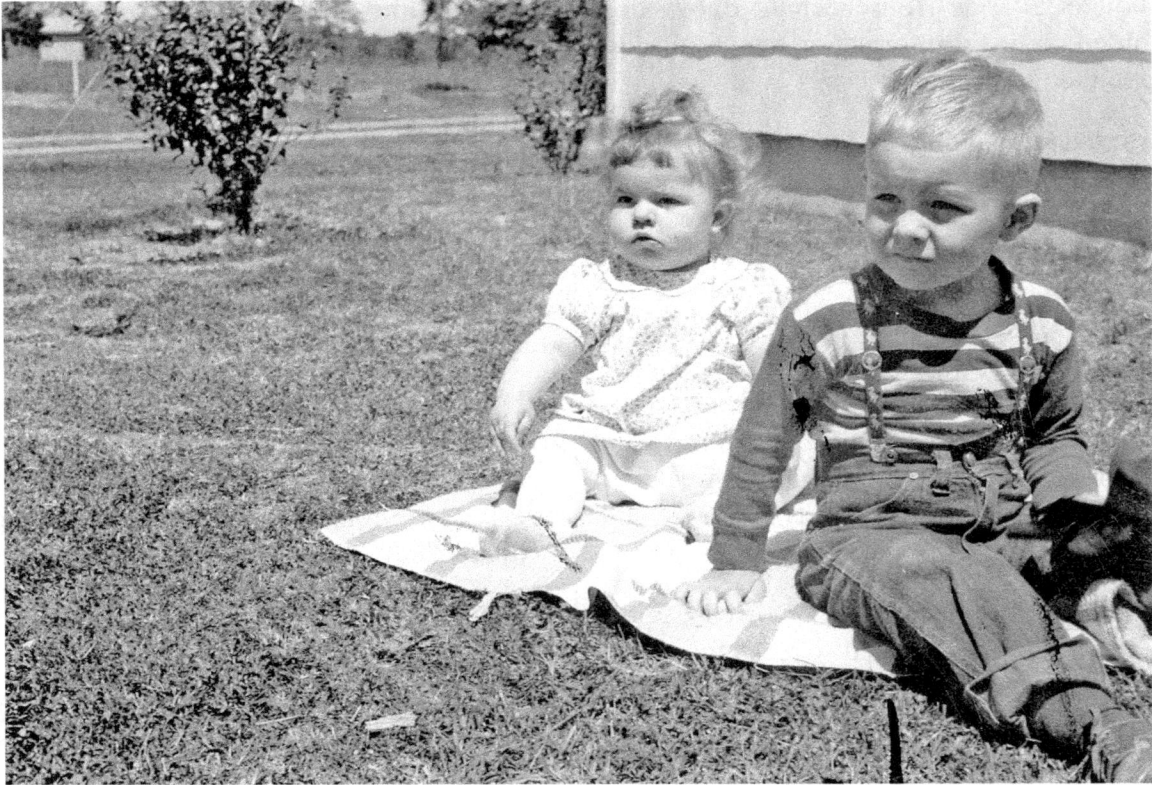

Peggy and David. Parker, Idaho. August, 1949.

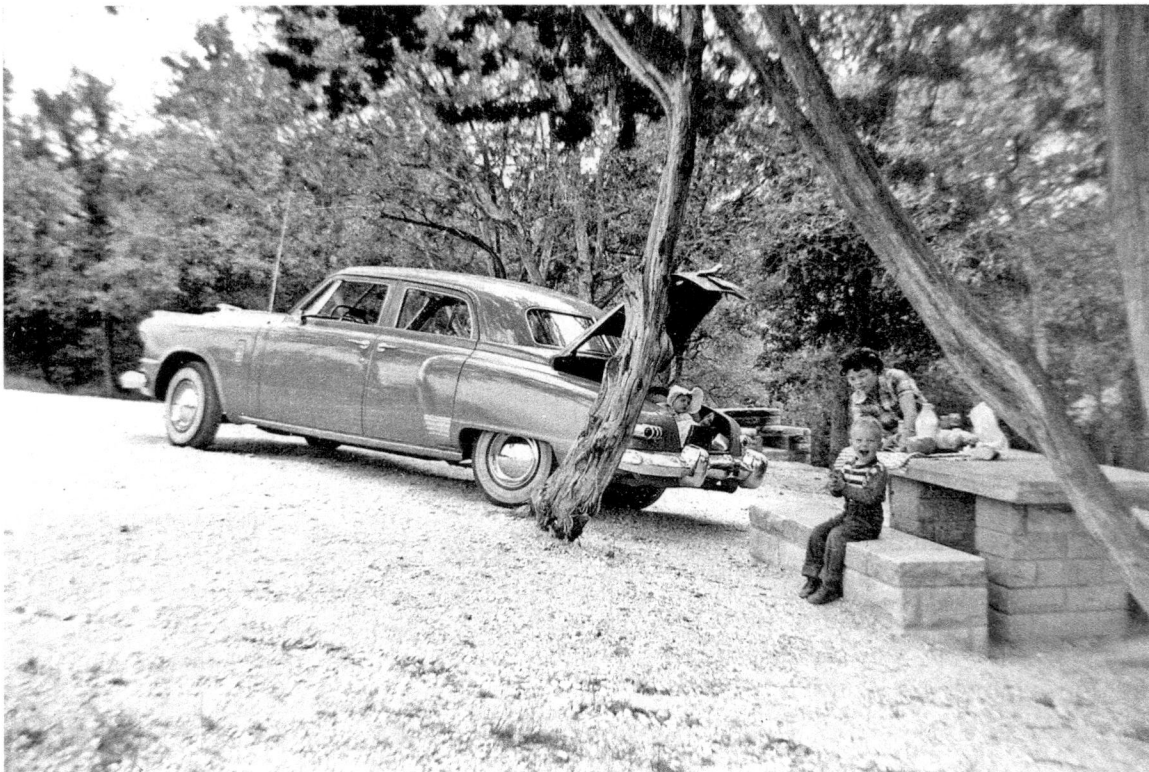

Picnicking with our new Studebaker. Peggy, David, and Jean. 1949.

Our second baby, Peggy Jeane Thomas, was born on March 20, 1949, at the hospital in St. Anthony, Idaho. We were thrilled with this new addition to our family.

Later that year, I was promoted and assigned to the new position of Work Unit Conservationist in Rexburg. We sold the house, barn and lot at Parker for $4,900 on July 5 and rented an old house in Rexburg. We also sold our jeep to Robert Ellis for $125 and bought a new Studebaker for $2,250. We also entered into an agreement with Walter to rent with a purchase option 80 acres of land near Arlee, Montana. (Walter gave up the lease as it was a sub-marginal operation. We recouped a part of our investment.)

Groceries went up to an average of $68 per month in 1949. Since I was in the Naval Reserve, I received orders in October to proceed to the Naval Air Station at Spokane for two weeks of flight duty.

Opening a new SCS office in Rexburg was a new challenge which I accepted with enthusiasm. I had a good group of District Supervisors and good cooperation from the agricultural community.

I enjoyed my work with the Soil Conservation Service in Rexburg and St. Anthony. The work was mostly outdoors – surveying for land leveling, staking out contour ditches, range surveys and general farm and ranch planning. We took pride in our work, seldom reaching home before dark. Our Yellowstone Work Unit received merit citations at the District and State levels.

Two minor incidents cost me some extra paperwork. The first was a hernia I developed during field work in 1947, which sent me to the hospital for 11 days. The second problem related to the time the pickup tipped over on an icy, snow-packed road. Jean and David were with me and thanks to the slow speed and deep snow no one was injured.

While I was in Rexburg, my former professor at the University of Idaho, Dr. Vernon A. Young, wrote to inform me that a small group of Range Professionals were trying to form a Scientific Society. I told him I would help and thus became a Charter member of the American Society of Range Management. At that time I had no idea that the Society would grow to over 2,000 members and I would eventually become President of the Texas Section and later, President of the International Society. These contacts and the work with the Forest Service and Soil Conservation Service helped instill in me a "Conservation Ethic" that shaped my entire professional career.

Medicine Lodge Ranch: End of an Era

"This place has seen better days."

I remember an old expression my Dad used when we visited some of the abandoned dry farms in Clark County after the Depression. As we looked at run-down buildings, cropland turned back to sagebrush and fences falling down, Dad would say, *"This place has seen better days."* Seen better days! Now Jean and I can use the same words as we revisit the Crooked Creek Ranch or our place on Medicine Lodge Creek.

My brothers Daniel and Walter took over the farm and ranch operation on Medicine Lodge after the war. They stayed with the marginal operation for a few years and eventually sold or traded the ranch to engage in other endeavors. The roof of the big barn fell in first – then other buildings collapsed. The orchard dried up and died. The old log house where four of Dan and Mary's boys and a cousin were born held out longer. Now, there is little evidence that a thriving homestead existed – a homestead based on many long hard days and months of sweat and tears. Certainly, the appropriate comment today about the Medicine Lodge Ranch is that *"this place has seen better days."*

Abandoned Medicine Lodge Ranch. Summer, 1970.

Medicine Lodge Ranch. Summer, 1976.

Gerald standing beside the only structure remaining on the Medicine Lodge
Ranch in June, 2006. This was the old shop.
Four of the Thomas boys were born on the ranch – Daniel
Gerald, Byron, and Walter – and my cousin Isla Byrne Johnson.
A part of my soul resides here forever.

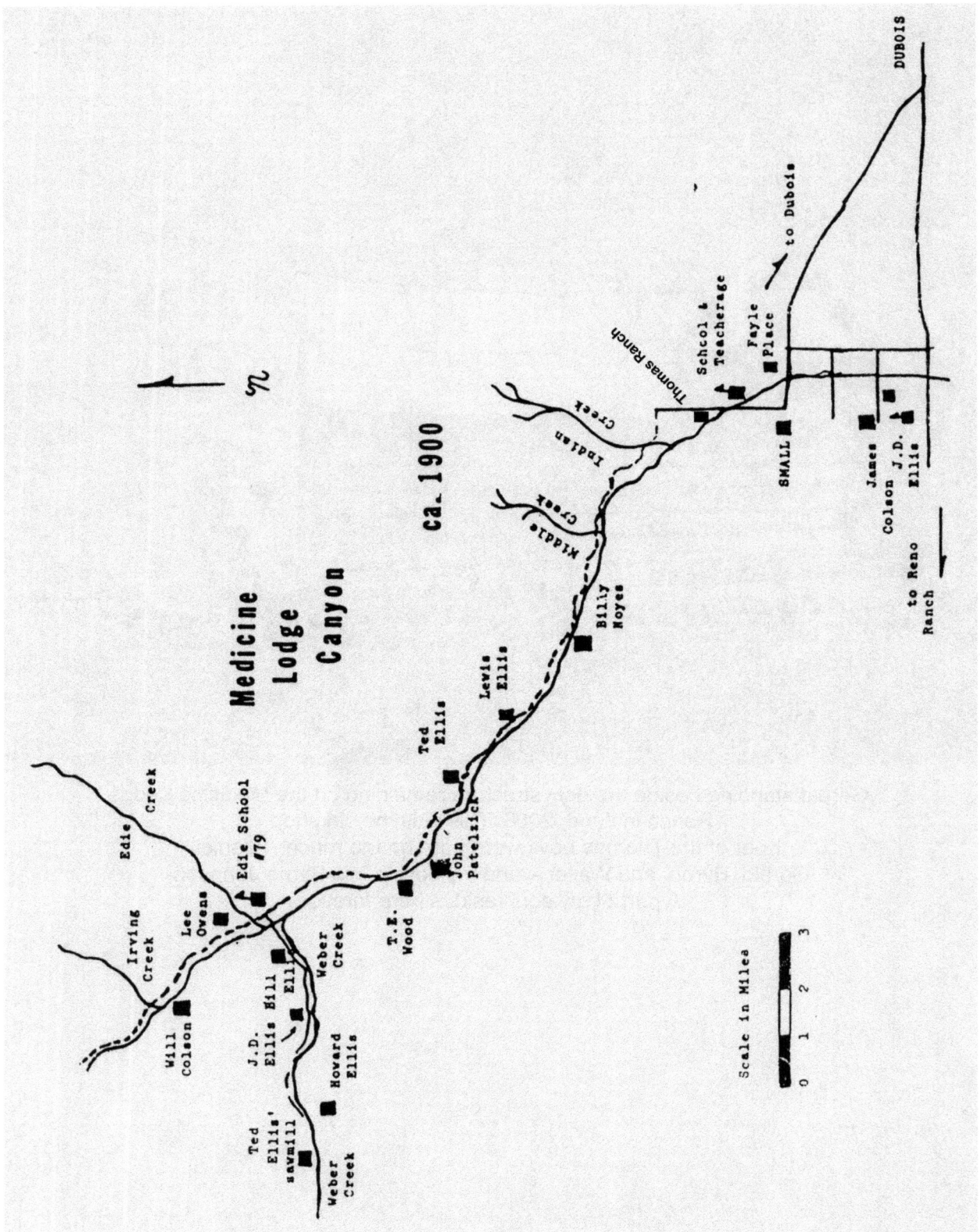

Map of Medicine Lodge Creek Canyon showing the homesteads in 1900.
Map courtesy of Eugene Ellis.

Chapter 16 | Conversion to a Texas Aggie

"Heading south after a reload."

The Road Southeast

1950 was a memorable year for our family. I had been considering the possibility of going to graduate school while I was in the Navy and this desire increased with post-war employment. Jean and I discussed the implications of this move even as our family responsibilities increased. I was settled into a challenging and satisfying position with the Soil Conservation Service (SCS). However, there were two factors that favored a move. One was the GI Bill, which promised some financial help with education. The other was a policy of the SCS that allowed for educational leave with return employment almost assured.

Several SCS administrators urged me to consider going to Washington State University with a major in Agronomy. I made plans for this option when I was again contacted by my old professor, Dr. Young. He said, *"It would be a mistake for you to change majors and go to WSC. You must come to Texas A & M. I have moved here and started the first PhD program in Range Science in the Nation. Surely you want to be a part of this exciting development."* Dr. Young convinced me to take the road southeast instead of northwest.

Moving all of our earthly possessions from our rented home in Rexburg was not an easy task – made harder by our decision to leave in the middle of a severe winter. We made a 4-wheel trailer out of the Model-A Ford we had bought from my brother. I did the carpenter work and we hired a welder to attach a tongue, remodel the chassis and fasten a trailer hitch to the Studebaker.

We loaded everything we owned in the trailer. No, not everything! We took the old kitchen stove Jean had found at the dump back to the dump. We left a few things at the Crooked Creek Ranch including some of my Navy flight gear. But we still had a heavy load including our new refrigerator loaded with elk meat. We also had the sewing machine, beds, tables, chairs, home-made desks, canned fruit and miscellaneous other items.

After we had hooked the homemade trailer onto our Studebaker sedan, we bid goodbye to our friends, bundled up our two kids and started merrily down the road. It was a cold February morning with about two feet of snow on the level. The highway was icy but most of the snow had been pushed to the side of the road.

We had covered only a few miles from Rexburg when the weld on the trailer hitch broke causing the trailer to swerve from side to side and finally tip over. The high snow bank on the side of the road prevented a major disaster. Our possessions were scattered widely. There was a hole in the washing machine; buttons everywhere; some damage to furniture but our refrigerator was relatively unharmed.

After the trailer tipped over, we got out of our car and surveyed the damage. Before long a car came down the highway, the occupant looked over our situation with sympathy and took word back to our SCS friends in Rexburg. Two SCS pickups then came to our rescue, loaded our possessions and hauled us back to town. Park Hook, one of my SCS employees and his lovely wife put us up at their home and helped us get things in order. Two days later, with a newly welded hitch and some other repairs we again headed for Texas. Roy Shipley, my former SCS boss, recalled this accident in a letter to me dated February 24, 1959:

Texas Aggie bonfire with the "eyes of Texas" on top. 1950. This was a tradition practiced every year before the football game against the University of Texas, until an accident in 1999 resulted in the death of 12 people.
In my day, the outhouse was "borrowed" from an unsuspecting "donor."

"College View" Veterans' Housing, February, 1950. Our building checked.
Texas A&M, College Station, Texas.

David and Gerald. Behind our Veterans' apartment.
Texas A&M, College Station, Texas. 1950.

Peggy and David, back porch, Veterans' apartment. David crawled
under this porch once and was badly stung by a scorpion.
Texas A&M, College Station, Texas. 1950.

Jean, Peggy, and David. Texas A&M, College Station, Texas. 1950.

Naval Reserve Training as a member of Attack Squadron VA-702.
VA-702 was the successor to VT-4. The squadron flew Douglas Skyraiders.
All members except another pilot and myself were called to active duty in Korea.
College Station, Texas, 1949.

"As we reviewed the biographical sketch relating to your accomplishments, the day you started south with all earthly possessions in the old trailer comes to mind. It was a sad day indeed for the lot of us to see your trailer and household effects scattered with reckless abandon on the road. It must have been even sadder for you and Jean. No doubt a less determined pair than you and Jean would have turned back and missed the opportunity that is now yours."

The highway from Idaho to Texas A&M was mostly icy and snow-covered. We barely made the Malad Pass with chains and we had to take an alternate route across Wyoming.

We found a room in an old motel in College Station with an unvented gas heater, rented a cold storage locker for our elk meat and contacted Dr. Young about entering Graduate School at A&M.

Dr. and Mrs. Young were really good to us. Mrs. Young wanted to move Jean and our two kids out of the motel with unvented heat as soon as possible and insisted that Dr. Young use his influence to get us into student housing. Student housing was crowded but, after a few days, Dr. Young arranged for a ground floor apartment in the Veterans' housing complex. That was a great relief! We could now settle down to the hard work of graduate studies.

Married student housing was adequate and the rent was only $26 per month. My GI allowance of $120 started in March of 1950. We sold our last horse for $20 and our cow for $109. My research assistantship of $100 did not start until the fall semester but Dr. Young paid some wages for my fieldwork at the Texas Range Station at Barnhart. Our grocery bill in 1950 was averaging $69 per month. My GI uniforms were getting thin and Jean and the kids needed new clothes. We purchased a sewing machine for Jean and I bought a new camera and a shotgun. Our records show total expenditures for the year at $4,088 against an income of $3,912.

Status in the Naval Reserve

"I had missed a recall to active duty during the Korean War."

With the move to College Station, I was "Transferred from the Command, Thirteenth Naval District to the Command, Eighth Naval District." I was assigned to Attack Squadron VA-702, Naval Air Station, Dallas. I started flying as a "Weekend Warrior" with VA-702 in March 1950. Finding time for the trip to Dallas was difficult, but I made a little extra money.

The squadron was flying the new Douglas AD "Skyraider." One weekend in July, I reported for duty but had trouble locating any other pilots. I finally found the Skipper of the Squadron. He stated that VA-702 had been called to active duty for the Korean War as of July 19, 1950. I asked about my status. He informed me that the Squadron only needed 20 pilots and since I was the last one to join, I would not have to go *"Unless someone flunks their physical."* As it turned out, 20 surprised Weekend Warriors were not given a physical but were now on full-time active duty, placed aboard an aircraft carrier in the Pacific and soon in combat.

I was left behind with one other officer who was a test pilot for Chance-Vought Aircraft Company. The two of us we were transferred to VA-701 but I was never able to train with the new Squadron due to my summer research work at Barnhart. On January 25, 1951 I was released from VA-701 "as you live out of the Dallas area."

I had missed a recall to active duty in the Korean War by a quirk of fate. Thus, I was allowed to continue my graduate work.

The Texas Range Station

"Dig a new hole for the outhouse."

I had just settled down to my 1950 spring courses at Texas A&M when Dr. Young informed me that my research for the MS degree would be to study the pastures on the Texas Range Station near

Texas Range Station, near Barnhart, Texas. 1950.

First Priority: *"Dig new hole for outhouse."* Peggy and David watching.
Texas Range Station, Barnhart, Texas. 1950.

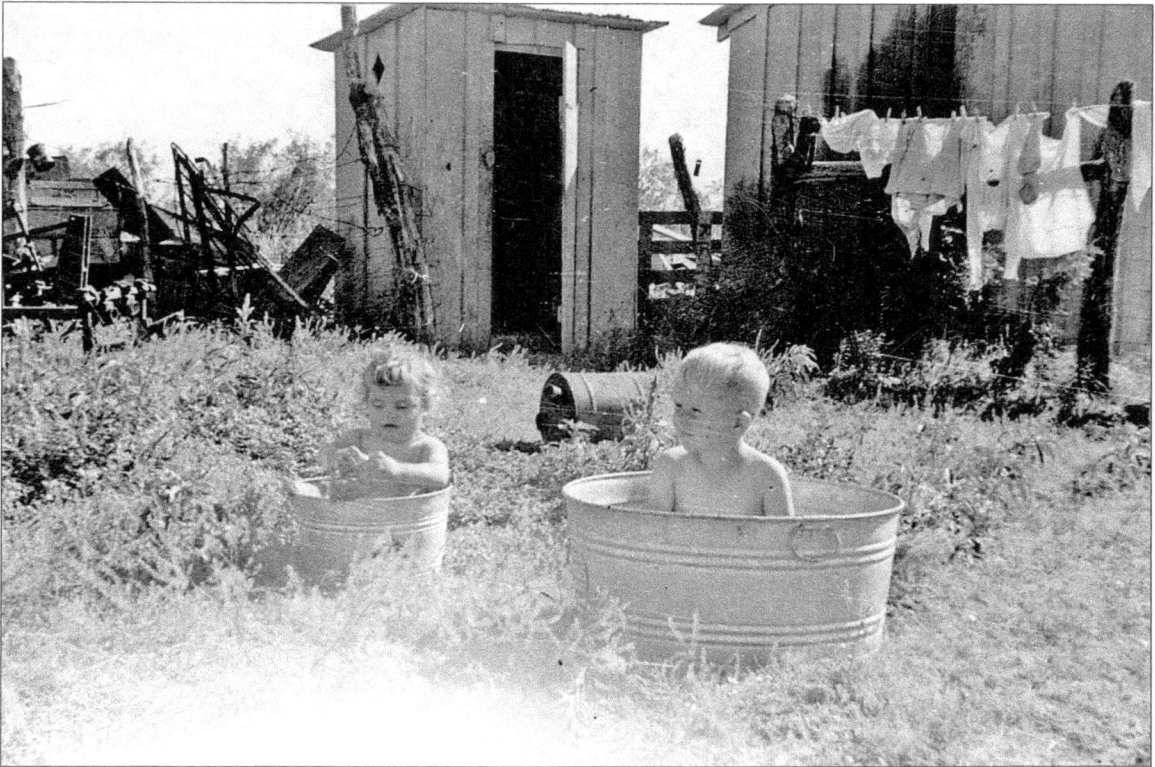

Peggy and David bathing in tubs at the Range Station. 1951.

The one-room cabin at the Range Station. 1951.

The stock tank we used for swimming and bathing. The water was usually
cold with some moss accumulation.
Texas Range Station, Barnhart, Texas. 1951.

Barnhart and determine the effects of sheep and cattle grazing on the vegetation. He was eager to take me out to look over this experimental ranch. Dr. Young stated that there was a nice one-room cabin on the Station that would be "just great" for your wife and two kids:

"You may have to spend several summers out there to complete your studies. There is a mesquite tree by the cabin that throws lots of shade and you can bathe in the stock tank."

Then, with his customary enthusiasm, Dr. Young stated that I would need to *"dig a new hole for the outhouse."* With the help of David and under the watchful eyes of Peggy we dug through a hard layer of caliche to a depth of about five feet. With the help of the ranch manager we eased the old two-holer over onto the new location.

I figured the new pit would have capacity for about 10 more years of graduate student research. Dr. Young seemed satisfied next time he paid us a visit.

The facilities at Barnhart consisted of the one-room cabin with a shed for equipment on one end. The outside was clapboard with a corrugated metal roof. There was one light bulb in the ceiling. We brought our camp stove for cooking. We did not have a refrigerator so Jean made a cooler out of an orange crate with a gunnysack over the top and a wick to suck water from a pan at the base. The old-timers used this system before refrigeration and it kept the milk and butter cool. When Mrs. Young found out we did not have a refrigerator at Barnhart the first year she insisted that Dr. Young buy one the next year.

The drought of the 1950s was severe in West Texas. No doubt this dry spell brought some rattlesnakes into headquarters. Jean and the children had some interesting experiences with these snakes. However, in all the time I spent on my hands and knees measuring the vegetation in the pastures, I never encountered a single rattler.

When we needed a bath at the Range Station we rolled out the wash tubs or jumped into the stock tank. The water in the tank was usually cold with some moss accumulation. As an alternative we stretched a hose out in the sun and took a quick rinse before the warm water ran out. The next person had to wait for more solar heat from sunshine on the hose.

About once a week we took our clothes to the washeteria in Ozona. One wash day Peggy caught her arm in the wringer. Jean forgot about the quick release so she reversed the wringer and ran the arm back through. That meant a worrisome visit to the hospital. Fortunately the arm was flexible and the injury not too serious.

We did not spend much on entertainment. However, Jean wanted the kids to be exposed to art and culture so we bought a second-hand piano in College Station and hauled it to Barnhart in the homemade trailer that we had towed from Idaho. We covered the piano, other furniture and supplies with a tarp but it rained so hard on the way to the Range Station that the base of the piano filled with a foot of water. The water did not seem to affect the sound. We sold the piano later for about the amount that we had paid. I should note, however, that none of our children ever took up the piano or any other musical instrument in spite of Jean's efforts to expand their horizons.

I really enjoyed my fieldwork at the Texas Range Station. There was so much to learn about the vegetation, the soils, the livestock, the climate and the overall environment. What a great opportunity Dr. Young had provided for me!

I collected enough data in 1950 and 1951, with the proper statistical analysis, to qualify for my Master of Science Thesis. Consequently, with more than enough course work completed, I was awarded the MS degree in Range Management at Texas A&M in June 1951.

Peggy and David in front of our home on Popular Street.
College Station, Texas. 1952.

Marianne Thomas at 6 months.
Born at College Station, Texas, March 30, 1953.

Teaching and Research at Texas A&M

"A new addition to the family and a promotion."

After completing the MS degree, Dr. Young strongly urged that I stay on for a Ph.D. He offered me a position on the faculty. My assignment was to teach full time during the regular term and continue the research at the Texas Range Station.

College teaching was a new experience for me. I found the students eager to learn and I tried hard to carry Dr. Young's interest in Range Management and his enthusiasm into the classroom. I took my classes on field trips to Texas ranches and we visited experiment stations. I utilized the basic ecology and plant science principles learned from my previous professors. Background with the Forest Service and Soil Conservation Service helped keep me aware of the need to apply range science principles and practices to field conditions.

My lectures about Range Condition, plant succession, and key species (such as side-oats grama and little bluestem) must have impressed my students because, on the occasion of the birth of our new daughter on March 30, 1953, my students met me at the door, escorted me to a chair and proceeded to tell me that they had a name for my new baby. *"We should call her Little Bluestem since she will be a key species in determining your future range condition."* At least the students did not propose the scientific name *"Andropogon scoparius."* In spite of the recommendations of my class, Jean and I named our new addition, Marianne – a combination of traditional family names. We had a bargain with the delivery cost of $178.

In 1952, I was full time teaching in the spring and fall terms. We had to move out of the Veterans' Barracks so we purchased a small house on Poplar Street in College Station. During the summer we went back to Barnhart with the reduced salary of a Graduate Assistant. Our total earnings of $5,909 exceeded expenditures of $4,893. Jean made a note on our 1951 budget that we still owned 3 cows and 4 calves in Idaho after our Guernsey cow had died

at Medicine Lodge. That year we were still paying back the money we had borrowed on our GI insurance to buy our car. In a letter dated November 27, Jean informed the family that:

"Byron dropped us a note to say he had received his degree at Johns Hopkins [in Geology]. Gerald is still doing research at Barnhart – we will have to go Christmas again. He will have 4 years data when he finishes – more than any one. Dr. Young thinks he should go out to Barnhart again next summer.... He has to work so hard. We have to scrimp like crazy to live too."

Dr. Young promoted me to a 12-month teaching/research assignment in 1953. On January 27, I wrote to R. N. Irving, Idaho State Conservationist for the SCS to:

"Request another extension of leave-without-pay for educational purposes. It appears that I am still more than a year away from the PhD.... Please advise me if another leave extension is possible. Again, I want to say that I will resign only if you feel I am preventing some other person from obtaining a position with the Soil Conservation Service." (The leave was approved.)

We returned to Idaho in the summer to visit our folks for the first time since leaving Rexburg. We received the last payment from Wendell Rudd on the Parker house and my old SCS buddy Ron Wilson paid off on a loan of $629 that we made to him to go into the sprinkler irrigation business in 1950. With an annual income of over $6,400 we felt that we could now afford an investment of $225 for the Encyclopedia Britannica.

Mother saved many of our letters home while we were in Texas. In a letter to the folks in January 1954, I wrote, *"I still have a night and day job to finish my PhD in June. Next semester, starting in February, I can devote more time to my dissertation."* I pointed out that I had to go back to graduate school full time to complete the requirements for the degree. My salary went from $428 per

Gerald in "cap and gown" following graduation from Texas A&M,
May 21, 1954. College Station, Texas.

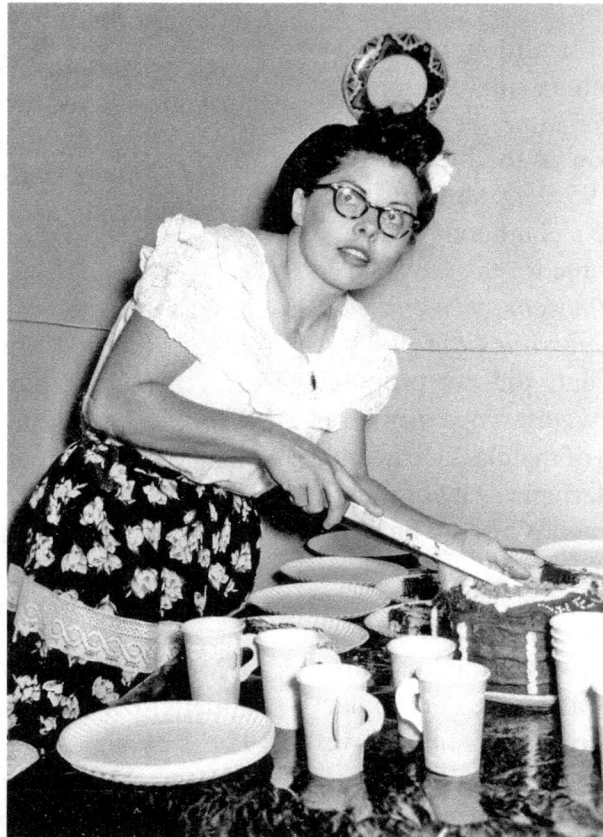

Jean cutting the cake at the surprise graduation party she gave me.
May 21, 1954. College Station, Texas.

month to $170. I also pointed out that *"Marianne was growing and lots of fun"* and *"Jean has been working too hard again."* (Jean typed my Master's thesis and my dissertation. In those days, no typing mistakes or corrections were allowed. The original and three copies had to be perfect.)

In another letter on May 7, 1954, Jean informed the folks that:

> *"Gerald passed his last oral today. Now in two weeks he should graduate…. I believe I will give him a surprise party to sort of celebrate…. When I think of him crawling around out at Barnhart reading 300 plots, four or five times each year for four years in the dust and heat. Also all this school work! He deserves something special"*

Sure enough, Jean organized a fantastic graduation party for me after the doctorate was conferred on May 21, 1954. Graduate students, friends and neighbors gathered for the occasion. I was the 10th person to receive a PhD in Range Science in the United States. Dr. Young gave me a full-time faculty position, I resigned from the Soil Conservation Service, pulled out my Civil Service Retirement funds and embarked on an exciting career with Texas A&M.

My brother Byron brought his wife and family to College Station several times to visit us while I was at A&M. Byron was helping Matheson Chemical Company get in the oil business and soon began branching out on his own. His PhD from Johns Hopkins gave him a good start.

Due to full-time employment in 1955 our income jumped to $6,066. We felt safe in adding a new room to the back of the house on Poplar Street. I did most of the work after hours and weekends. We made our usual trek to Idaho in July to see the Ellis and Thomas families.

With the move to Texas, I was assigned to the Research Reserve (Company 8-3) at College Station. On May 12, 1953, I was promoted to Lieuten-

ant Commander. Assignments in 1954 took me to the Nuclear Science Seminar in Idaho Falls, Idaho with Security Clearance and the West Coast Research Seminar in California.

I supervised my first graduate student, Martin Gonzalez from Chihuahua, Mexico in 1955. Martin agreed to conduct his research at the Texas Range Station. I assigned him to a project on Tobosa Grass and he agreed to help run the other pasture studies. Jean and I became well acquainted with Martin and his wife Carmen. They invited us to visit them at Martin's father's ranch in Chihuahua over the Christmas holidays. This was an enjoyable experience. Martin later finished a PhD at Utah State, became Director of the La Campana Experimental Ranch in Mexico, and was a featured speaker at my Inauguration as President of New Mexico State University. He was the first foreign President of the Society for Range Management.

Agricultural Research in West Texas

"To the windy High Plains."

In 1956, after the first semester of teaching and a few trips to Barnhart, I was surprised when Dr. Robert D. Lewis called me into his office to discuss a new position he had created in the Texas Agricultural Experiment Station. This job would be called Research Coordinator for West Texas. I had great respect for Dr. Lewis and, even though I hated to leave the Department of Range & Forestry, I accepted Dr. Lewis` offer effective June 1, 1956. We agreed that I could still keep up with the research at Barnhart and supervise graduate students. The primary purpose of the new job was to strengthen the research of 13 experiment stations and to improve relations with Texas Tech and other organizations and agencies in West Texas.

A move to Lubbock with an office at the Lubbock Experiment Station was required. We sold our house in College Station and moved the family into the windy High Plains of Texas. We bought a house at 4402 45th Street, enrolled the kids in school, transferred our membership to Westminster Presbyterian Church and started on a new and ex-

Thomas family. Longview, Texas, 1954.

Marianne and Jean. College Station, Texas. 1954.

David, Marianne, and Peggy. College Station, Texas. February, 1955.

David, Marianne, and Peggy. College Station, Texas. Christmas, 1955.

Our 14-foot camper trailer, purchased for $1,038. South Dakota, 1957.

Our new house in Lubbock, Texas. 4402 45th Street. 1958

citing challenge for the family and for my professional career. (The first time we went through Lubbock, Texas in a wind storm we thought, *"Who in their right mind would live in this place!"*)

For Naval Reserve Training in 1956 I was ordered to report on November 25 to the Nuclear Reactor Seminar at Oak Ridge, Tennessee. We decided to drive so the family could enjoy another trip. We rented a furnished Government apartment and Jean promptly checked the kids into school. To our surprise, the school accepted our kids for the 14-day period. On December 11, Jean informed my folks that; *"The children have really enjoyed school here and have had lots of new experiences. We went to the Smoky Mountain National Park Sunday. Near the top of the mountain we found snow."* I added a note to Jean's letter:

"I've been very busy in my new job in Texas. We have such a big State and so much to do. Right now we need more research in agriculture than ever before. We are losing many of our best men to private industry. Salaries are too low to hold good men."

No major changes in my work took place in 1957. Our groceries were now costing us $109 per month. We purchased a small trailer house (14-foot) in March for $1,038. The trailer was not self-contained but we could squeeze our family of 5 in it by careful management. Also, I could use it in some of my travels in West Texas.

The trailer house really proved its worth for our trip to the Black Hills of South Dakota where I had a Range Society meeting in July. This gave us an opportunity to visit my former VT-4 buddy Bob Ruth and family. We stopped on the return trip in Idaho and Montana. (Side note: Mother had saved a letter from my brother, William dated June 2, 1957. He is aboard the ***USS YORKTOWN*** with a schedule which includes Hong Kong, Japan, Philippine Islands, etc. William is the third son of Dan and Mary Thomas to serve in the Navy. He says he only has 251 days more to serve.)

In March of 1958 I was involved in a Federal review of agricultural research and teaching programs at A&M. I used my new trailer house and parked at the Sunset Trailer Court. I wrote to Jean that, *"The trailer house is working out fine. Back to the bachelor days… scrambled eggs for breakfast, scrambled egg sandwich for lunch and toast and scrambled eggs for supper."* From College Station I drove to Corpus Christi to consult with Dr. Clarence Cottam on the research program for the Welder Wildlife Foundation.

March 14: Jean informed the folks that:

"I just found out that David is as near sighted as can be – couldn't even see the blackboard so took him to the doctor and he is now wearing glasses… He is a Boy Scout now and… he received his tenderfoot badge. Peggy's Blue Bird Group meets at my house now. Peggy will be 9 on March 20th and Marianne will be 5 on March 30th. I am glad you have a TV. We don't have one yet but would except for the children…."

I was offered a position with the Southwest Research Foundation in San Antonio with a substantial pay increase. I turned the job down not knowing at that time that I was being considered for the Dean of Agriculture position at Texas Tech College. A firm offer soon came through.

Initially I was not interested in a move to Texas Tech. I discussed the offer with Dr. Lewis. He took me up to visit with Chancellor M. T. Harrington. In the discussion that followed, I was told that A&M would match the Tech offer and I would be named an Associate Director of the Texas Agricultural Experiment Station. However, after some meetings on the Texas Tech campus and visits with the Tech Board of Directors, I decided to accept the Dean position at Texas Tech. A new challenge lay ahead. Texas Technological College was not a Land Grant College and, therefore, did not have the State and Federal support for the agricultural sciences traditional to Land Grant status.

THE TEXAS A.&M. SYSTEM NEWS — *April 1956*

A GRIN FOR DR. YOUNG—Dr. Vernon A. Young, right, head of the Department of Range and Forestry at Texas A. and M., smothers a grin as he receives—for the fourth time in a row—a plaque stating that his department produced the outstanding student in range management in the state. Awarded by the Texas Section of the American Society of Range Management, the plaque could go to any of several schools in the state which offer the subject. It has been offered for four years, and has never been off the A. and M. campus except to be engraved each year. Dr. Gerald Thomas of Dr. Young's department presents the plaque for the ASRM.

Dr. Young was the most important influence in my professional life. He provided critical guidance in my career decisions, was always available when I needed advice or help, was a pioneering Range and Forest scientist, a remarkable leader, and a warm and generous friend.

Chapter 17 | Dean of Agriculture

"They withdrew the only grant that we had in the School of Agriculture."

Research and Public Service

I was appointed Dean of Agriculture, Director of Farms and Professor of Range Management at Texas Technological College at Lubbock, Texas in the summer of 1958. We were living in Lubbock at the time so no move for the family was necessary. Also, my previous position with the Experiment Station had provided a good opportunity for me to become acquainted with the people and programs of Texas Tech. Jean also became an important part of the College community. She hosted many socials and developed friendships which followed us later to New Mexico.

One of my first priorities as Dean at Tech was to seek funding for research. I was convinced that research was the key to developing quality programs and graduate studies in the College. In my previous position with A&M I had helped formulate policies for cooperative research with Tech.

Before the actual funding for this work, Tech had only one significant research project supported by outside funding. This was a livestock feeding study to test cottonseed meal as a supplement. The research was supported by a $1,200 grant from the Cottonseed Crushers Association. Immediately after I hired Ralph Durham to head the Animal Science Department he raised questions about this project. His first decision was to feed whole cottonseed as a part of the study. The Cottonseed Crushers did not want whole cottonseed fed to livestock since they were in the business of buying seed at low prices, grinding it and selling a finished product. Consequently, when they could not get Ralph to change his mind, they withdrew the only grant that we had in the School of Agriculture. That left us completely dependent on the cooperative program with A&M.

An indication of the progress in research and public service programs is quoted here as a part of a report I presented to the Texas Tech Board of Directors on December 9, 1967:

"We started immediately to enlarge the research program and to hire young, energetic faculty members with research orientation. As might be expected, this change in emphasis from 'traditional programs' met with some resistance. We now have over 187 active research projects and preliminary investigations. These studies are being conducted in seven departments and at the 14,000-acre research farm near Amarillo. This work is supported in part by over 60 different companies or individuals."

In regard to service and outreach, *"The School of Agriculture is now sponsoring or co-sponsoring over 25 conferences and short courses. Several of these are state-wide meetings and some are national in scope."* Since water was the most critical resource in the region, we organized the "West Texas Water Institute" and cooperated actively with regional and state organizations concerned with water issues.

Several academic departments were strengthened in line with more research orientation and graduate work. It was also appropriate to add a Department of Range and Wildlife Sciences. The final achievement came when we received approval for the PhD in several Agricultural Science Departments. The Texas Tech College of Agricultural Sciences became the first non-Land Grant College in the nation to offer the doctorate in agriculture. (Note: Texas Technological College became Texas

Visiting the Parthenon in Athens. September 3, 1959.

Testing the community water supply in Northern Greece. September, 1959.

Tech University in 1969 and the various "Schools" became "Colleges."

International Involvement: A new Dimension

"An assignment to Greece."

In 1959 I was contacted by the Grain Sorghum Producers Association for a possible assignment in Greece. At that time Texas Tech did not have a policy or a program relating to the international dimension. The University had no contractual or cooperative relationships with foreign universities, the US Agency for International Development (USAID) or other government agencies. Foreign assignments were not officially discouraged, but the acceptance of an assignment would require the use of vacation time.

In September I made the trip to Greece, by way of Paris. After several days in Athens, I proceeded to American Farm School in Thessaloniki, where I visited numerous Greek agricultural operations and consulted with both American and Greek Ag economic advisors.

My work in Greece convinced me that our College of Agriculture could play an important role in the so-called "War on Hunger." It was apparent that Greece was a country in transition between relatively primitive agriculture and improved technology. This unique combination of the ancient and modern influenced all aspects of economic and social life. But it was the continuing impact of tradition and culture that slowed the process of change.

After the assignment to Greece, I continued to encourage the University to move toward a positive approach to the international dimension. But change came slowly in the West Texas environment. We moved from the requirement of "vacation time" to "leave without pay." I participated in 10 foreign assignments while at Texas Tech.

Defining a role in the international arena for Texas Tech came eventually with the formation of ICASALS (the International Center for Arid and Semi-Arid Land Studies). The concept for this new international focus came from discussions between the new President Grover E. Murray and the Inauguration Committee that I co-chaired. Later Texas Tech joined with other universities in the Consortium for International Development (CID), the Southwest Alliance for Latin America (SALA) and the Organization for Tropical Studies (OTS).

There is no doubt that an international assignment will broaden the education of university faculty, staff and students. Such an experience with foreign cultures, governments and economic systems will not only change the individuals view of this complicated world but it will give them a greater appreciation of our own government and way of life. A worthwhile goal would be to expose every faculty member and student to an international experience.

Academic Freedom and Tenure

"A challenge to tenure policies."

As a new administrator at Texas Tech I experienced my first challenge to defend academic freedom by supporting a controversial faculty member. Later, I challenged tenure policies that were used to protect an incompetent faculty member.

I was called before the Board of Directors and the President of Texas Tech on several occasions to defend the actions and policies of Dr. Ralph Durham, Head of the Department of Animal Husbandry. Dr. Durham had made strong statements against some traditional and widespread practices of the livestock industry. Durham had evidence, obtained through research, that the accepted livestock judging procedures were neither the best for the producers (leading toward less efficiency in lean meat production) nor for consumers (too much fat for good health). Some of the Tech board members and many of their friends were purebred cattle producers who stood by the old traditions. Dean Emeritus W. L. Stangel, as general chairman of the Fort Worth Livestock Show, also supported the traditional approach to shows. I had to admit that Durham was not very diplomatic in his approach to change, but his concepts were correct. At any rate, I was successful in preventing Durham's

The Babtistas family, which I visited several times during my Greek trip. The oldest son, left, was a graduate of the American Farm School at Thessaloniki, Greece. September, 1959.

On the trip home from Greece, I stopped in Paris. Of course, I took advantage of the opportunity to visit the Eiffel Tower. September 27, 1959.

termination and upholding, what I considered, an issue of academic freedom.

When I hired Ralph Durham he was already a controversial figure in animal science circles. We heard the story of his challenge to the swine producers while at Iowa State. He was in charge of the swine-testing program for the University Extension Service. He noted that, after the annual standard feeding tests to check boar performance, the swine producers took their boars home and still sold them on the basis of pedigree and not on performance. Consequently, Ralph decided it was time to bring about change. At the annual field day, when all of the important swine producers gathered to hear the latest results and brag about their boar's pedigree, they were shocked to learn that Ralph had castrated the low performers and tossed the testicles in the pens. The uproar after this event had reverberations throughout the swine industry. This was typical of the Durham approach.

Although tenure is designed to protect academic freedom, it can also be used to maintain mediocrity or protect downright incompetence. I experienced this aspect of tenure also at Texas Tech when I supported a department head's decision to terminate a tenured faculty member. The department head and I faced the fired faculty member's attorney for two days of intense hearings. At that time we were not offered legal help from the University. From this experience I learned that termination of a tenured professor was difficult, particularly when coworkers (who admitted privately of his incompetence) came to his defense. This tenure hearing vividly demonstrated the need for adequate documentation on worker performance and carefully planed "due process" procedures.

I started teaching a course in Agricultural orientation developing notes which later became a book entitled, **"Progress and Change in the Agricultural Industry."** In addition, I taught an advanced course in Range Management in the Department of Agronomy. I was soon convinced that we needed to create a Department of Range and Wildlife Science and we worked toward that end with Dr.

Thad Box and John Hunter as our key organizers. Enrollment in the School of Agriculture increased rapidly since we drew students from Eastern New Mexico as well as Texas.

Chihuahuan Moonshine – Sotol

In July, 1959, I was invited by my former graduate student Dr. Martin Gonzalez to attend the dedication of the Rancho Experimental La Compana in Chihuahua, of which he was the new director. I was not surprised by Martin's rapid advancement, as he was a natural leader. Martin suggested I bring Jean and the kids and he'd show us around Chihuahua, and then take us to visit his parents' cattle ranch.

While visiting the ranch, Martin and his father escorted us to a small village in the nearby mountains. Without this escort we would not have been welcome, because the village was the site of the illegal production of a potent whiskey distilled from the Sotol plant (*Dasylirion wheeleri*), called Sotol.

Sotol is a yucca-like Chihuahuan Desert plant. It is gathered using pack mules from the surrounding hills. The plant is dug up and trimmed to a ball about 8-12 inches in diameter. These balls are thrown into a hole in the ground and covered with dirt. Heat from an outdoor oven is piped into the covered holes. After an appropriate length of time, the dirt is removed and the balls, now very soggy, are tossed into a mule-powered grinder.

The juice from the Sotol was then manually transferred to an open trough that lead to fermenting tanks built into the side of the hill. In this case, the trough went right past the outhouse. In the tanks after some additional processing, the resulting liquid was bottled and sold on the illegal market.

We asked the Mexican in charge, a former General, what the alcohol content was. He said it was "about right." Martin's father said it was drinkable only if you add some fruit or a snake's head to the bottle and let it sit for about a year. Even then, Sotol is a "he-man's drink."

David, Dr. Martin Gonzalez, and Peggy. Chihuahua, Mexico. July, 1959.

The Soto distillery. The many goats on the site added their own unique
contribution to the final product. Chihuahua, Mexico. July, 1959.

Chapter 18 | A Shake-Down Period: 1960 - 64

"We broke out our first TV."

1960: Selected Journal Notes

Our family moved from 4402 45th Street to 3805 27th in Lubbock in early 1960 and we became increasingly involved in university and local affairs. I served as President of the Texas Section of the Society for Range Management, on the Board of the Lubbock Rotary Club, the Session of Westminster Presbyterian Church, and in the Research Reserve of the Navy. I had many speaking engagements and frequent radio and TV interviews. Jean adapted readily to the social responsibilities of a Dean's wife. David had a large paper route and was active in the Lubbock Chess Club. Peggy and Marianne were attending public schools.

On January 17, my brother William (Bill) married Eunice Irene McAlear in Polson, Montana. Dad and Mother and my brother John were present for the ceremony, but we could not attend.

We borrowed money in June to invest in an oil well (Butler #2) under development in East Texas by my brother Byron. We lucked out and the well produced oil for several years.

Russian rockets in Cuba presented a crisis for our country and the Congo gained independence from Belgium.

We took our usual trek to Idaho and Montana in 1960 by combining vacation with a review of Range Research at Montana State University. We have always considered visits with the Ellis and Thomas families enjoyable and important, particularly for the sake of our children. This year was special since the family honored Grandma Sarah Evans in Ronan.

Dr. Robert C. Goodwin was named President of Texas Tech in 1960. He had been acting President since Dr. Edward N. Jones retirement. I selected Dr. Willie Ulich from Texas A&M to head our Department of Agricultural Engineering.

Oscar Knudson, a former graduate student at Texas A&M, and his wife Amalia visited us from Argentina October 13-25. We enjoyed their visit and kept some contact after they returned to Argentina.

Dr. Frank Gould, Texas A&M, asked me to prepare an Ecological Summary of the vegetation of Texas for his new book on Texas Plants.

We invited Ralph Durham's family and Harry and Beth Lane to Thanksgiving dinner.

1961: Selected Journal Notes

"Range meetings and flight training."

We developed a cooperative research program with Monty Moore of the Post/Montgomery Estate for range research utilizing graduate students. This tie with the Ranch proved to be a valuable asset to our programs in range and wildlife.

Jan 30-Feb 3 -- I attended the Range Society meeting in Salt Lake while serving on the National Board.

Feb 6-17 -- Naval Reserve training at the National Security Seminar included meetings with Secretary of the Navy John Connally. Also, I received orders for flight training at Corpus Christi, Texas. This was my first opportunity to check out the controls of a Navy jet although I was not qualified to solo.

On Feb 20th I helped David deliver papers in the snow. We pushed 19 cars out of snowdrifts.

Eunice Irene (McAlear) and William Thomas. Married January 17, 1960.
Polson, Montana.

Gerald and Byron at site of Butler #1, discovered and developed by Byron.
This successful well launched Byron's career as an independent oil producer.
Near Longview, Texas, June, 1960.

Gerald and Lt. F. W. Grant. Naval Reserve Training.
Corpus Christi, Texas. April 3, 1960.

Lubbock's "Family of the Year." 1962.

I was surprised to meet my former Torpedo 4 crewman, John Holloman, when I spoke to a group of cotton ginners on March 13. John was operating a gin in New Mexico. We had not seen each other since April, 1945.

My cousin, Dean Thomas from Dubois, Idaho flew into Reece Air Base in an F-105 for a surprise visit on April 19.

In July the family loaded up the car and camp trailer for the Range Society Meetings in Calgary, Canada. We combined this trip with a vacation visit to family in Idaho and Montana.

We dedicated a new Plant Science Building for the College of Agriculture on Oct 21.

Nov 16 -- With Elo Urbanovsky's help we presented a request to the Killgore Foundation for a half-million dollars to build a beef cattle center at our Pantex farm.

Mother, Dad, John Foster, Daniel and Betty came into Lubbock for Christmas and we took two cars to Longview, Texas to visit Byron and Mary.

1962: Family Ties and Selected Notes

"Family ties and our first TV."

Byron informed us in January that we hit a dry hole in our latest oil venture. We had invested $6,000 in that project.

I served as General Chairman for the Annual Meeting of the Society for Range Management in Corpus Christi (Jan 21-29). The weather was bad but the program went well. Field trips to the King Ranch and to Monterrey, Mexico added to the effectiveness of the meetings.

Our family was nominated for, "Lubbock Family of the Year" and we purchased our first TV in December (The children said we were the last family in Lubbock to get a TV). Jean and I both served a term on the Session of Westminster Presbyterian Church.

On May 11th we were surprised when a car load of women (Mother and sisters Beulah, Gertrude, Flora, Mona and Elsie) stopped by our home for a visit. These brave ladies were on a trip which would eventually lead to Webster, Kansas to check out their roots.

Naval Reserve training in San Diego at the North Island Naval Air Station provided an opportunity for us to visit relatives in California, including Bill and Gene Harwell, Roy and Dorothy Lingo, Guy and Boonie Lingo, Vernie and Dot Officer and the Junior Evans family.

We purchased a large lot on the Flathead Lake in Montana in September. Mother had helped us find a good location at a reasonable price on "Big Arm" facing south.

We broke out that first TV for Christmas and Byron and Mary drove in from Longview.

1963: Kennedy Assassinated/Other Notes

"A Good Neighbor trip to Mexico."

Jan 4 -- Elo Urbanovsky and I meet with Governor John Connally, Preston Smith and others to review the Texas State Parks Plan and the Status of Agriculture. Elo and his students had invested a lot of time and effort on the State Park Plan – even to the point of impressing Lady Bird Johnson.

The Turner Case is on the front burner. I supported Ralph Durham in firing an incompetent tenured professor. We went through intensive hearings facing one of the best legal teams in Lubbock. This case generated additional controversy over Durham and we were surprised when the former Dean supported Turner.

Feb 1 -- We held our first "West Texas Water Conference" in Lubbock. I followed up with a presentation on the need for a "West Texas Water Institute" to focus on research and education relating to the critical water issues in the area.

Mary and Dan. Lubbock, Texas. December, 1961.

Visit by my Mother and her sisters. From left: Flora, Elsie, Beulah,
Mary, Peggy, Gerald, Marianne. Lubbock, Texas. May 11, 1962.

Our cousin, Phyllis Laird from Dubois, Idaho stopped in for a visit on April 9. She is active in the National Wool Growers Association.

Several changes were made in the Animal Science arena. Professor Ray Mowery, long-term and well-known leader in animal husbandry died. We hired Dr. Sam Curl in the Animal Science Department, moved Dr. George Ellis to head the Pantex Farms and held a retirement party for J. P. Smith, long-term Director of the Research Program at Pantex.

Apr 20-24 -- I served on the Southern Accreditation Evaluation Team at Ruston, LA for Louisiana Polytech.

Jun 11 -- I was promoted to Lt. Commander and scheduled to take over command of the Lubbock Research Reserve Unit when the Navy discovered that I fell in a special category that required that I be terminated from the Active Reserve (without retirement or other military privileges). It seems that I had over 20 years of total Reserve service without enough "annual active duty points.") This was somewhat of a shock since I had also taken several special correspondence courses and remained active in our Reserve Unit. However, I was too busy at the time to question the decision.

From June 29-July 13, Frank Gonzalez, Dr. Walter Parr and I organized a "Mexico Good Neighbor Project." We took two bus loads of young people and adults on an extensive trip through Mexico. We carried introductory letters from Governor John Connally and the Mayor of Lubbock. Of special note were the visits with the Governors of Nuevo Leon, Coahuila, San Luis Potosi, Aguascalientes, Durango and Chihuahua. We had police escorts into several cities. We delivered 5,000 books to the University of Chihuahua, one

of our dentists pulled some teeth and we started a "Cattle Bank" program.

On July 18, I received the Honorary State Farmer Award from the FFA.

Our two-week vacation was in August. We hooked on our little camp trailer, stopped at the Crooked Creek Ranch and talked Jean's Mother and Dad into joining us for the trip to Montana. We spent time on our new Flathead Lake lot and visited with relatives and friends.

Dr. Joe Schuster, from Texas A&M, accepted a position in the Range and Wildlife Department.

Dub Waldrip's wife Dottie died of cancer on Sept 24. I went to Seymour, Texas to serve as a Pall Bearer at the funeral. We have been friends with the Waldrip's since graduate school at Texas A&M.

President John F. Kennedy was assassinated in Dallas on November 22 and Governor Connally was wounded. Thad Box and I were enroute to Loredo, Texas when we heard the news. The nation was in a state of shock. The Mexico border was closed. We went on to the Sonora Experiment Station where we heard that Lee Harvey Oswald had been arrested and shot by Jack Ruby. All offices were closed on Nov 25th but I went ahead with a scheduled speech (with modifications) at Ladies Night for the Lubbock Agriculture Club.

Dec 13-14 -- Served as M. C. for the banquet of the Texas Section, SRM with Ace Reid as the main speaker.

After the usual 3-day deer hunt with Roy Davis, et. al., at the Wardlaw Ranch in South Texas and a check on progress at the Killgore Beef Cattle Center, I returned home for Christmas and New Years vacation.

Photo taken from the shore of the Flathead Lake lot purchased September 15, 1962.
The photo shows a rainbow following a lake squall.

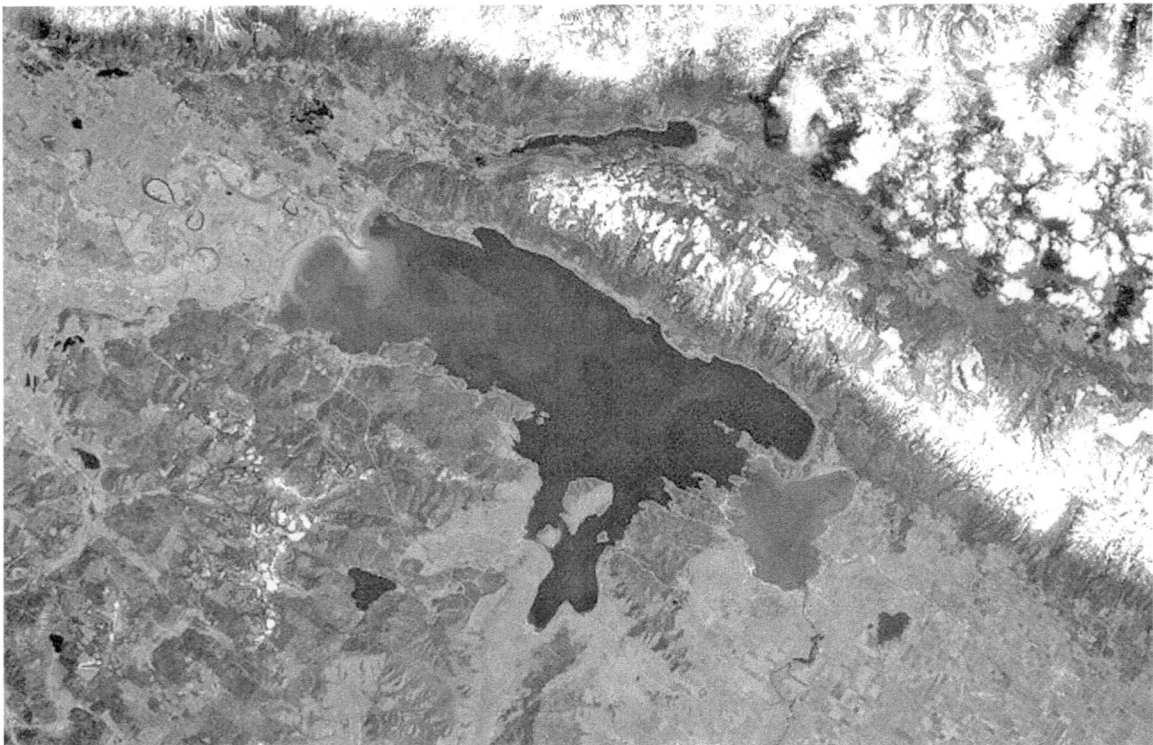

Satellite image of Flathead Lake (Montana). Flathead lake is the largest natural freshwater
lake in the western United States. The surface area is approximately 191.5 square miles.

Chapter 19 | Family Traditions

"Our most important family tradition."

In 1951, we had our first opportunity to take a vacation. Jean and I agreed almost without discussion that we wanted to spend it visiting our families in Idaho and Montana. The next year we again spent our limited free time traveling to Idaho and Montana, a three-day drive each way. Shortly after that, we realized what a valuable experience it was for our kids. Living so far from their grandparents, aunts, uncles, and cousins meant that unless we took them back to visit often, they would never know them.

So began what might be our most important family tradition. Every year, our main vacation priority was to return to visit our families. In this way, our kids learned to know the places where Jean and I grew up: Crooked Creek Ranch, Medicine Lodge Ranch, Lidy Hot Springs. They knew the surrounding places in Idaho where our many relatives lived, such as Dubois, Mud Lake, Roberts, and Idaho Falls. In Montana, they learned to know Ronan, where my parents had retired, Polson, and perhaps most of all – Flathead Lake. We all fell in love with the lot that we had purchased on Flathead.

(After I graduated from A&M, if we were in a position to afford it and had the time, we'd take a second, usually short vacation, to other places.)

In later years, when our kids were young adults, they missed a few trips north. But when they got older, they often joined us with their families, introducing a third generation to their Idaho and Montana relations.

Last year Jean was unable to go, because of serious illness, but David and I made the trip, completing 58 years of this family tradition. It is my hope and wish that my grandkids, and eventually their children, will continue to feel this deep attraction to their extended relatives, and to the places to which Jean and I will be forever tied.

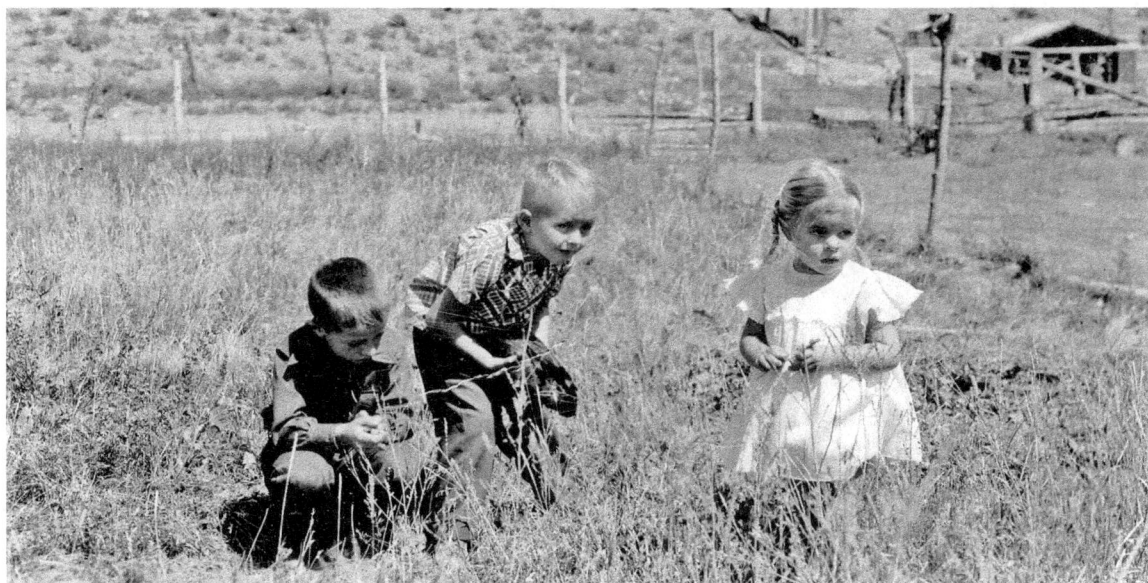

Cousin Dan Moore, David, and Peggy. Crooked Creek Ranch. 1951.

Dan Moore and David. Crooked Creek Ranch, 1952. Dan was killed August 31, 1969 in a tragic accidental fall just before his twenty-fourth birthday.

My brother Walter's family with Dan Thomas (standing). Betsy, Walter, Candy, and Willes. Ronan, Montana, 1953.

Jean's brother Robert with his two eldest, Andy and Penny. January, 1956.

Visiting my VT-4 buddy Bob Ruth and his family.
Bob Ruth, David Ruth, Marianne, Gerald, David, Jean, Peggy, Claramae Ruth.
Deadwood, South Dakota, July, 1957.

Garbage Can Cafe and Lookout Resort, Flathead Lake, September, 1957.
My Mother and her sisters Gertrude and Beulah ran the cafe for two years.
They did everything from cooking to waiting tables. Mr. White, the owner, had a
fabulous collection of antiques and Western memorabilia, accumulated over a
lifetime. When he died, the resort was closed and the collection sold.

Postcard showing extent of the Garbage Can Cafe and Lookout Resort.

Gertrude, Jean, Dan, Marianne, Peggy, David, and Mary.
Garbage Can Cafe and Lookout Resort, September, 1957.

David, Marianne, and Peggy. Padre Island, Corpus Christi, Texas. 1958.

A visit with Byron's family. Back row: David, Andrew, Peggy, Patti, and Barbara. Front: Marianne and Judy. Longview, Texas, 1960.

Marianne, Peggy, and David. Jackson Lake, Wyoming, July, 1961.

Lamar Ellis, Rees Thomas (Dan's brother), Dan, and Franklin Sullivan (Gertrude Ellis' brother). Crooked Creek Ranch. July, 1961.

Jean, Dan, Marianne, Mary, Peggy, and David.
Grand Teton National Park. August, 1961.

A picnic in the timberland owned by Dan and Mary Thomas.
Standing: Dan, Mary, Peggy, Jean. Sitting: Eunice, William, Marianne.
Ronan, Montana, 1962.

Eunice, William, and Kirk. San Francisco, March, 1964.

Lamar and Sandy Ellis and their children Jim and Mike. Mack Ellis, at left.
Crooked Creek Ranch. August, 1966.

Gertrude and Mack Ellis, Crooked Creek Ranch. August, 1966.

Visiting the Jay and Lois (Ellis) Hawker ranch, Mud Lake, summer, 1966.
Back row: Jay, David, Peggy, Gerald, Marianne, Jean.
Front: Ben, Jan, and Jill Hawker. David's VW shown on left.

Dan and Mary Thomas. Ronan, Montana. July 1967.

Lamar Ellis and Dan Moore with the mobile grain cleaning machine
that Lamar designed and built. Summer, 1968.

Gertrude and Mack's five children. Weldon, Robert, Lamar, Gertrude, Jean,
and Lois. Crooked Creek Ranch. Summer, 1978.

Dan and Mary's six boys – the last time they were all together.
John, William, Walter, Byron, Gerald, and Daniel.
Mary Thomas' funeral. Ronan, Montana. December 10, 1986.

Chapter 20 | Expanding Horizons

"Fourteen states and Africa."

A Break from Texas Tech

In February 1964 I took leave from Texas Tech to accept an assignment with the Cooperative State Research Service of the US Department of Agriculture. My job description included reviewing research programs on forage crops and range ecology in USDA and the Land Grant Colleges. This was a great opportunity for me to study programs in my professional field. I worked closely with Dr. Thomas Ronnigan and other scientists in CSRS under the overall supervision of Administrator Ted Byerly. I was the only Range Scientist in CSRS.

The team reviews took me to 14 States (Kansas, Missouri, Nebraska, Illinois, Ohio, Maryland, Nevada, California, Florida, Oklahoma, Colorado, Pennsylvania, Connecticut and New Mexico). I was able to schedule several stops at Lubbock to check by the Dean's office and attend some functions such as the dedication of the Killgore Beef Cattle Center at PanTex on March 12.

I had the privilege of watching the funeral procession for General Douglas MacArthur in Washington on April 8, 1964 – an impressive tribute to the leader who made so many headlines during WWII and Korea.

On May 29, I stopped in Lubbock to pick up Jean and the kids in our Ford station wagon for a short stay in the Washington area. We rented an apartment in Alexandria, Virginia and took enjoyable tours to the White House, Gettysburg, the Smithsonian museums and a short trip to the World's Fair in New York City. Congressman George Mahon and his wife escorted us around the House and Senate buildings. David was able to hone his chess skills by playing in the Eastern Chess Open.

During office time in the USDA building I completed an article for the Agricultural Scientist Magazine entitled, *"Rangelands: Our Billion-Acre Resource."* My assignment with CSRS ended on August 28, 1964. I turned in a final report to Administrator Byerly and returned to my position as Dean with a new salary of $17,200.

I was back to Texas Tech for the fall term noting that I was not very impressed with Barry Goldwater's speech on October 8 even though my brother Byron was a fan of Goldwater. Then, on November 3rd, the papers announced the election of L. B. Johnson and Hubert Humphrey.

We held our Annual Pig Roast on November 17. The Ulich family joined us for Thanksgiving. We celebrated Christmas at home and I joined Roy Davis and others for the usual deer hunt at the Wardlaw Ranch in South Texas.

1965: Africa and Selected Notes

The College of Agriculture had good support from the West Texas Chamber of Commerce and I participated in Chamber meetings in Del Rio and Cuidad Acuna as a part of INFOCADE 65. We were now more involved in state-wide water planning as a partner with A&M and UT-Austin. In January I cut several radio tapes and TV videos on "Water."

In May I took some Campfire Girls, including Peggy, to Palo Duro Canyon and tried, without much success, to teach them about the vegetation. David bought a Volkswagen and he graduated from Monterrey High on May 27.

On May 7 we interviewed Bobby Rankin for the position as Director of our research and out-

Angola Study Team. Gerald, Ralph Durham, John Jaques, and Nino Lopez Alvez.
Angola, July, 1965.

A cart pulled by a team of nine oxen with a police guard. Angola, July, 1965.

reach program at PanTech Farms. Bobbie was a student of mine at Texas A&M. He declined the job and later served with distinction as Head of the Animal and Range Science Department at NMSU. Thus, our friendship and professional interactions continued.

May 29 -- Texas Tech awarded honorary degrees to George Dupree and Governor John Connally.

Angola: First Exposure to Africa

We started our family vacation with car and trailer in July. However, I had to leave the family in Idaho to accept an assignment in Portugal and Angola, Africa. I asked Dr. Ralph Durham to accompany me since we were to make recommendations on a joint Portuguese/American livestock venture. This study was sponsored by Companhia Mineira do Lobito and an American businessman. The mining company furnished a small airplane to facilitate the visits to experiment stations and ranching areas in Angola. This was before Angola gained its independence from Portugal. Our study lasted from July 15 to August 8, including stops in New York and Lisbon. Some notes on this project follow.

In 1965, Angola was a colony of Portugal. This relationship dates back to the 1400s. We were emphatically told that *"Angola is a part of Portugal and it does not want independence. We cannot understand why some groups are sponsoring unrest in our country. Furthermore, there is no discrimination against the natives."*

We were informed that the capitol, Luanda, was the last African port to be closed to the slave trade.

Following the trip to Portugal and Angola, I prepared a final report for Mr. Hinn and Sr. Machado of Mineira do Lobito. We stated that the resource base for the two ranches we had located (one was nearly a half-million acres) was good and the ranches were probably economically feasible but we expressed concern over the political and social situation. We were particularly apprehensive about the Portuguese policies which allowed land occupied by the natives to be taken under private control.

Shortly after our visit a revolution started and some ranchers were killed. This was the beginning of the move toward independence for Angola. Independence was gained in 1975 and some 350,000 Portuguese, the country's main traders, exporters, and importers fled, impairing the ability of the country to function economically. Real progress in Angola still waits on peace and a stable government.

On July 7, Nuno Lopez Alvez with his wife, Teresa, came to Lubbock to discuss our recommendations for ranching development in Angola. Nuno had been our contact for the study in Angola.

Oct 20 -- Organizational meeting for the "Institute for New Uses of West Texas Cotton" – a joint effort between our Ag College, the College of Engineering and private industry.

In November, I was elected President of the Texas Agricultural Workers Association.

Congressman George Mahon visited our home on December 18 to discuss the status of my new book on American Agriculture. We enjoyed the Christmas break in Lubbock with the family.

Visiting the US Capital. Peggy, David, Jean, and Marianne. June, 1964.

Visiting Mount Vernon, George Washington's home near Alexandria, Virginia.
David, Jean, Marianne, and Peggy. June, 1964.

Chapter 21 | Texas Tech Gets a New President

"Dad and Mother came to Lubbock by bus."

Texas Tech Begins Rapid Growth

One of the first notes in my journal in 1966 was: "Dull outlook for Viet Nam."

On January 4, I addressed the joint meeting of the Soil Conservation Supervisors and the Society for Range Management in Denver,

Dad and Mother came into Lubbock by bus on February 26. We took them to visit Byron and Mary in Longview while I attended a meeting on water at Texas A&M. My parents left for home by bus on March 11.

May 10 -- I addressed the Honor Society of Phi Kappa Phi at Texas A&M. This speech was later published in the Phi Kappa Phi Journal. *"Diversified Excellence: The Challenge in Variation."*

Jean and I held a dinner for Dr. George Ellis on May 25 as he resigns from the position as Head of the Animal Science Department. Peter Hurd was awarded an Honorary Degree from Texas Tech on May 28.

In June, David won the Chess Championship of Lubbock for the first of many times. We were surprised at his success, as he had developed his skill at chess privately, on his own, without any outside training. A few years later he won the Texas Open Chess Championship. In 1974, he achieved international success by playing in the World Chess Olympics in Nice, France. He was not representing the United States, however, but Lebanon, where he was living at the time.

As usual, our vacation in the summer to Idaho and Montana was combined with attendance at the Great Plains Agricultural Council meetings in Bozeman, Montana.

I was appointed Chairman of the Inauguration Committee for Grover Murray, the new President of Texas Tech, in June and we started planning for the concept of ICASALS – the International Center for Arid and Semi Arid Land Studies. Dr. Robert. C. Goodwin's last day as President of Tech was August 31. I enjoyed my association with President Goodwin and was pleased that Dr. Murray came in with new ideas and enthusiasm.

In September 1966, Dr. George Ellis and I were hired as consultants to make recommendations on forest, range and livestock management on the "Baca/Valles Caldera" Ranch near Los Alamos by Pat Dunnigan, owner of the ranch. Playboy Magazine was hosting a conference for "playgirls" at the same time, which served as a distraction to our fieldwork. Dunnigan later released the ranch to the Federal Government and Valles Caldera became a unique conservation reserve.

Sep 11-13 Washington, DC – Congressman George Mahon helped us with introductions to key personnel at the National Science Foundation, the Agricultural Research Service and the Department of Interior for developing research contacts for Texas Tech. Also, I visited with Marjorie Merriweather Post at the famous Hillwood Estate. I record this visit because of the historical role Charles William "CW" Post played in West Texas agriculture.

A Visit to Hillwood

"Mrs. Post is not available."

On September 12, 1966, President Grover E. Murray, Dean of Engineering John Bradford and I were in Congressman George Mahon's office in Washington DC on a visit to promote programs at Texas Tech. I asked Mr. Mahon if he had a phone

David with Midge and his Lubbock Chess Champion trophy. June, 1966.

David with the 3-D chess set he built. June, 1966.

I could use to call Marjorie Merriweather Post. He stated firmly that no one could reach Mrs. Post except perhaps the White House. I said I still wanted to try. The first person I reached by phone at the Hillwood Estate stated that *"Mrs. Post is not available."* I went on to explain that I was Dean of Agriculture at Texas Tech and that we had been doing research with graduate students on the Post-Montgomery Ranch and I was sure Mrs. Post would like a report. He referred me to another person who repeated that Mrs. Post was not available. I went through the same story again about our research on her ranch in West Texas. The second person then referred me to Mrs. Post's private secretary. After another explanation of my mission, I was abruptly informed that *"Mrs. Post wants to see you. Can you come out to Hillwood?"* I explained that the President of the University and the Dean of Engineering were with me. *"Bring them along,"* I was instructed.

Congressman Mahon was very surprised, but he congratulated me for reaching Mrs. Post. The three of us took a taxi to the magnificent Hillwood Estate. Mrs. Post gave us a very cordial welcome. For the next four hours, including an elegantly served lunch, we visited with Mrs. Post. She gave us a personal tour of Hillwood.

Marjorie Merriweather Post was one of the most impressive ladies that I have ever met. She was elderly at the time, I believe close to eighty, but she had a straight back, an impressive posture, and a keen interest in our discussion of her ranching operations near Post, Texas.

Mrs. Post soon took over the conversation with fascinating accounts of her father's early attempts to establish a viable agricultural enterprise in West Texas. (Post founded his empire based on his coffee substitute Postum and his production of Post Toasties, Grape Nuts and other cereals.) Two of Mrs. Post's stories bear repeating. They are roughly as follows:

(1) When my father first bought the land around what is now Post, Texas, he divided part of it into 160-acre blocks. He sold these to families who wanted to farm at no interest and long-term payments. He located the farmstead buildings where the corners of the land came together. He thought this would prevent loneliness. But, father was wrong! The kids got into fights; the chickens got mixed up and other problems developed so most of the families moved back toward the center of their land.

(2) My father believed that he could make it rain in West Texas. He conducted the first rainmaking experiments in the country. His experiments were based on accounts from the Civil War. Soldiers reported that it often rained after a big battle. So my father took his cowboys, loaded up wagons with dynamite, and placed large charges all along the cap rock between the High Plains and the Rolling Plains. He had everyone synchronize their watches and set the blast off at the various locations at a specific time.

No rain came after this big blast. So my father got to thinking that the Civil War was not one simultaneous explosion, but a series of explosions during the battles. In the next experiment, my father replenished the dynamite supplies, and set the blasts off with a preset differential. It rained within 24 hours. Yes my father believed he could make rain with enough dynamite. (Note: Some scientists confirm the reports on rain during the Civil War. They say the black powder explosions may have had the same effect as the silver iodide used in weather modification research today. However, dynamite does not produce the same effect.)

Mrs. Post also told us about her father's love of cooking – particularly cooking with mesquite wood. But, Post also had "stomach trouble" – and he could not drink coffee. This distaste for coffee motivated Post to create Postum – still for sale today. In the early experiments which resulted in Post Toasties, Mr. Post tried marketing the product

Mack and Gertrude Ellis. Crooked Creek Ranch, August, 1966.

John and JoAnn serving in the Peace Corps on the island of Truk,
Federated States of Micronesia. January, 1967.

as "Elija's Manna." Criticism from churches arose, so he called the product Toasties. In order to stimulate sales, he also packaged the same Toasties in a different box under another name so that consumers would have a choice and this stimulated sales.

Marjorie accompanied her third husband, Joseph E. Davies, to the Soviet Union, where he served as the American Ambassador (1937-1938). This was during Stalin's reign of terror and his administration was determined to erase remnants of the Csar's regime. Mrs. Post told us that she and the Ambassador were invited to look over confiscated art works, jewelry and furniture stored in a warehouse near Moscow and to purchase any that they wanted. She and the Ambassador collected many items such as jade and paintings from the floor and the balcony and piled them up in the middle of the storage shed. The Soviets weighed the pile of materials and sold them to the couple by weight. Materialism was certainly not in vogue for the USSR at that time.

When I first conceived the idea of approaching Mrs. Post for a possible large contribution to Texas Tech, I laid some groundwork with Monty Moore, manager of the Post-Montgomery Ranch. Monty gave me Mrs. Post's phone number but he warned me that I probably could not get through to her. Furthermore, he cautioned me against any mention of an Assistant Professor Post that was working at Texas Tech in the Music Department. Monty said this Professor Post was a descendant of an illegitimate relationship of Post. (It is my understanding that before Marjorie Merriweather Post passed away, she invited this professor and his family to visit at her home in the Adirondacks and that she finally accepted him as a part of the family.)

After our visit with Mrs. Post at Hillwood, I learned from Monty Moore that Mrs. Post was scheduled to fly into Lubbock for a visit to her properties and to attend a ceremony in Post. She was to stay in a motel in Lubbock. Consequently, Elo Urbanovsky and I assembled a huge dry floral arrangement made up of various strains of grain sorghum for her visit. We placed this large spectacular arrangement in one room of the motel. With this gift we attached a history of grain sorghum with emphasis on the fact that Post was instrumental in bringing the early varieties of grain sorghum to West Texas.

Unfortunately, I was never able to follow-up on my contacts with Mrs. Post on that "large contribution" to Texas Tech. However, the range research program at the Post-Montgomery Ranch has continued.

On September 20 I was involved in a car wreck. I was the third car back in a 4-car accident. Received a bad whip lash as I was hit from behind. Therapy was required and neck problems have plagued me since.

Oct 31-Nov 1 -- Served as General Chairman for the Inauguration of President Grover E. Murray and the initiation of ICASALS. Speakers included Secretary Udall (USDI), Secretary Ripley of the Smithsonian, Governor John Connally, John Ben Sheppard and others.

I visited my Torpedo Four turret gunner John Holloman at the Lubbock Hospital. He had been in and out of a coma but he recognized me. He died soon after my visit.

The Headlines in the Lubbock paper on December 17 read, *"Tech gets $1 Million for brush research under Dr. Gerald Thomas."* Our contacts are starting to yield results.

1967: Yearbook Dedicated, A Pioneer Lost

In early January, 1967, my brother John and his wife JoAnn began their Peace Corps service on the Pacific island of Truk, of the Federated States of Micronesia, an experience they have told me many times was one of the most enjoyable and rewarding of their lives. They had joined the Peace Corps the previous year, and had had about 3 months training. This decision by my brother and his wife reflected that spirit of public service that was so prevalent among the young in the mid-60s.

My Torpedo 4 crewmen Donald H. Gress and John E. Holloman.
Aboard the **USS ESSEX**, 1944.

Jan 15 -- Meet with Asst. Secretary of Agriculture George Mehren and Dean Patterson of Texas A&M on cooperative research between Tech, A&M and the Agricultural Research Service. Tech is now recognized as a partner in all aspects of agricultural development.

Dr. Thad Box was appointed Director of ICASALS on my strong recommendation. He provided inspirational leadership to the program, but Tech later lost him to Utah State where he became Dean of the College of Natural Resources.

Jean flew to Idaho in February to visit her father who is seriously ill with cancer. He was moved from Idaho Falls to Salt Lake City.

In a surprise announcement on April 5, the editors of the '67 La Ventana *dedicated the student annual to Ag Dean Gerald Thomas."* The students designed a cover for the "Tyme Magazine" section of the yearbook naming me "Man of the Year."

On May 7 we dedicated "Stangel Hall" in honor of the former Dean of Agriculture. Dean Stangel was widely recognized for his support of the Fort Worth Livestock Show and for his leadership in traditional animal husbandry.

I was elected President of the Lubbock Rotary Club in March replacing Bob Nash. Then Jean and I received a paid trip to attend the Rotary International Meetings in Nice, France in May. We stopped in Portugal to follow up on my Angola report and we were invited to visit a ranch in Albacate, Spain. We also made stops in Paris, Zurich and Lucerne.

Jean and I were walking through a section of Paris, somewhat off the tourist path, when we decided to eat at a local café. At the checkout counter we were informed that the café did not accept travel checks or US currency. The manager was called and a discussion developed – most of which we did not understand. As a consequence, it was agreed that I would leave Jean as security while I went back to the hotel to obtain some French money. The owner was all smiles as he accepted my payment (and a tip). And I was glad to secure the release of my wife.

May 26 -- As tired parents we returned from Europe just in time for Peggy's High School Graduation.

Dr. Thad Box and I attended ICASALS meetings in Mexico City June 21-23. We discussed our programs with American Embassy and Mexico agriculture officials.

We took our family vacation at the end of June (with car and trailer) to Idaho and Montana. Mack Ellis was not well but he went on a camping/fishing trip with us to Irving Creek. We also visited Daniel and Betty where they were farming on Lost River.

While I was attending the Tenth Anniversary of the La Compana Experimental Ranch in Chihuahua I received a call from Jean (now in Idaho) about her father. I flew to Idaho Falls. Mack S. Ellis passed away on August 10, 1967. Memorial Services were held at the Dubois Baptist Church. The family and our country lost a hard working, honest and dearly loved pioneer.

Nov 16 -- An invitation to address the Kiwanis Club at Lovington, New Mexico provided an opportunity for me to visit Dr. Walter Hopkins, one of our former Torpedo 4 pilots.

Dec 10-13 -- I joined a tour of the California Water Project sponsored by WATER INC with stops at Sacramento, Modesto, Bakersfield, Tehachapi, and Long Beach.

Dec 21 -- Received the 50th Anniversary Federal Land Bank Medal for "Outstanding Service to American Agriculture." We spent Christmas in Lubbock and on the 29th we joined the Al Couch family at Tres Ritos, New Mexico.

The cover of the 1967 *La Ventana*, the Texas Tech Student Year Book.
The book was formatted as if it was a news magazine.

Chapter 22 | At Home and Abroad

"The President of Chad comes to Lubbock."

Professional Challenges and Rewards

On January 15, 1968 I was invited by Harold Hinn, Texas Tech Board of Directors, to meetings in Mexico City concerning world food problems. From February 23-March 2 I visited Guatemala, Honduras and Costa Rica for the Organization for Tropical Studies (OTS).

I was appointed Interim Executive Vice-President by President Murray effective February 1. Dr. Murray asked me to stay in the position, but I told him I would rather move back to the Dean's office in June. Murray then appointed Dean Kennedy as VP.

In March we joined Al and Norma Couch for the purchase of land at El Valle, New Mexico from Jose Aguilar. On the return trip we were snowed in at Clines Corners. We spent the night in our car and the service station. We tried to help other motorists since we had some food supplies. Everyone was locked out of the café and those inside were not allowed back in if they left.

March 29-April 13 -- Travelled to Peru as the agricultural representative of the Texas Partners for the Alliance for Progress. Edward Marcus of Neiman-Marcus in Dallas, chaired the group. We visited with President Fernando Belaunde Terry at the Palace in Lima. We were escorted around the agriculture sector by Father Robert Lejan, a Catholic Priest. He stated that one of the biggest problems was population growth and his group was actively promoting birth control. Also, the men took every afternoon off to drink "Chi Cha" – made from potatoes and grain – usually chewed by the women to help with fermentation. Chi Cha took away most of the desire to work.

While we were in Peru President Johnson announced that he would not seek another term. This shook up some of the US delegation, especially since one member of our team, Jim McCrocklin, was Chairman of the LBJ Texas Reelection Campaign.

The delegation also visited Machu Picchu, one of the most fascinating places in the world because of the unique setting in the rugged mountains of Peru and the mystery surrounding its history and culture.

April 20-26 -- Addressed the International Symposium on Arid and Semi-arid Lands, Monterrey, Mexico at the invitation of Martin Gonzalez.

North Africa: 1968

A consulting assignment to Algeria, Libya, Chad and Turkey occupied the time between August 25 and September 26. Dr. James Osborn from the Department of Agricultural Economics, joined me on this trip. A summary of this experience follows.

Algeria

Our study in Algeria consisted of two parts:

- Examine the country from the standpoint of underground water development for agriculture.

- Check into the possibilities for desalting water in the desert. Most of our travel was in the desert areas.

Northern Algeria is fairly well developed. It has served for many years as the vacation land for the French. The vast grape plantations furnished

One of the wonders of the ancient world: Machu Picchu. Said to have been built as the private estate of Inca emperor Pachacuti (1438–1472). April, 1968.

Machu Picchu. April, 1968.

Camel and Ox hitched to a plow. Algeria. September, 1968.

Ruins of Timgad, built by the Roman Emperor Trajan about 100 AD. Shown here is the Arch of Trajan. The city had disappeared from history until its excavation in 1881. Located near Batna, Algeria. September, 1968.

Another shot of Timgad, Algeria. September, 1968.

Oxen pumping water near Fort Lamy, Chad. September, 1968.

quality wines for the European continent. However, since independence (gained from France after a bitter struggle which began in 1954 and did not end until 1962) Algeria has lost access to the vast European markets. As a result there is a huge surplus of grapes. Diversification is gradually taking place but a shift from a Colonial dominated economy is not an easy task.

The range lands of Algeria are severely overgrazed and badly eroded. We saw many nomads moving toward the desert with camels, goats, and donkeys. The animals were surviving largely on crop aftermath. We were told that the established tradition of nomad rights to crop aftermath could not be changed. Hay stacks and straw stacks were covered with a thick clay layer to protect against nomadic livestock.

Our visit to Algeria was sponsored by Sonatrach, the National Petroleum Company of Algeria and our tour guide was Hamocide Heoul, a Texas Tech graduate married to Pat Parnell of Paducah, Texas.

Chad

We finished our assignment in Algeria on September 10 and flew to Fort Lamy, Chad. We were invited by President Ngarta Tombalbaye of Chad to give him some advice on agricultural development in his country. Since housing was very limited in the capitol Fort Lamy, arrangements were made for us to stay with the American Ambassador at the Embassy.

Chad, formerly a part of French Equatorial Africa, was proclaimed an autonomous republic in 1958. The new republic experienced several political crises in the next several years. Tombalbaye became Chad's first President after Independence in 1959. A country more than twice the size of Texas, Chad had a per capita GNP of $150 in 1968.

We covered as much of Chad as possible in spite of travel restrictions imposed because of disturbances in the country. A British missionary with a float plane and a small Peace Corps group on Lake Chad helped us get into the rural areas.

While in Chad we had the opportunity to become acquainted with President Tombalbaye. During our discussions on Agriculture, I invited him to visit Texas. He enthusiastically stated that he would do so. I did not take his affirmation too seriously at the time. Consequently, I was surprised to get a call from Washington DC on October 1. The State Department informed me that President Tombalbaye was in Washington and wanted to visit Lubbock. I was invited to stay overnight at Blair House and accompany the Chad President, with several members of his Cabinet to Lubbock.

I spent the next several days showing President Tombalbaye around West Texas. He had brought several gifts for me and some of the other hosts. He gave me a brass sculpture made from shells left over from the French Foreign Legion. He also conferred on me the honor of a Chadian "Knight" (Chevalier).

But the most unusual gift was a freshly skinned, untanned cheetah hide. Even at that time the cheetah was considered an endangered species. The President wore a cap made from cheetah skin. Cheetah was the symbol of royalty and this gift from President Tombalbaye was a royal honor. After he left Texas, I tacked the cheetah hide on the wall of our garage. I did not know what to do with it since cheetah skins were banned in international trade. The hide hung on my garage wall for over a year before I decided to send it off to a tannery. I was certain that I would be arrested for owning the hide and that the tannery would identify the hide as an endangered species. Surprisingly, the hide came back, beautifully tanned, with a bill, but no questions.

After his visit to Texas Tech, President Tombalbaye returned to Chad. During the next several years, I read news releases about the President and continued unrest in the country. Tombalbaye had been trained in a Christian mission, exposed to some education in France, and moved into the power structure of Chad through an unusual set of circumstances. To survive as a Christian leader in a country predominantly Moslem, Animist or Pagan

Examining long-horn cattle. Chad. September, 1968.

Our host said we needed camp meat, so we headed into the bush. I spotted and
shot this spiral-horned antelope. Notice how huge the animal is, stretching over 12 feet
and weighing roughly 1,200 pounds. Angola. September, 1968.

Gerald, President Tombalbaye, and Chadian official.
Lubbock, Texas. October 6, 1968.

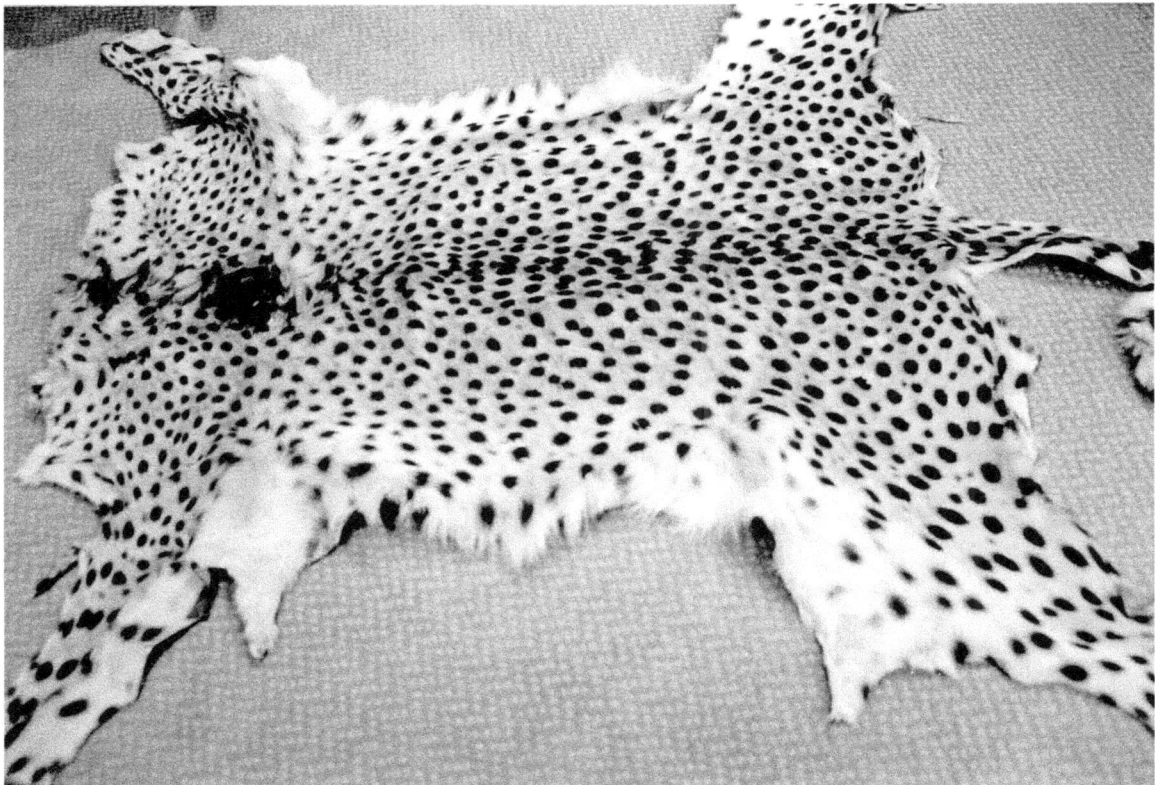

Cheetah hide given me by President Tombalbaye after tanning.

Le Chancelier de l'Ordre National du Tchad

certifie que par Décret du 18 novembre mil neuf cent soixante huit

Le Chef de l'État

a conféré à Mr DEAN Gerald Thomas

le grade de Chevalier de l'Ordre National du Tchad

Fait à Fort Lamy le 9 décembre 1968

Vu, vérifié, scellé et enregistré n° 2975
Le Secrétaire de la Chancellerie

Le Chancelier

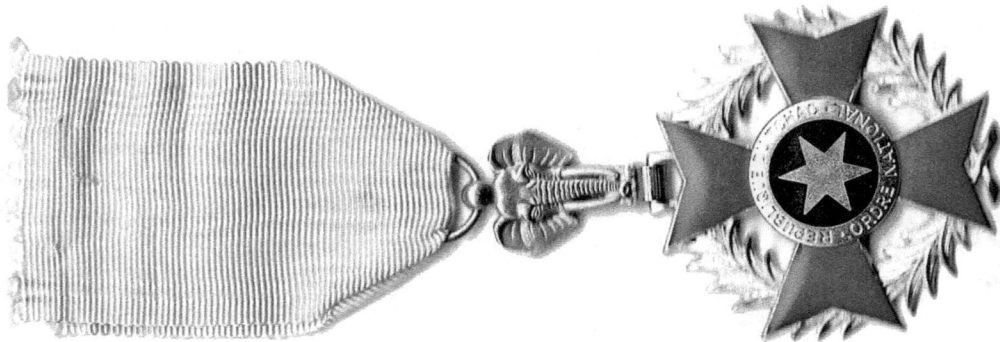

During President Tombalbaye's visit to Lubbock, I was honored by being made a Chevalier of the Ordre National du Tchad.

would be difficult under the best of circumstances. Papers reported that the President reverted back to his early exposure to witchcraft, became a victim of the Occult, and started killing or jailing those who appeared to be against him.

Tombalbaye's regime ended with a military coup. *"Soldiers seized him on a Sunday morning. They told him to climb aboard a truck with other prisoners. 'C'est fini' he said 'it is finished.' And he walked away 'until a burst of gunfire caught him,"* reported the *New York Times*.

After I moved to NMSU I met with a student by the name of Tombalbaye. I asked him if he was related to President Tombalbaye. He said, *"Yes, he was my uncle."* When I asked about the President, he stated that soldiers came into his uncle's house and shot the entire family. In the confusion of a revolution, it would be easy to get different stories. One has to wonder which is correct.

Libya

Our contacts for agricultural development in Libya were dependent upon the implementation of Armand Hammer's contract with King Idris which committed a portion of the oil revenue of Occidental Petroleum to the agricultural sector. Hammond agreed to drill for water and develop agriculture at Kufra which was the birthplace of the King and Queen. (King Idris was overthrown by a military coups on September 1, 1969, and Maummar el-Quaddife became dictator.)

Turkey

The cooperative agreement with Ankara University was developed as a result of Dr. Ahmet E. Uysal's assignment to the faculty of Texas Tech. His specialty was Turkish folklore. As we approached the small village our friend pointed to the central adobe oven and enthusiastically explained, *"Look they are bringing some fresh bread out of the oven. You will have to try this delicious bread. It is the best in Turkey."* After tasting the bread it became obvious that the fuel used in the oven was cow chips – not an uncommon fuel in rural areas of Turkey and Greece.

In December of 1968, I received a call from Utah State requesting that I visit the campus to consult on agriculture and consider the position of Dean of the College of Natural Resources. The reception at USU was friendly, but I declined a firm offer as Dean.

I presented a paper that Dr. Thad box and I had prepared to the American Association for the Advancement of Science in Dallas on December 30 entitled, "Social and Ecological Implications of Large Scale Water Transfer to the Arid Zones."

1969: A College Becomes a University

After several years of debate, the Texas Tech Board of Directors voted to change the name of Texas Technological College to Texas Tech University – thus retaining the Double-T. Also, in 1969, our College of Agricultural Sciences received approval to offer the Ph.D. in several areas of study.

Our daughter, Peggy Jeane, married Royace O'Neal on January 10, 1969, in Lubbock, Texas. Peggy will turn 20 in March. She was a striking beauty in her long wedding dress.

President Tombalbaye invited me to Chad's National Celebration in January but I had too many conflicts with the schedule.

I appointed Dr. Joe Schuster as Chairman of the Department of Range and Wildlife Sciences in January of 1969.

Feb 21 -- My brother John and his wife, JoAnn, stopped by for a rare visit.

Mar 26 -- Elo Urbanovsky and I went to New York City to visit Nelson Rockefeller and then on to Washington, DC where we made Elo's multi-screen presentation on Texas Parks & Recreation.

May 31 -- Byron and Mary came to Lubbock for their son Byron Andrew Thomas' graduation from Texas Tech.

At the Texas and Southwestern Cattle Raisers Association June 6 meeting in Abilene and Throckmorton, Jean and I had the opportunity to

Peggy's Wedding. Marianne was Maid of Honor.
January 10, 1969. Lubbock, Texas.

meet briefly with President Lyndon B. Johnson and Lady Bird. Mrs. Johnson walked up to Jean and cordially asked, *"How are you, Jean?"* as if they were long-time friends. She was adept at reading name tags.

PhD Approved for Tech Agriculture

The Texas Coordinating Board for Higher Education approved our PhD program in several areas of Agricultural Science – a first for a non-Land Grant University in the Nation. Our enrollment in Agriculture has now passed many of the Land Grant Colleges.

Aug 31 -- Dan Moore, Lois' son, died after falling from a roof in Idaho. Jean and Peggy flew to Idaho Falls for the funeral. This was devastating for Lois and it hit our family hard, particularly David as he was very close to Dan. Lois had lost Dan's father shortly after marriage in a plane crash while he was in the Air Force.

In the fall of 1969, I received several calls from New Mexico informing me that the Presidency of New Mexico State University was open due to the retirement of Dr. Roger B. Corbett. At that time I was not interested in moving from Texas Tech. We were launching our new PhD programs, working on the Algerian project and I was busy with teaching and administrative duties.

Nov 12-15 -- Back to Costa Rica for meetings of the Organization for Tropical Studies.

On December 1, a Republican delegation, including Ann Armstrong, came in to ask me to consider running for Congress against George Mahon, Chairman of the House Appropriations Committee. I declined.

Over the Christmas Holidays Jean, Marianne and I drove to California to visit my folks in Hemet. Walter, John and William joined us for a work session to repair Mother's house.

I completed the manuscript for the text book, *"Progress and Change in the Agricultural Industry,"* which was published by Wm. C. Brown and Co. in 1969.

Wedding photo. Gerald, Jean, Peggy, Royace O'Neal, Mrs. O'Neal.
January 10, 1969. Lubbock, Texas.

Chapter 23 | 1970: The Road Turns Westward

"The Regents were examining a couple."

On January 5, 1970, Justin Smith (College of Law), Frank Councelman (Director of ICASALS) and I flew to Alger via Paris to negotiate a contract with SONATRACH Petroleum Company for agricultural development in Algeria. We held discussions with Mr. Ghozali, President of SONATRACH and other representatives of the Company. President Ghozali said he wanted to move as rapidly as possible toward the establishment of 6-8 demonstration farms in Algeria. We prepared a draft contract for consideration. On January 10, Frank Schultz (a Dallas oil man with interests in Algeria) held a fancy reception for us at the St. George Hotel where we met about 20 other Americans and several Algerians interested in the project. When we returned to Texas Tech we encountered political resistance to the project. Eventually the project was terminated.

Back at Texas Tech, I kept busy with my duties as Dean. My graduate class in Range Science now had 10 students. As President of the Southwest Alliance for Latin America (SALA), I made a trip to Washington, DC with representatives of the University of Oklahoma and Colorado State to meet with Government Agencies about possible support for our work in South America. In May, I traveled to Nicaragua, Panama, Colombia and Venezuela on behalf of SALA.

Thad Box and I presented a paper on "Ecology and Use of Water Resources" to the West Texas Chamber of Commerce in February. I noted that it was well received – a change in public awareness about environmental issues. The board of directors at the meeting gave me a special plaque for "Founding the West Texas Water Institute."

At the annual meeting of the American Society for Range Management held in Denver on Febru-

ary 10, I was recognized with an award for "Contributions to the Art and Science of Range Management."

Toward the Land of Enchantment

Friends in New Mexico finally convinced me to submit biographical material to the search committee at New Mexico State University. I was surprised in late February of 1970 to receive a call requesting that I come to the campus for an interview. Jean and I drove to Las Cruces for the interview on February 17. Without the knowledge of the press, I met with the Board of Regents, the Deans and the Search Committee in "pleasant and penetrating discussions." Jean was also involved in various meetings. It was obvious that the Regents were examining a "couple," although no mention could be made of this as possible criteria for employment. We left Las Cruces knowing nothing of the competition or the status of the search process.

In another surprise call, I was asked by Dick Reeves, President of the Board of Regents of NMSU to meet in a closed session on March 7 at Rogers Aston's home in Roswell, New Mexico "to discuss further details of the position as President of NMSU."

The meeting in Roswell was pleasant. I was surprised to be offered the Presidency at a salary of $32,000 with house, utilities, a maid, a university car and miscellaneous benefits. The reporting time would be August 1, 1970. I was overwhelmed by the support of the Regents. I accepted the assignment and called Jean.

The Regents then requested that I drive directly from Roswell to Las Cruces and prepare for the official announcement to the University community. As a part of this process, I was asked to remain

Royace and Peggy standing in the remains of their second floor apartment.
Lubbock, Texas. May 12, 1970.

Photo showing the extent of the tornado damage to Royace and Peggy's
apartment building. Lubbock, Texas. May 12, 1970.

somewhat under cover until March 9 when I was to address to the faculty, staff and students of New Mexico State University – my first exposure to the Land Grant University of New Mexico.

South America and a Crisis in Lubbock

From May 3-12, I was on an assignment as Agricultural Consultant and member of the Board of Directors of the Southwest Alliance for Latin America in the countries of Nicaragua, Colombia and Venezuela. On May 8, our team met with Ambassador Jack Vaughn in Bogotá about general Latin American development problems. The Ambassador was particularly concerned about student unrest related to the Viet Nam War. The South American papers were carrying headlines, "US in State of Crisis" due to the invasion of Cambodia. In sympathy with US students many South American universities went out on strike. Even secondary schools in Venezuela were closed. I also visited with Robert B. Anderson, son of one of New Mexico's wealthiest oilman about his work with the Peace Corps in Colombia. I was informed by the American Embassy that Jean was trying to contact me but we failed to connect.

In the Dallas airport, waiting for a flight to Lubbock, I met Andy Jumper, a Lubbock minister. He said, *"Do you suppose we have a home to go to? The phones are out and this is the first flight to Lubbock since the tornado."* Thus, I learned about the disaster at home. There was no transportation at the Lubbock airport so the Jumpers took me home. Jean briefed me on the tornado and Peggy's status. She had no idea where David was since he left before the storm.

The next day, May 13, we drove through National Guard and police checkpoints to examine the ruins of Peggy and Royace's apartment.

Downtown Lubbock was a disaster – no phones, water supply curtailed, electricity still out in many sections. Peggy's apartment was completely destroyed. No one from our family was hurt but the death toll in Lubbock reached 26.

On July 16, 1970, W. J. "Dub" Waldrip, Manager of the Spade Renderbrook Ranch with friends from Texas Tech organized a "going away" party for us at the Lubbock Country Club. A news release in the Lubbock Avalanche Journal stated, *"The few Tech friends who started out to honor Dr. Thomas mushroomed to a crowd that jam-packed the ballroom."* There were Tech officials and professors, state representatives, farmers, ranchers, neighbors and friends from a wide section of Texas and even a few from Mexico, the Dominican Republic and Algeria. This group of friends established an endowment in the College of Agricultural Sciences for an "Agriculturist of Distinction Award" in my name.

The Viet Nam War was continuing as I was leaving Texas Tech with student unrest as a major problem on most university campuses. By the end of May 1970 nearly one third of some 2,500 US colleges and universities had experienced some kind of protest activity. Texas Tech and NMSU remained calm. Nevertheless, I was asked to attend a meeting of University Presidents on August 5-7 to respond to the theme, "How to keep the Universities open this fall."

We sold our home in Lubbock and in July, 1970, Jean and I loaded up our belongings and took the last segment of a winding road to Las Cruces, New Mexico. On December 31, I recorded in my journal, *"New job, new home, new problems and new opportunities."*

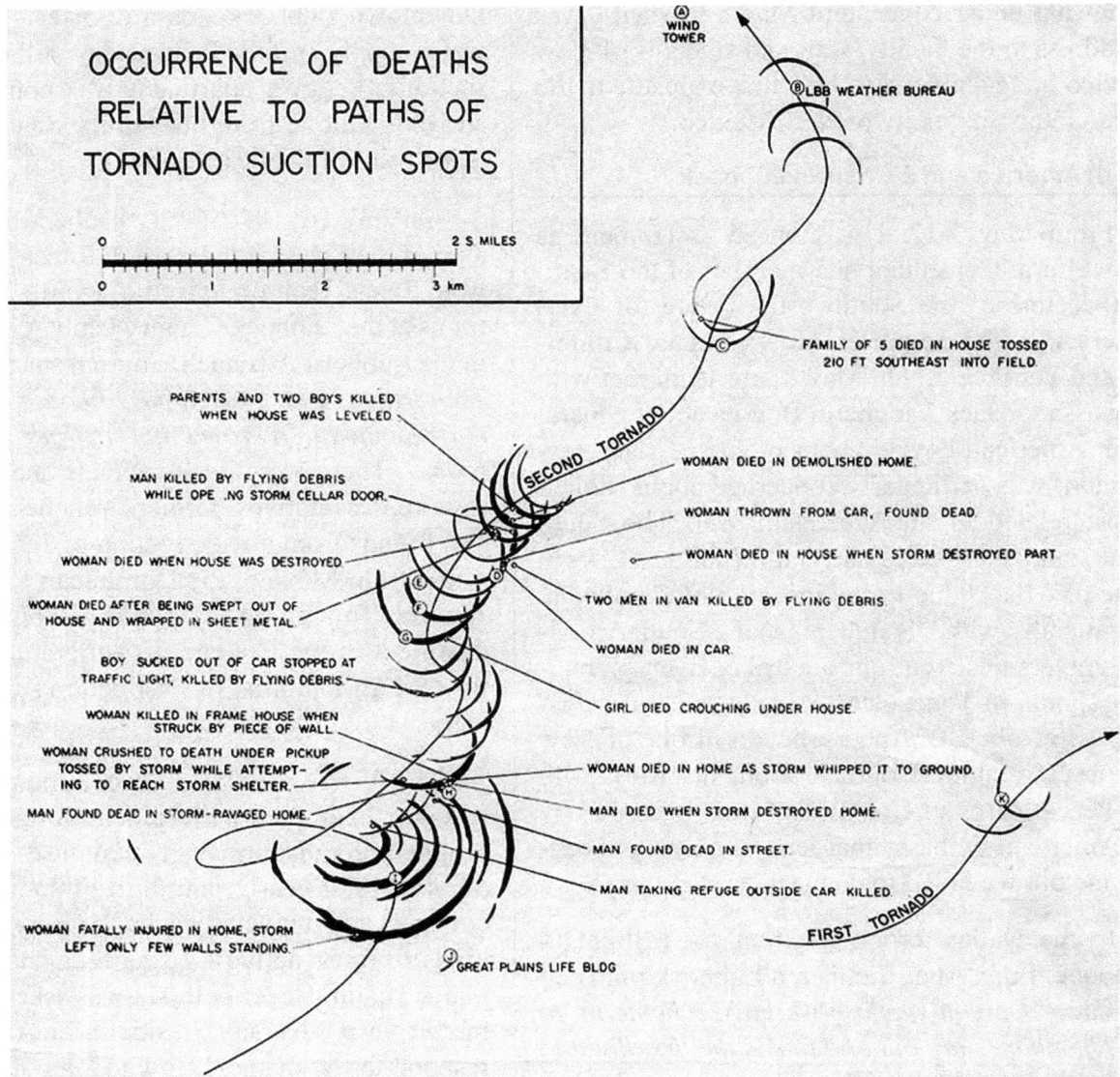

OCCURRENCE OF DEATHS
RELATIVE TO PATHS OF
TORNADO SUCTION SPOTS

0   1   2 S. MILES
0   1   2   3 km

Ⓐ WIND TOWER

Ⓑ LBB WEATHER BUREAU

Ⓒ FAMILY OF 5 DIED IN HOUSE TOSSED 210 FT SOUTHEAST INTO FIELD.

SECOND TORNADO

PARENTS AND TWO BOYS KILLED WHEN HOUSE WAS LEVELED.

MAN KILLED BY FLYING DEBRIS WHILE OPE .NG STORM CELLAR DOOR.

WOMAN DIED WHEN HOUSE WAS DESTROYED.

WOMAN DIED AFTER BEING SWEPT OUT OF HOUSE AND WRAPPED IN SHEET METAL.

BOY SUCKED OUT OF CAR STOPPED AT TRAFFIC LIGHT, KILLED BY FLYING DEBRIS.

WOMAN KILLED IN FRAME HOUSE WHEN STRUCK BY PIECE OF WALL.

WOMAN CRUSHED TO DEATH UNDER PICKUP TOSSED BY STORM WHILE ATTEMPT-ING TO REACH STORM SHELTER.

MAN FOUND DEAD IN STORM-RAVAGED HOME.

WOMAN FATALLY INJURED IN HOME, STORM LEFT ONLY FEW WALLS STANDING.

WOMAN DIED IN DEMOLISHED HOME.

WOMAN THROWN FROM CAR, FOUND DEAD.

WOMAN DIED IN HOUSE WHEN STORM DESTROYED PART.

TWO MEN IN VAN KILLED BY FLYING DEBRIS.

WOMAN DIED IN CAR.

GIRL DIED CROUCHING UNDER HOUSE.

WOMAN DIED IN HOME AS STORM WHIPPED IT TO GROUND.

MAN DIED WHEN STORM DESTROYED HOME.

MAN FOUND DEAD IN STREET.

MAN TAKING REFUGE OUTSIDE CAR KILLED.

FIRST TORNADO

Ⓙ GREAT PLAINS LIFE BLDG

Analysis after the Lubbock tornado showed that the city was actually hit by two tornadoes. It was the second tornado which was devastating, killing 26 people injuring more than 1,500, and doing 250 million dollars of damage.
The second tornado was rated F5, the highest rating. The map shows the locations of the deaths. Analysis by Dr. Theodore Fujita, University of Chicago. The man killed by flying debris while opening his storm cellar door is the jeweler who sold Royace and Peggy their wedding ring.

Chapter 24 | A New Mexico Welcome

"We moved into the President's home on campus."

Jean and I were overwhelmed with the welcome we received in New Mexico. We moved into the president's house on campus and started adjusting to the new life.

My appointment to the presidency of NMSU generated more favorable press coverage than I had anticipated. The people of New Mexico had strong feelings about "their Land Grant College" and they wanted to get acquainted with their new CEO. Consequently, in 1970, I delivered 36 talks at various locations in New Mexico, eight in Texas and four in other States. I met my obligations to present technical papers to the American Institute of Biological Sciences, American Society of Agronomy, Federal Land Bank Association, Texas Dietetics Association, American Society of Range Management, and the La Campana Range Conference in Mexico.

The official Inauguration was scheduled as a part of "Homecoming" on November 13-15, 1970. A regional symposium was held featuring the diversity of cultures in New Mexico and my interest in the environment. We were fortunate to have outstanding speakers – Jack Campbell, Former Governor; Robert Lewis, Governor of the Zuni Pueblo; Father Angelico Chavez, Franciscan historian and poet; and Dr. Ira Clark, well-known historian and water authority. I invited Dr. Martin Gonzalez from Chihuahua as a special speaker.

In addition to representatives from other Universities, Jean and I were pleased to welcome my parents, relatives from Idaho and former associates from Texas A&M and Texas Tech. We were also surprised to see five fellow Navy pilots including our Executive Officer from Torpedo Four with their wives. This group served as the base for later VT-4 reunions and as an incentive for me to complete my book, *"Torpedo Squadron Four: A Cockpit View of World War II."*

After serving 14 years as President and First Lady of New Mexico State University, we have semi-retired and planted our roots firmly in the Land of Enchantment. Our "Winding Road" will terminate here.

Organ Mountains, east of Las Cruces, New Mexico.

Hadley Hall, New Mexico State University, Las Cruces, New Mexico.

The Regents who hired me. Rogers Aston (Roswell), Avelino Gutierrez (Albuquerque), Seaborn Collins (Las Cruces), Dick Reeves (Albuquerque), R. L. Ahrens (Farmington), and Malcolm Garrett (Clovis). NMSU. May, 1970.

Gerald and retiring NMSU President Dr. Roger B. Corbett. NMSU. March 12, 1970.

Presidential Inauguration, NMSU. November 13, 1970. Las Cruces, New Mexico.

Five of my VT-4 buddies and their wives at my Inauguration.
Back row: Walter Hopkins and Lee Hamrick. Middle Row: Jean, Betty Barnett,
Bee Hamrick, Lyn Souza, and ClaraMae Ruth. Front: Gerald, Buck Barnett,
Will Souza, and Bob Ruth. NMSU. November 14, 1970.

Epilogue

"What do you want for those pigs?"

As I write these final words, I face two thresholds.

One is the story of Jean's and my move to Las Cruces, to become first lady and president of New Mexico State University. I'm not going to tell that story here, partly because that story has been told in my book *"The Academic Ecosystem: Issues Emerging in a University Environment,"* and partly because it's a different kind of story. I loved my job as president of NMSU, and I know Jean felt the same about her duties. Being president was a constant challenge, with difficulties arising every day. Most of these difficulties current academic leaders continue to face, but some were unique to the 70s, such as Viet Nam war protests and an attempted fire-bombing of our on-campus residence while we were sleeping.

When I joined NMSU, the institution had about 900 faculty and employees and 10,000 students. It grew to 1,700 faculty and employees, five campuses, and 19,000 students. Making decisions for so many people, and for an institution that was founded in 1888, was a demanding responsibility. NMSU is organized with executive authority residing in the president and the Board of Directors in charge of policy. So, in theory, the Board would decide on the institution's policies and the president would run the university in conformity with those policies. Some Board members did not see their role as limited to policy, however, and that was one of the on-going challenges of being president.

I made controversial decisions – but I made all decisions with the best interests of NMSU as my goal. I never made a decision without consultation.

I was fortunate to have a good administrative team, especially the Administrative Council.

Leading requires consulting. But there is another aspect of leading, delegating decisions and authority. When I was serving in Air Group 4 during the war, we had responsibility thrust upon us, because decisions had to be made quickly, by those facing imminent repercussions. We were all unprepared for the responsibilities we were given, but we accepted it and it served us well. If you are a leader, give responsibility to those working for you.

From my parents, I learned and was given so much. What I have tried to practice in my life is open and honest communication, and integrity. My Dad always dealt fairly with people, even to the extent that it often disadvantaged him, and that was a characteristic all his brothers had. Here's a story that David told me about my Dad. When he was about 16 years old, on a visit to Montana, David went with Dad to buy a couple of weaned pigs to fatten and sell. Dad leaned over the fence looking at the 16 or so piglets that were being offered and asked the seller:

"What do you want for those pigs?"

The seller replied, *"Sixteen dollars a piece."*

"What about that bigger one there? He must be from another litter."

"I reckon the same."

"I'll tell you what," Dad said, *"I'll give you twenty for that big one, and I want those two littler ones by the trough too."*

My Administrative Council – our last meeting before my retirement.
Standing: Gus Freyer, E. J. "Buck" Waid, and Gerald Burke. Seated: Bruce Streett, Eddie Groth, Harold Daw, Donald Roush, Gerald, Dick Wells, Robert Kirkpatrick, and Peggy Elder. NMSU. May 1, 1984.

The other threshold Jean and I face is the end of life. I had a stroke several months ago that I'm still recovering from and Jean is not well.

Today I look at life more reflectively than I have at any time since I was flying combat missions from the *USS ESSEX*.

What is important to me, after 91 years?

My parents, to whom I owe an incalculable debt. I don't have to close my eyes to feel their presence. Strong, honest, hardworking.

Medicine Lodge Ranch, the land I grew up on. A place that still resides in me.

My war experiences, my war buddies. Men on whom my life depended, men who helped me survive the war.

Jean. From the moment we fell in love she has been my helper and companion. Her strength, her loyalty, her faith in me, have been everything.

David, Peggy, Marianne, now in their 50s and 60s. Years of every kind of experience. Highs and lows, pride and disappointment, success and failure. But a wonderful, wonderful blessing.

My grandchildren Amy and Ethan, and my great grandchildren, still infants, Kynlee Pope and Lair and Lake Vickery. The future.

My many, many friends.

Gerald Thomas
July 3, 2010
Las Cruces, New Mexico

My retirement banquet was attended by my Mother and three of my brothers and their wives. Back row: Eunice and William, Walter and Betsy, David, Betty and Daniel. Front: Gerald, Mary, and Jean. NMSU, Las Cruces, NM. May 3, 1984.

Thomas Family Roots

Gerald W. Thomas Family Tree - Four Generations

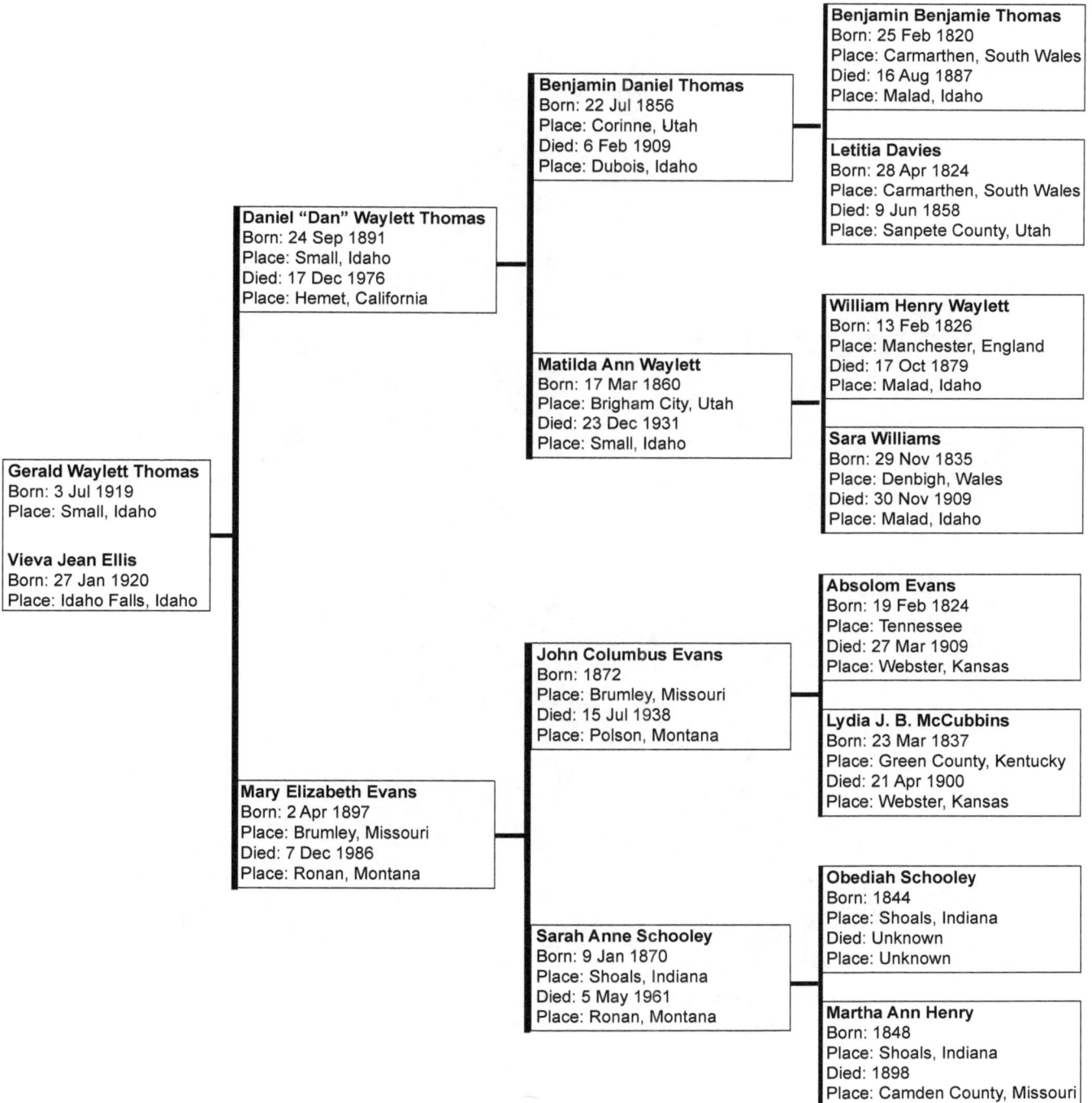

Gerald Waylett Thomas
Born: 3 Jul 1919
Place: Small, Idaho

Vieva Jean Ellis
Born: 27 Jan 1920
Place: Idaho Falls, Idaho

Daniel "Dan" Waylett Thomas
Born: 24 Sep 1891
Place: Small, Idaho
Died: 17 Dec 1976
Place: Hemet, California

Benjamin Daniel Thomas
Born: 22 Jul 1856
Place: Corinne, Utah
Died: 6 Feb 1909
Place: Dubois, Idaho

Benjamin Benjamie Thomas
Born: 25 Feb 1820
Place: Carmarthen, South Wales
Died: 16 Aug 1887
Place: Malad, Idaho

Letitia Davies
Born: 28 Apr 1824
Place: Carmarthen, South Wales
Died: 9 Jun 1858
Place: Sanpete County, Utah

Matilda Ann Waylett
Born: 17 Mar 1860
Place: Brigham City, Utah
Died: 23 Dec 1931
Place: Small, Idaho

William Henry Waylett
Born: 13 Feb 1826
Place: Manchester, England
Died: 17 Oct 1879
Place: Malad, Idaho

Sara Williams
Born: 29 Nov 1835
Place: Denbigh, Wales
Died: 30 Nov 1909
Place: Malad, Idaho

Mary Elizabeth Evans
Born: 2 Apr 1897
Place: Brumley, Missouri
Died: 7 Dec 1986
Place: Ronan, Montana

John Columbus Evans
Born: 1872
Place: Brumley, Missouri
Died: 15 Jul 1938
Place: Polson, Montana

Absolom Evans
Born: 19 Feb 1824
Place: Tennessee
Died: 27 Mar 1909
Place: Webster, Kansas

Lydia J. B. McCubbins
Born: 23 Mar 1837
Place: Green County, Kentucky
Died: 21 Apr 1900
Place: Webster, Kansas

Sarah Anne Schooley
Born: 9 Jan 1870
Place: Shoals, Indiana
Died: 5 May 1961
Place: Ronan, Montana

Obediah Schooley
Born: 1844
Place: Shoals, Indiana
Died: Unknown
Place: Unknown

Martha Ann Henry
Born: 1848
Place: Shoals, Indiana
Died: 1898
Place: Camden County, Missouri

Gravestone of Benjamin Benjamie and Susanah (Roberts) Thomas
(second wife). Malad Cemetery, Malad, Idaho.

Children of Benjamin Daniel and Matilda Ann (Waylett) Thomas

Benjamin Daniel Thomas
  Born 22 Jul 1856 (Corinne, Utah)
  Married 6 Mar 1880 in Malad, Idaho
  Died 6 Feb 1909 (Dubois, Idaho)

Matilda Ann Waylett
  Born 17 Mar 1860 (Brigham City, Utah)
  Died 23 Dec 1931 (Small, Idaho)

Children:

Ella Mae Thomas, born 20 Oct 1880 (Malad, Idaho), died 24 Oct 1920
William Henry Thomas, born 9 Aug 1882 (Malad, Idaho), died 7 Dec 1961
Leah Thomas, born 12 Aug 1884 (Small, Idaho), died 28 Sep 1964 (Dubois, Idaho)
Letitia Thomas, born 10 Nov 1886 (Small, Idaho), died 1 Feb 1973
Daniel "Dan" Waylett Thomas, born 24 Sep 1891 (Small, Idaho), died 27 Dec 1976 (Hemet, California)
Rees Waylett Thomas, born 16 Sep 1893 (Small, Idaho), died 15 Aug 1971 (Idaho Falls, Idaho)
Sarah Mabel Thomas, born 5 Jan 1896 (Small, Idaho), died 18 Feb 1973
George Dewey Thomas, born 23 Dec 1897 (Small, Idaho), died 12 Jan 1970
Benjamin Hobson Thomas, born 23 Dec 1897 (Small, Idaho), died 29 Oct 1967 (Idaho Falls, Idaho)

Children of John Columbus and Sarah Anne (Schooley) Evans

John Columbus Evans
  Born 1872 (Brumley, Missouri)
  Married 2 Jul 1893, (Brumley, Missouri)
  Died 15 Jul 1938 (Polson, Montana)

Sarah Anne Schooley
  Born 9 Jan 1870 (Shoals, Indiana)
  Died 5 May 1961 (Ronan, Montana)

Children:

Amos Ezra Evans, born 5 Jul 1894 (Camden, Missouri), died 28 Mar 1937 (Ronan, Montana)
Mary Elizabeth Evans, born 2 Apr 1897 (Camden, Missouri), died 7 Dec 1986 (Ronan, Montana)
Flora Maye Evans, born 11 Feb 1899 (Camden, Missouri)
Beulah Grace Evans, born 13 Aug 1902 (Webster, Kansas), died 21 Sep 1997 (Ronan, Montana)
Laura Elsie, born 22 Jan 1906 (Webster, Kansas)
Lettie Gertrude, born 5 Jan 1907 (Webster, Kansas), died 8 Jul 1997 (Cashmere, Washington)
John Bunyon, born 13 Mar 1909 (Webster, Kansas)
Mona Lucille, born 6 May 1911 (Webster, Kansas), died 22 Sep 1992 (Ronan, Montana)

Gravestone of Benjamin Daniel and Matilda Ann (Waylett) Thomas
Dubois Cemetery, Dubois, Idaho.

Gravestone of Sarah Anne (Schooley) Evans
Ronan Cemetery, Ronan, Montana.

Jean Ellis Family Tree - Four Generations

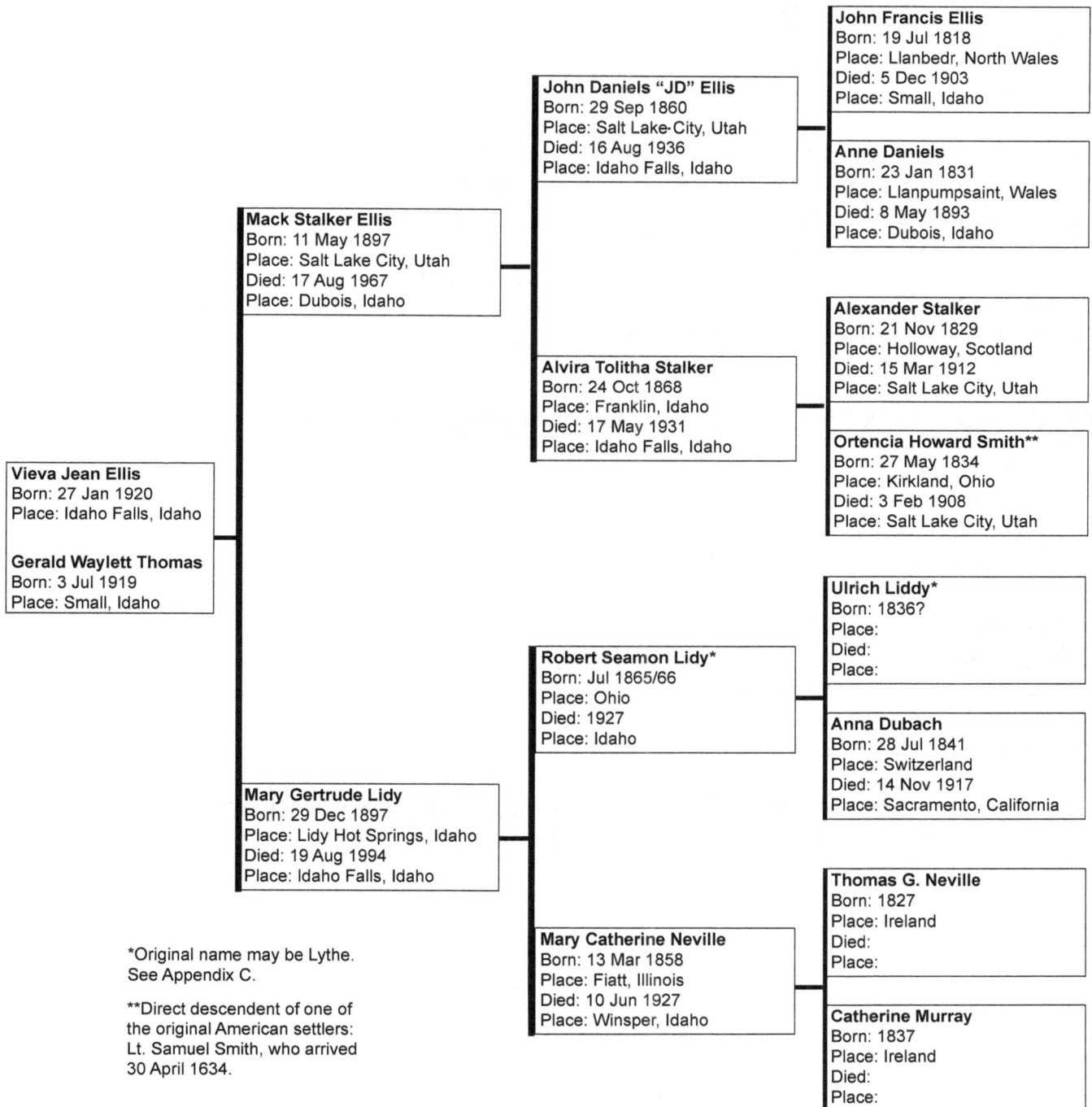

John Francis Ellis
Born: 19 Jul 1818
Place: Llanbedr, North Wales
Died: 5 Dec 1903
Place: Small, Idaho

John Daniels "JD" Ellis
Born: 29 Sep 1860
Place: Salt Lake City, Utah
Died: 16 Aug 1936
Place: Idaho Falls, Idaho

Anne Daniels
Born: 23 Jan 1831
Place: Llanpumpsaint, Wales
Died: 8 May 1893
Place: Dubois, Idaho

Mack Stalker Ellis
Born: 11 May 1897
Place: Salt Lake City, Utah
Died: 17 Aug 1967
Place: Dubois, Idaho

Alexander Stalker
Born: 21 Nov 1829
Place: Holloway, Scotland
Died: 15 Mar 1912
Place: Salt Lake City, Utah

Alvira Tolitha Stalker
Born: 24 Oct 1868
Place: Franklin, Idaho
Died: 17 May 1931
Place: Idaho Falls, Idaho

Ortencia Howard Smith**
Born: 27 May 1834
Place: Kirkland, Ohio
Died: 3 Feb 1908
Place: Salt Lake City, Utah

Vieva Jean Ellis
Born: 27 Jan 1920
Place: Idaho Falls, Idaho

Gerald Waylett Thomas
Born: 3 Jul 1919
Place: Small, Idaho

Ulrich Liddy*
Born: 1836?
Place:
Died:
Place:

Robert Seamon Lidy*
Born: Jul 1865/66
Place: Ohio
Died: 1927
Place: Idaho

Anna Dubach
Born: 28 Jul 1841
Place: Switzerland
Died: 14 Nov 1917
Place: Sacramento, California

Mary Gertrude Lidy
Born: 29 Dec 1897
Place: Lidy Hot Springs, Idaho
Died: 19 Aug 1994
Place: Idaho Falls, Idaho

Thomas G. Neville
Born: 1827
Place: Ireland
Died:
Place:

*Original name may be Lythe.
See Appendix C.

**Direct descendent of one of
the original American settlers:
Lt. Samuel Smith, who arrived
30 April 1634.

Mary Catherine Neville
Born: 13 Mar 1858
Place: Fiatt, Illinois
Died: 10 Jun 1927
Place: Winsper, Idaho

Catherine Murray
Born: 1837
Place: Ireland
Died:
Place:

Children of John Daniels "JD" and Alvira Tolitha (Stalker) Ellis

John Daniels Ellis
  Born 29 Sep 1860 (Salt Lake City, Utah) (Stalker was John's second wife)
  Married 27 Aug 1893 in Franklin, Idaho
  Died 16 Aug 1936 (Idaho Falls, Idaho)

Alvira Tolitha Stalker
  Born 24 Oct 1868 (Franklin, Idaho)
  Died 17 May 1931 (Idaho Falls, Idaho)

Children:

Bessie Lisle Ellis, born 18 Jul 1894 (Small, Idaho), died 23 Nov 1958
John Howard Ellis, born 17 Sep 1895 (Small, Idaho), died 28 Nov 1941
Mack Stalker Ellis, born 11 May 1897 (Small, Idaho), died 10 Aug 1967
Elias Daniels, died as an infant 1899 (Small, Idaho)
Leila Anne Ellis, born 17 Nov 1901 (Small, Idaho), died 31 Jan 1968
Francis Gordon Ellis, born 27 Jun 1903 (Small, Idaho), died 4 Aug 1971 (Gold Beach, Oregon)
Helen Ellis, died as an infant 8 Aug 1907 (Salt Lake City, Utah)
Fremont Ellis, born 1910

Children of Robert Seamon and Mary Catherine (Neville/Sullivan) Lidy

Robert Seamon Lidy
  Born 16 July 1859 (Sedalia, Missouri)
  Married Feb 1897
  Died 1927

Mary Catherine Neville/Sullivan
  Born 13 Mar 1859 (Fiatt, Illinois) (Lidy was Mary's second husband)
  Died 10 Jun 1927 (Winsper, Idaho)

Children:

Mary Gertrude Lidy, born 29 Dec 1897 (Lidy Hot Springs), died 19 Aug 1994 (Idaho Falls, Idaho)
Arthur Lidy, born 1899, died as infant 1901 (Lidy Hot Springs)

Appendix C | An Investigation into Robert Lidy's Origins

The Initial Clues

The origins of Jean's Grandfather, Robert Lidy, are obscure and mysterious. Numerous efforts by family members and researchers to locate any ancestors have failed.

The only clues to his origins are those provided by his daughter Gertrude (Jean's mother) in an undated, transcribed oral account. Here's what she says:

> "My Father, Robert Seamon Lidy, was born in Sedalia, Missouri, July 16, 1858. Actually his surname was Liddy, but when he came West he decided to drop one 'd.' His mother and father were divorced when he was young boy. His Grandmother Liddy raised him and his Father took his older brother Albert to live with him. As the years passed, there was no trace of Albert or his Father."

> "Dad left home when he was 17 and came West to the Teton Mountains, hunting and trapping for a living, for several years. Then he spent some time in Butte, Montana where he worked with dynamite. He came to Camus in 1890."

Based on these details, attempts to locate Robert Lidy (or Liddy) in ANY state in the 1860, 1870, or 1880 censuses failed.

There it stood until a letter that had been saved by Gertrude was rediscovered. The letter was written to Robert Lidy by a brother informing him of his Mother's recent death.

The Letter

Here is the text of the letter:

Sacramento, Calif
11/17/'17

Dear Robert:

> *With broken hearts we are sending this message to you. Yesterday while you were following your daily task in far away Idaho, we laid mother away.*

> *A little over two weeks ago, mama took cold; and for a few days it threatened to become serious. But through the aid of the doctors, she seemed to be making good headway. However, her strength was gradually slipping away and on last Wednes-*

> *day, Nov. 14, at about eleven o'clock she bid a silent good bye to this world and said good morning in Heaven. Her end came without a struggle and she was well prepared. God called in a most tender voice and she answered with a nod. We laid the body away in a beautiful spot where the morning and evening sun will warm the sod. A host of friends covered the spot with nature's sweetest flowers and God has stationed two angels to watch over the remains.*

> *We know that this message will bring sorrow to you. But you may find comfort in the thought that mother's garments of eternal life were whiter than snow. And she is now resting peacefully and sweetly in His Almighty arms.*

> *Please let us hear from you, at least, occasionally, so that we may always keep in touch with each other.*

> *Dear mama was seventy eight years old the 28th day of last July and during these last forty years Albert and you have occupied a very warm and sacred place in her loving heart. You cannot easily imagine how eagerly she read your letters and how she looked for them with such a longing heart. And so often she wondered what had become of Albert Do you know?*

> *May God bless you and your loved ones. And may we have a family reunion some day in heaven.*

> *With love from us all to you all and especially to you.*

> *From Father, sister and brother, Theodore L. Harder, Sacramento, California*

2207 G St
Sacramento, Calif

From this we learn:

- His mother died November 14, 1917 (the letter is dated 11/17/17)
- She was born July 28, 1839
- Robert does have a brother named Albert
- She apparently hadn't seen Robert and Albert for 40 years

Sacramento, Calif.
11/17/17

Dear Robert:

With broken hearts we are sending this message to you. Yesterday while you were following your daily task in far away Idaho, we laid mother away.

A little over two weeks ago mamma took cold, and for a few days it threatened to become serious. But through the aid of three doctors, she seemed to be making good headway. However, her strength was gradually slipping away. and on last Wednesday Nov. 14 at about eleven o'clock she bid a silent good bye to this world and said good morning in Heaven. Her end came without a struggle and she was well prepared. God called in a most tender voice and she answered

First page of letter written by Theodore L. Harder to Robert Lidy informing Robert of his mother's death on November 14, 1917.

- The letter writer's name is Theodore L. Harder and he's living in Sacramento, California
- Robert's father and sister are living

Harder Family

Based on the information provided by the letter, Theodore's family can be located in the 1910 census in Sacramento. They are in the 1900 census living in Portland, Oregon, also. To summarize the data in these two censuses:

- Ferdinand T. Harder, head, born March 1840, in Germany, Minister
- Anna Harder, wife, born July 1841 in Switzerland
- Amelia M, daughter, born March 1876 in Missouri
- Theodore L. Harder, son, born May 1879 in Kansas

In the 1920 census, Amelia is living with her father, her mother is gone (having died), and Theodore has married and moved into his own home.

Working backwards from this data, the Harders are found in the 1880 census in Elmendaro, Lyon County, Kansas:

- F. Harder, head, age 40, born in Prussia, Minister
- Anna Harder, wife, age 40, born in Switzerland
- Amelia, daughter, age 4, born in Missouri
- Theodore, son, age 1, born Kansas

No sign of Robert or Albert Lidy, though.

Robert Found

If Anna Harder is Robert and Albert's mother, and she's in Kansas in 1880, it makes sense to look for the boys there too. And it was at Sedalia, Kansas that Gertrude said Robert Lidy was born.

No sign of him in Kansas, however.

How about Missouri, where Amelia was born?

Sure enough, there he is in Green River, Pettis County, Missouri in the 1880 census:

- Dubazh, Godfip, head, age 43, born in Switzerland, farmer
- Dubazh, Margaret, age 70, born in Switzerland
- Ludy, Robert S., nephew, age 14, born in Ohio, farm hand (at 14!)

That this is really Robert Lidy is confirmed by examining the earlier 1870 census for this family:

- Dubsch, Gottleib, head, age 30, born in Switzerland
- Dubsch, Nicholas, age 73, born Switzerland
- Dubsch, Margaret, age 65, born Switzerland
- Dubsch, Lethy Ann, age 28 born Switzerland

- Dubsch, Albert, age 11, born Ohio
- Dubsch, Robert, age 5, born Ohio

There is a slight variation in the recording of the surname, but this is clearly the same family. In 1870 we have Robert and Albert living in a household headed by Gottleib. Also living in the home are Gottleib's parents Nicholas and Margaret. Lethy Ann is probably Gottleib's sister and Robert and Albert's mother.

In 1880, Lethy Ann and Albert are gone and Nicholas has died. Robert, age 14, is living "with his grandmother" as Gertrude said. He evidently leaves home shortly after this census is taken.

If we refer back to the 1880 census for the Harder family, we can see that Ferdinand and Anna have 4-year-old Amelia, suggesting they were married about 1875, and giving an approximate date when Anna would have left the Dubsch household.

Note that both censuses agree that Robert and Albert are born in Ohio.

Albert Found

Albert leaves the Dubsch family some time after 1870. Where does he go? Gertrude said that he was taken by his father after their divorce.

Albert turns up in the 1880 census in Cambridge, Gurnsey County, Ohio. He is boarding with a Longsworth family: G. S. Longsworth, which includes a wife, four sons, and a grandmother. Albert is listed as:

- Liddy, Albert, age 22, born Ohio, parents born Germany, working as a blacksmith.

If Albert left with his father to return perhaps to the area in Ohio where he and Robert were born, there is no trace of the father.

Note that Albert is spelling his surname as Liddy, with two d's, which Gertrude said was the original name.

Albert appears again in the 1900 census, in Perry, Tuscarawas County, Ohio (Perry is about 25 miles north of Cambridge, where he was in 1880):

- Liddy, Albert L., head, age 40, born May 1860, Ohio, blacksmith
- Liddy, Harrieta A., wife, age 43, born Dec 1856, Ohio, parents born Ohio
- Liddy, William R., son, 14, born March 1886, Ohio
- Liddy, Ionas E., daughter, 8, born Oct 1891, Ohio

Albert is married with a 14-year-old son, William R., and an 8-year-old daughter, Ionas E., indicating he married about

1886. His wife is slightly older and is born in Ohio.

Albert died October 7, 1901, as his obituary reveals:

> *Albert F. Liddy died at his late home on East Gomber avenue about 11 o'clock today after a short illness of abscess on the brain. Deceased was born in Newcomerstown [Ohio] in 1859 and was married to Harriet Parkinson in 1884 and to them were born two children, one son and one daughter. Deceased has resided in Cambridge [Ohio] about nine years and for years had been employed at his trade that of blacksmith, in the tin mill. He had been sick about three weeks and his death has cast a gloom over not only his family but a large circle of friends. – Cambridge Jeffersonian, October 10, 1901.*

Albert's death warrant lists his father as Urlich Liddy, our first clue as to his and Robert's father's name. To date, a search of the census records has failed to locate a Urlich Liddy, but a Urlich Lythe, born 1836, appears in the 1870 census for Tuscarawas County, Ohio – and that's probably him.

Albert's wife Harriette died September 3, 1949 in Cambridge, Ohio. Her obituary:

Oldest Resident of Cambridge Is Dead

> *Services for Mrs. Harriette Ann Liddy, 99, Cambridge's oldest resident, were conducted Tuesday at 10:30 a. m. at the Bundy funeral home by Rev. Louis M. Swartz, pastor of the First Presbyterian church. Interment was in Norwood cemetery.*
>
> *Mrs. Liddy, who would have been 100 years old on Dec 23, died Saturday at 6 p. m. at the home of her son, William R. Liddy, 1236 E. Gomber Ave. Her husband, Albert F. Liddy, blacksmith at the tin mill, died several years ago.*
>
> *The nonagenarian was born Dec 23, 1849 at Antrim [Ohio], a daughter of John and Charlotte Agy Parkinson, and was a life long resident of this community. The Parkinson name is well known in*

> *the early history of Cambridge and Guernsey county.*
>
> *A devout member of the First Methodist church and Class 12 of the Sunday school, Mrs. Liddy is survived by one son, at whose home she died; one daughter, Mrs. Edgar Prince, Calgary, Canada; two sisters, Mrs. Alice Aten and Miss Nan Parkinson, Bedford, O., four grandchildren and five great grandchildren. Two brothers and three sisters are deceased. – Daily Jeffersonian, September 6, 1949.*

Both Albert and Harriette are buried in the Northwood Cemetery, Cambridge, Ohio.

Ohio death records indicate that Albert's son William R. Liddy died May 15, 1971 in Cambridge. William's wife Edna M. Liddy died October 28, 1971. They also are buried in the Northwood cemetery in Cambridge.

Summary

Theodore Harder's death certificate gives his mother's (Anna) surname as Dubach. The Dubsch and Dubazh spellings in the 1870 and 1880 censuses are probably transcription errors.

Robert was born in Ohio in 1865 or 1866.

The current best guess is that Robert and Albert's father's surname was Lythe. Note that the person we are assuming is their mother is listed as Lethy Ann Dubsch in the 1870 census. This probably means that Lethy (Lythe) is her married name.

Harriette's obituary makes it clear that she has grandchildren and great grandchildren. So far, none have been located. It's likely that they have a photo of Albert and maybe Robert and Albert's father. They also may know why their father and mother separated.

Gertrude wondered all her life about her father's origins. This investigation is dedicated to her and to Anna, Robert and Albert's mother.

Notes:

Mary Schumaker, Secretary, Sedalia Public Library, Sedalia, Kansas; Sarah A. Olsen, Genealogical Researcher, Waldport, Oregon; and Cal Traylor, Las Cruces, New Mexico provided critical help in this research.

Index

Doc 45 Publications

Torpedo Squadron Four – A Cockpit View of World War II, Gerald W. Thomas, paperback, 280 pages, 209 photos, e-book available.

Torpedo Squadron Four – Photo Supplement, Gerald W. Thomas, e-book, 120 pages, 120 photos.

La Posta – From the Founding of Mesilla, to Corn Exchange Hotel, to Billy the Kid Museum, to Famous Landmark, David G. Thomas, paperback, 118 pages, 59 photos, e-book available.

Giovanni Maria de Agostini – The Astonishing World Traveler Who Was A Hermit, David G. Thomas, paperback, 196 pages, 59 photos, 19 maps, e-book available.